Kristy Beers Fägersten
Language Play in Contemporary Swedish Comic Strips

Language Play and Creativity

Editor
Nancy Bell

Volume 3

Kristy Beers Fägersten
Language Play in Contemporary Swedish Comic Strips

—

DE GRUYTER
MOUTON

Copyright and permissions
Berglins copyright Jan and Maria Berglin. Used by permission.
Elvis copyright Tony Cronstam. Used by permission.
Fucking Sofo and *Vi ses i Sofo* copyright Lena Ackebo. Used by permission.
Lilla Berlin copyright Ellen Ekman. Used by permission.
Pondus copyright Frode Øverli, distributed by Strand Comics. Used by permission.
Rocky copyright Martin Kellerman, distributed by Strand Comics. Used by permission.
Stockholmsnatt copyright Pelle Forshed and Stefan Thungren. Used by permission.
Zelda copyright Lina Neidestam. Used by permission.

ISBN 978-1-5015-2718-0
e-ISBN (PDF) 978-1-5015-0511-9
e-ISBN (EPUB) 978-1-5015-0505-8
ISSN 2363-7749

Library of Congress Control Number: 2020932143

Bibliographic information published by the Deutsche Nationalbibliothek
The Deutsche Nationalbibliothek lists this publication in the Deutsche Nationalbibliografie; detailed bibliographic data are available on the Internet at http://dnb.dnb.de.

© 2022 Walter de Gruyter Inc., Boston/Berlin
This volume is text- and page-identical with the hardback published in 2020.
Typesetting: Integra Software Services Pvt. Ltd.
Printing and binding: CPI books GmbH, Leck

www.degruyter.com

Acknowledgements

This book would not be possible without the comic art that preceded it. As the creators of the comic strips analyzed throughout the chapters, Lena Ackebo, Jan and Maria Berglin, Tony Cronstam, Ellen Ekman, Pelle Forshed and Stefan Thungren, Martin Kellerman, and Lina Neidestam, all deserve particular acknowledgement. Their individual contributions to Swedish comic art are remarkable, but collectively they have succeeded in creating a national brand of comics which is unique on the international comic art scene. It is my hope that this book will serve to introduce contemporary Swedish comic strips to new audiences and bring these and other Swedish creators much-deserved attention and appreciation.

This book would also not be possible without the permission of the creators to reprint a selection of their comic strips. I am forever grateful to each of them for their kindness, enthusiasm, and generosity. I would like to extend my gratitude especially to Maria Berglin, Tony Cronstam, Pelle Forshed, and Håkon and Hege Strand (on behalf of Martin Kellerman) for sharing their digital files with me.

I am grateful to the Wennergren Foundation for supporting work on this book by funding a research sabbatical at the University of Michigan. Thank you to the staff at the Department of Germanic Languages and Literatures and especially to Johannes von Moltke, former Head of the Department, for hosting me. Special thanks go to Johanna Ericsson, Director of Scandinavian Studies, for welcoming me so enthusiastically and for helpful discussions of the material. Thank you, Kimb and Ebi, for sharing your home with me and Tintin.

I would like to acknowledge the Foundation for Baltic and East European Studies (*Östersjöstiftelsen*), whose funding partially extends to this book, the Publications Committee at Södertörn University, and the Swedish Academy for early support of this research.

I am immeasurably grateful for all the reviewer comments, critiques, questions, and compliments and for the careful, involved reading that yielded them. Any lingering errors are my own fault. Finally, I would like to thank Nancy Bell, Professor of English at Washington State University and Series Editor of Language Play and Creativity at Mouton de Gruyter, for seeing the potential of my research to be developed into a book and for encouraging me along the way.

Contents

Acknowledgements —— V

List of Figures —— IX

1 Language play as humor in comic strips —— 1
    1.1   Introduction —— 1
    1.2   What is language play? —— 2
    1.3   Language play and humor —— 4
    1.4   Humor in comic strips —— 7
    1.5   Language play in contemporary Swedish comic strips: Chapter overview —— 10

2 Vällkamm to Sviden —— 14
    2.1   Highlighting Swedish humor —— 17
    2.2   Contemporary Swedish comic strips —— 19
    2.3   A comic a day —— 23
    2.4   The central role of language in Swedish comic strips —— 28

3 Schwädu hupp jöördi hoo —— 35
    3.1   Sweden's linguistic capital —— 36
    3.2   Sweden's Mark Twain? —— 44
    3.3   Dialect humor —— 45
    3.4   The sounds of Sweden: West, south, and north —— 47
    3.5   Visualizing variation —— 56

4 Gracias de nada! —— 62
    4.1   The other languages of Sweden —— 64
    4.2   Neighboring languages —— 67
    4.3   Visualizing the struggle —— 71
    4.4   German-language play —— 74
    4.5   Spanish-language play —— 81
    4.6   The multicompetence underlying incompetence —— 87

5 In English, please —— 90
    5.1   English code-switching in Swedish comics —— 95
    5.2   The impact of media —— 108
    5.3   The Swedish variety of English —— 117

6 Are you completely @# ☠ fucking crazy? —— 125
- 6.1 English-language swearing in Swedish —— 126
- 6.2 Swearing in the media —— 129
- 6.3 Swearing as code-switching —— 141
- 6.4 Swearing as the 'other' —— 144
- 6.5 New norms of English-language swearing —— 153

7 Face the facts —— 155
- 7.1 Creative English —— 158
- 7.2 Performing the native speaker —— 164
- 7.3 Many Englishes —— 166
- 7.4 Anglicisms in Swedish —— 178
- 7.5 Lingua ludica —— 188

Bibliography —— 191

Index —— 201

List of Figures

Figure 1	Vällkamm to Sviden	14
Figure 2	Tippikal Svedish kalltjör	14
Figure 3	Swedish humor	18
Figure 4	Of course we can talk seriously	25
Figure 5	*Fucking Sofo*	29
Figure 6	*Rocky* #2948	30
Figure 7	*Rocky* #2949	30
Figure 8	*Stockholmsnatt*	31
Figure 9	*Lilla Berlin*	31
Figure 10	*Fucking Sofo* trio	32
Figure 11	*Rocky* at night	33
Figure 12	*Rocky* #3436	33
Figure 13	*Rocky* #3437	34
Figure 14	*Rocky* #3438	34
Figure 15	Schwädu hupp jöördi hoo	35
Figure 16	Who now?	38
Figure 17	Östermalm	41
Figure 18	Söööder!	42
Figure 19	E du go ellör?	48
Figure 20	Ångörreeed!	49
Figure 21	Sån läjvnadsgläjdje!	51
Figure 22	Precis sum i Möllan!	52
Figure 23	Varför int'?	55
Figure 24	Titti! In mimmit!	57
Figure 25	Nill mattobinen!!!	58
Figure 26	Tired of consonants	60
Figure 27	Hu-alllah mu-hackbar	65
Figure 28	Alhadr moqtadrrr al-sadrrr!	66
Figure 29	Ett nei er ett nei!	68
Figure 30	Ö and consonants	70
Figure 31	Al dente	71
Figure 32	Katastrofani idioto!	72
Figure 33	Sieg heil!	75
Figure 34	Ten …	77
Figure 35	They're like vhat?	78

https://doi.org/10.1515/9781501505119-204

Figure 36	Spray it don't say it!	82
Figure 37	El Robocopo!	84
Figure 38	Gracias de nada!	86
Figure 39	In English, please	92
Figure 40	Laxpink ... ?	94
Figure 41	How primitive ...	96
Figure 42	Here we go again ...	99
Figures 43–45	Punchline English in *Lilla Berlin*	102
Figure 46	Take me now	103
Figure 47	That's how we scroll ...	104
Figure 48	No further questions your honor!	105
Figure 49	I have no further questions your honor ...	106
Figure 50	Now that's what I want!	109
Figure 51	One cat to rule them all ...	111
Figure 52	Nobody puts Mattias in a corner!	112
Figure 53	It's better to fade away	113
Figure 54	It's better to sell out	114
Figure 55	Jack Shit! ATF!	114
Figure 56	Cops!	116
Figure 57	Oops	118
Figure 58	Ajm bissi bissi bissi	119
Figure 59	It's wery cold and wet	120
Figure 60	Aj dånt tink så!	121
Figure 61	Shit vacation	127
Figure 62	A fucking eternity	128
Figure 63	Ow, damn it!	130
Figure 64	Oh cock and piss!	131
Figure 65	Fitta	132
Figure 66	A true "original"	133
Figure 67	Are you crazy?	134
Figure 68	Turn it down!	135
Figure 69	Bronx	136
Figure 70	Yeah fo sho!	139
Figure 71	Fuck! Vroom!	142
Figure 72	Fucking fuck!	143
Figure 73	Fucking fags!!!	145
Figure 74	Fuck you Charlotte	147
Figure 75	Guppy	148
Figure 76	Fuck you!	149
Figure 77	Subject: Romantic film	151

Figure 78	Maddafakka!	152
Figure 79	Lanzarote	152
Figure 80	Sock it!	159
Figure 81	Bros goes before hoes!	160
Figure 82	I say toast!	161
Figure 83	You poofta!	164
Figure 84	I'm loving these shoes?	165
Figure 85	Fück öff	167
Figure 86	Dis is for dis	169
Figure 87	Yez!	170
Figure 88	This good bar?	172
Figure 89	Hello papa!	174
Figure 90	Have you heard	175
Figure 91	*Rocky*: Face the facts	179
Figure 92	*Berglins*: Face the facts	180
Figure 93	Fucking brejk	180
Figure 94	Give me a break	181
Figure 95	Chicken race!	183
Figure 96	A little something like this …	184
Figure 97	What's up, homeboy?	186

1 Language play as humor in comic strips

1.1 Introduction

This book represents an investigation of language play in contemporary Swedish comic strips. In and of itself, language play promises to be an entertaining enough subject to appeal to the interests of a general audience. A focus on language play in the Swedish language may serve to limit this audience somewhat, while adding comic strips to the mix results in a study that must be considered a niche endeavor. However, the more targeted an area of inquiry, the more in-depth knowledge there is to be gained and, in its turn, further applied, extrapolated, and built upon. Such is the premise (and potential) of this book. Indeed, language play in contemporary Swedish comic strips is just one of countless niche areas waiting for their moment in the spotligt of academic exploration. This book features investigations of contemporary Swedish comic strips as fascinating and rich sites of innovative linguistic practices, focusing on humor derived from language play – a phenomenon common to all languages.

The overall purpose of the book is to highlight language play, linguistic creativity, and conversational playfulness in Swedish comic strips as examples of practices as yet unobserved and unaccounted for in theories of humor as applied to comics scholarship. Focusing on specific strategies of language play and linguistic creativity, such as the use of eye-dialect, regiolectal spelling, word play, and code-switching for the purpose of imitating Swedish dialects, mocking foreign language proficiency, invoking English-language popular culture, or swearing in multiple languages, the chapters of this book will familiarize the reader with contemporary Swedish comic strips as well as the Swedish language and linguistic culture. In this way, *Language play in contemporary Swedish comic strips* aims to appeal to readers interested in humor or comics, or those curious about how linguistic innovation, creativity, language play, and even language contact each can further the modern development of language, exemplified by the case of Swedish. Before turning our attention to the content of Swedish comic strips, however, we first need to explore the concept of language play and the relationship between language play and humor.

1.2 What is language play?

Before focusing on language play specifically, let us consider play in general. Play is a social and free activity (in the sense that it is entered into voluntarily) that takes place within a framework of rules and orderliness, but outside the realm of "ordinary" life, and neither motivated nor rewarded materially (Huizinga 1980: 13). Play is active and enacted for its own sake, and play aims at pleasure, entertainment, recreation, or other positive effect (Rieber, Smith and Noah, 1998; Smith and Pellegrini 2008). Furthermore, play is a "behaviour not primarily motivated by human need to manipulate the environment (and to share information for this purpose) and to form and maintain social relationships – though it may indirectly serve both of these functions" (Cook 2000: 227). Cook claims that play is "a major component of life" which, quite simply, has "something to do with enjoyment and relaxation" (Cook 2000: 227).

As a specific form of generic play, language play should share some of the same characteristics. Indeed, language play, too, is an activity entered into freely which distinguishes itself from ordinary language usage, is social in nature, is motivated by enjoyment, and aims to entertain. Cook (2000: 5) defines language play as "the patterning of linguistic form, the creation of alternative realities, and the social use of both of these for intimacy and conflict." Accordingly, language play can take place on precisely these different levels, i.e., linguistic form, semantic meaning, and pragmatic use, manifesting as, for example, play with phonology, orthography and grammar; play with meaning; and play with communicative conventions, respectively, where this form of play should first and foremost be understood as creative manipulation.

Sherzer (2014: 727) uses the term 'speech play' to refer to "the manipulation of elements and components of language, in relation to one another, in relation to the social and cultural contexts of language use, and against the backdrop of other verbal possibilities in which speech play is not foregrounded." Sherzer notes that speech play can be purposeful or accidental (and can potentially go unnoticed), but that manipulation of the linguistic system often indicates a deliberateness uncharacteristic of "ordinary" language use. While he acknowledges that speech play can be observed to various degrees in all speech (more on this below), its close association with conventionalized forms of linguistic manipulation such as wordplay, jokes, or riddles renders it extraordinary. Sherzer does not explicity contrast the terms 'speech play' and 'language play', nor do there seem to be any significant differences. 'Language play', however, emerges in the literature as the established term; throughout the remainder of this book, the term 'language play' is thus used exclusively.

Norrick (2017) focuses on the role of language in language play, namely, as the object of play or, in contrast, as the medium of play. Where language is the object of play, the context is usually one of a game, such as *Scrabble*, or game-like activities, such as solving crosswords. Language as the medium of play refers to play activities operationalized via language, such as teasing, joking, or humorous self-disclosures (Norrick 2017: 11). This dichotomy of language with regards to play, that is language as object versus language as medium, can be compared to the approach to language play as playing with a language versus playing in a language (Bell 2012; Bell and Pomerantz 2015; Vandergriff and Fuchs 2009, 2012). Similar to language play where language is the object of play, play with a language normally involves some sort of overt manipulation of language or linguistic form. The most common example of play with language is wordplay or punning, but Bell (2012: 190) notes that "any level of language may be manipulated, including phonology, syntax, or pragmatics, for instance by inventing a new word or subverting a ritual [...]." In comparison to language play where play is the medium of language, play in a language also refers to the use of language to take part in a play activity, including real game-play, as well as the acts of telling jokes or recounting funny stories (Bell 2012).

From the perspective of language play as "extraordinary", performance plays a central role. As such, language play is closely connected to verbal art, that is, "a concern with the form of expression, over and above the needs of communication" (Bascom 1955: 247), "a focus on the message for its own sake" (Jakobson 1960: 356), or "a focus on the aesthetic use of language, both oral and written" (Sherzer 2014: 727). With regards to verbal art, performance in its turn is "conceived of and defined as a mode of communication" (Bauman 1975: 9). According to Bauman, verbal art as performance, and performance as communication, both invoke a performance frame with particular interpretive parameters:

> Performance involves on the part of the performer an assumption of accountability to an audience for the way in which communication is carried out, above and beyond its referential content. From the point of view of the audience, the act of expression on the part of the performer is thus marked as subject to evaluation for the way it is done, for the relative skill and effectiveness of the performer's display of competence. Additionally, it is marked as available for the enhancement of experience, through the present enjoyment of the intrinsic qualities of the act of expression itself. Performance thus calls forth special attention to and heightened awareness of the act of expression and gives license to the audience to regard the act of expression and the performer with special intensity. (Bauman 1975: 11)

Language play can thus be conceived of as a form of both verbal art and performance which draws attention to itself, the interpretation of which is directed by "play" as the communicative goal. Crystal (1998: 180) has argued the importance of ludic language in interaction for linguistic development, noting that language play "commands our attention whether we laugh or not." In other words, language play may not be experienced as humorous, but it distinguishes itself from ordinary language and saliently invokes a "play" frame. According to Bateson (2006), communication requires a frame in order to be understood. A play frame corresponds to the metacommunicative message, "this is play," which encourages interlocutors to interpret talk and action as non-serious. The performance of language play can invoke such a play frame. This is not to say that all instances of language play render interaction non-serious, nor must serious discourse be devoid of language play. However, language play can serve to frame an interaction as play, or an interaction that is already framed as play may prove conducive to the occurrence of language play. I return to framing further on, to consider how the comic strip format also serves as a framing device.

In its essence, and in line with Bell (2012) and Norrick (2017), language play can be understood to denote the manipulation of language that is both deliberate and creative. As used throughout this book, the term also connotes the joyful spirit of play, as well as play for the express purpose of entertainment. This particular usage thus aligns with Crystal's (1996: 328) identification of language play, that is, "when people manipulate the forms and functions of language as a source of fun for themselves and/or for the people they are with." In this formulation, Crystal manages to capture additional aspects central to language play, namely, its occurrence as a socially contextualized performance (central to the definition proposed by Cook 2000) and its relation to pleasure, enjoyment, or positive affect (as highlighted by Sherzer 2014). Indeed, telling a joke, making a witty comeback, or engaging in wordplay would each be viewed as attempts at having fun or being funny, at entertaining one's addressees, or at producing a laughter response from them. Language play, it follows, can thus be considered a behavior that fills a humorous function. The relationship between langauge play and humor is explored in the next section.

1.3 Language play and humor

Inherent in language play is creativity. Indeed, language play is often actualized as the creation of novel linguistic forms or new semantic associations. However, creativity as recognizable innovation depends on pre-existing parameters, conventions, habits, or rituals. In other words, creativity is borne of rules:

> Creativity carries with it associations of freedom, agency and the unshackling of constraints. This is a beguiling but misleading view because creativity does not operate, unbounded, in an autonomous fashion. It is usually shaped by convention. It is about giving form to the material we draw on and transform, and this cannot be done without reference to existing rules, devices, codes and procedures. (Negus and Pickering 2004: 68)

It is by virtue of, and to a certain extent an awareness of, "rules, devices, codes and procedures", that deviation from or flouting of these becomes possible, whereby language play is also possible, in the form of being linguistically creative and also recognizing and responding to others' linguistic creativity. Without the existence of language-specific phonological, morphological, grammatical, or syntactical systems, for example, or without pragmatic or sociolinguistic conventions and rituals, there would be no framework to support a counter-culture of creativity.

Language play and creativity trade on deliberate linguistic manipulation. This manipulation results in something new or different, the distinction apparent only in tacit comparison or explicit juxtaposition. For example, the joke, "Why did the tomato run? To [kˈɛtʃʌp]!", involves language play in the form of near homophony. To appreciate the joke, one must be able to recognize that [kˈɛtʃʌp] sounds like both "catch up" and "ketchup". The lexical priming of "run" together with the infinitive marker "to" encourage the hearing of the verb phrase "catch up", while the use of "tomato" rather steers the listener towards the noun phrase "ketchup" – despite the grammatical infelicity. It is only in recognizing both of these competing interpretations that one can understand the joke and, ideally, find it humorous. Indeed, humor, in its most basic conceptualization, "derives from the juxtaposition of two odd, unexpected, or inappropriate elements in a particular context. The incongruity that results from this pairing must then be at least partially resolved in order for the contrast to be interpreted as funny" (Bell and Pomerantz 2015: 23). Many theories of humor position incongruity as a necessary condition for conveying humor. Warren and McGraw (2014: 52) argue that humor and its appreciation depend on an ability to manage "contrasting interpretations at the same time," and thus refer to incongruity and related concepts such as bisociation, juxtaposition, and script opposition as "simultaneity." Similarly, the script-based semantic theory of humor (SSTH) holds that any humorous text invokes two possible scripts which not only oppose one another, but also do so in a way that is incongruous with the receiver's expectations. A script is "a large chunk of semantic information surrounding the word or evoked by it" (Raskin 1985: 81); in the joke presented above, the use of "tomato" would invoke a script that would allow the hearer to access "ketchup," while the word "run" would trigger another script that includes "catch up". The opposition of these two scripts provides the necessary condition for humor: incongruity.

Incongruity alone, however, is insufficient for the perception of humor (Attardo 2014: 384). Any incongruity invoked must also be recognized and at least partially resolved[1] in order for humor to be perceived or experienced. Efforts to understand humorous incongruities have led humor theorists to focus on what is required of the receiver to resolve them, namely, the acceptance of given premises, a willingness to suspend disbelief, or an ability to surrender to the immediate context of the humorous text (Attardo and Raskin 1991). In so doing, opposing scripts, incongruities, and juxtapositions can be sorted out. Aiming to reveal how this actually takes place is the general theory of verbal humor (GTVH). The GTVH expands upon and further develops the SSTH by identifying script opposition as fundamental, but nevertheless not in and of itself responsible for creating humor. Script opposition is rather one knowledge resource, which interacts with an additional five knowledge resources: language, narrative strategy, target, situation, and logical mechanism (Attardo and Raskin 1991). Language as a knowledge resource comprises not just the language in which the humorous text is recounted (e.g., Swedish or English), but also the phonological, morphological, syntactic, lexical, and pragmatic features of the text. Denoting the genre of the humorous text or the category of joke, narrative strategy acknowledges the role of how a humorous text is organized and structured in its recounting. The target refers to the person or object that is victimized by the humorous text, the 'butt' of the joke, as it were. Not all humorous texts include a target, and thus this knowledge resource is optional. The situation refers to the context or the background of the humorous text. The logical mechanism refers to the reasoning required to make sense of the script opposition of the humorous text. In other words, it is via the logical mechanism that incongruity can be (at least partially) resolved. Much of humor appreciation hinges on the logical mechanism; as such it has been scrutinized as problematic (Davies 2004, 2011b; Hempelmann and Attardo 2011; Oring 2011, 2016). Some of the controversial issues include not only the many different manifestations of the logical mechanism (see for example a list provided in Attardo, Hempelmann and Di Maio 2002), but also the fact that the logical mechanism may even be absent. Thus, determining exactly which, if any, logical mechanism is invoked and understanding its interaction with the other knowledge resources constitutes the better part of past and present work with the GTVH.

---

[1] Ruch's (1992) 3WD model allows for the possibility of no resolution in 'nonsense' humor, but the *impression* of resolution nevertheless serves to reaffirm its essential role.

The knowledge resources proposed by the GTVH are hierarchical in nature such that language represents the lowest level and script opposition the highest level of knowledge resource. Higher level resources may determine or restrict lower level resources. As linguistic theories of humor, the SSTH and the GTVH are particularly applicable to identifiable types of humorous texts, such as canned jokes or riddles, as exemplified by the 'tomato' joke, above. Indeed, the main goal of the GTVH is to provide a framework for identifying and comparing joke types. Norrick (2014: 175) thus argues that such theories that focus more on 'joke' as a genre cannot account for conversational humor in the sense of 'joking' as a phenomenon of talk-in-interaction: "Humor in spoken language is based in interaction [and] involves gestures, play-acting, and imitations of voices and dialects – matters not addressed by theories of verbal humor." Norrick also proposes that the application of methodologies particular to discourse and conversation analysis as well as interactional sociolinguistics allows humor researchers to identify social and pragmatic functions of humor, such as identify formation, interpersonal (dis)affiliation, or interactional alignment.

The analyses featured in this book focus on language play as a source of humor in contemporary Swedish comic strips, where it is a feature of talk-in-interaction which is depicted visually in the comic strip format. Language play appears most often precisely in the form of "gestures, play-acting, and imitations of voices and dialects", and as such, it falls under this category of conversational humor which is generally outside the purview of SSTH and GTVH as linguistic theories of humor. Nevertheless, many of the examples share a common narrative template, namely one centered around a concluding punchline, and thus reflect a text type that is relevant to both the SSTH and the GTVH. In their turn, punchlines are predominantly based on an incongruity, one which often draws on the multimodality of the comic strip medium. This multimodality distinguishes comic strips as more complex than exclusively verbal or visual sources of humor, due to the potential variety of incongruous combinations. Incongruity thus emerges as a familiar touchstone of the analyses, and its resolution requires attention to not only to the propositional content of the text but also the actual visual form of the text (including, for example, spelling or lettering), and the remaining visuals as interacting features of the comic strips.

1.4 Humor in comic strips

As this book focuses on language play as a source of humor in Swedish comic strips, it requires that one accept the premise that comics can, in fact, be created with the intention of being humorous. While it might seem self-evident to some that 'comic' strips are comical, many comics scholars are keen to disabuse the general public from this very notion (Gardner 2012; McCloud 1993; Saraceni 2003), due to the fact that the term 'comics' continues to be used even to refer to serious, tragic, or violent works in a range of genres such as history, fantasy, or autobiography. However, although publications such as Art Spiegelman's *Maus* (1986) Alan Moore's *Watchmen* (1987), or Alison Bechdel's *Fun Home* (2007) are examples of such works that could broadly be considered comics, they are more aptly labeled as graphic novels, since their ultimate publication in book form distinguishes them from conventional daily or weekly comic strips. Indeed, the very first comic strips appeared in magazines, newspapers, and periodicals (Gardner 2012), and were, in fact, comical, hence the emergence of the terms 'comic strips' and 'comics', but also alternatives such as, 'cartoon strips', 'the funny pages', or simply 'the funnies' (Inge 1990).

The advent of graphic novels, also called 'graphic narratives', which has ushered in a modern development away from the traditional comics-as-humor template, actually serves to re-establish the connection between humor and the objects referred to as 'comics' or 'comic strips', particularly with regards to newspaper comic strips. All of the comics included in this book were originally published as comic strips in one or more of Sweden's daily tabloid or broadsheet newspapers, daily free newspaper, or bi-weekly free newspaper. According to Lefèvre (2000: 1), this "publication format and the caricatural style suggest a humorous content," which applies to each of the featured Swedish comics, all of which are humor strips centering around a punchline (or several), and thus adhering to at least one of Freud's accompanying factors for humor, namely, that there is an "expectation of the comic", whereby readers are "attuned to comic pleasure" (Freud 1905: 282–285, as cited in Raskin 1985: 12). In other words, regardless of whether such newspaper comic strips are meant to be (or reliably succeed in being) funny, a reader can be assumed to approach them with an expectation of humor and/or will consider the conditions of the comic strip context as favorable for humor.

At this point, it is fruitful to return to the concept of framing and how it may apply to comic strip analysis. Earlier, the act of engaging in language play was proposed as paramount to invoking what Bateson (2006) calls a "play frame", that is, the framing of an interaction as "this is play". Participants of a communicative interaction can signal to each other metacommunicatively that their actions acquire new meaning because they are within a frame of play. Signalling or invoking the play frame is thus crucial to achieving the desired interpretation of the communicative event as 'play'.

As a communication theory, framing "refers to the process by which people develop a particular conceptualization of an issue or reorient their thinking about an issue" (Chong and Druckman 2007: 104). In other words, how any issue (e.g., social, political, religious) is framed (e.g., as serious, absurd, dangerous) will affect how it is received and accepted. Comic strips provide their own frames, both literally in terms of panels and metacommunicatively in terms of a comical or humorous frame. The literal, visual frame imposed by the comic strip panels encompasses the contents of the strip, rendering each of the panels potential sites for humor. The comic strip's metacommunicative frame encourages the reader to think of the comic strip content as funny. Content, however, is multi-layered and includes the overall propositional content of the narrative (in other words, what the strip is about), the language used to instantiate the narrative, and the visual representation of both in the form of illustration, ballooning, and lettering. Each of these aspects of content can separately or simultaneously and collaboratively constitute the site of humor. For this reason, language play, for example, not only represents a source of humor on its own, but may also operationalize the humor of the propositional content such that the funniness of language play influences the reader's understanding of the propositional content as also funny.

In order to understand the role of comic strips specifically in both constructing and reinforcing humor, the connection between comic strips and humor must be made evident. The comics featured in this book are either single-panel comics (that is, panel gags or gag-a-day comics) or multi-panel comics structured around an incongruity or opposition serving as the source of humor. This is to say that humor results when a textual or visual cue encourages a likely interpretation of a narrative or a contextualized image, which is then challenged by new information that opposes the likely interpretation, rendering it incongruent. This incongruity results in "cognitive dissonance" (Yus 2003: 1308), which can only be resolved with an alternative, humorous interpretation: "The resolution of the incongruity, by finding an overall coherent sense of the whole text, together with the addressee's realization of having been fooled into selecting a specific interpretation, is supposed to trigger a humorous effect" (Yus 2003: 1309). Incongruity is particularly essential to the humor of comic strips, the multimodality of which allows for three possible kinds of opposition: within the texts, within the images, or between the text(s) and image(s) (Beers Fägersten 2014b: 156). As shown in the examples presented throughout this book, both text and image are used as resources in the reading and processing of comics (Cohn 2013; McCloud 1993), to formulate both likely and alternative interpretations.

1.5 Language play in contemporary Swedish comic strips: Chapter overview

The overall purpose of this book is to highlight language play and other expressions of linguistic playfulness in Swedish comic strips as practices yet unobserved and unaccounted for in theories of humor as applied to comics scholarship. To this end, the remaining chapters focus on presenting and analyzing examples of language play from a range of Sweden's most popular comic strips and according to different themes. Chapter 2, "Vällkamm to Sviden," begins an exploration of what constitutes Swedish humor by way of inviting the reader to consider the reigning stereotypes of Swedes and Swedish culture. The chapter continues by introducing the Swedish comic strips featured in this book and providing details on the creators, the comic strips' broad story lines, and their publication histories. All of the comic strips included are humor strips published as serial narratives in various Swedish broadsheet and tabloid newspapers. Definitions of the terms comic strip and serial narrative are thus provided, and the chapter also considers the relationship between the comic strips' serial publication and their shared focus on detailed depictions of talk-in-interaction. In Chapter 2, it is proposed that contemporary Swedish comic strips are so uniquely recognizable in the ways they foreground conversation as to constitute a national characteristic. Furthermore, the salient focus on dialogue creates the conditions for humor to be a recurrent and reliable function of language play and linguistic creativity.

Chapter 3, "Schwädu hupp jöördi hoo," explores Swedish humor as linguistic (self-)mockery, presenting examples of native accents and dialects of Swedish as well as non-dialectal variation. The concept of dialect humor is invoked in analyses of comic strips that derive their humor from poking fun at recognizable characteristics of the dialects of Sweden's capital city of Stockholm and the cities of Gothenburg in the west of Sweden, Umeå in the north, and Malmö in the south. The depiction of the accents associated with these regional dialects is achieved in the visual medium of the comic strip in the form of non-standard orthography recognizable as either re-spellings known as eye-dialects (Krapp 1926; Preston 1982) or regiolectal spellings (Androutsopolous 2000), also known as dialect spellings (Honeybone and Watson 2013). The visual aspect of the comic strip medium is thus used effectively to capture, in written form, the aural features of each accent. The use of eye-dialects and regiolectal or dialect spellings foregrounds the incongruity with regards to standard orthography, in its turn corresponding to the incongruity between standard and regional accents, which is mined for humor. Chapter 3 also presents examples of non-regional variation, where language play takes the form of creative imitation of imagined accents of Swedish.

1.5 Language play in contemporary Swedish comic strips: Chapter overview

Chapter 4, "Gracias de nada!" also highlights how non-standard orthography and visual representations of text serve to depict and co-articulate aural aspects of face-to-face communication. However, while Chapter 3 focuses on language play enacted for Swedish dialect humor and other humorous portrayals of linguistic variation in Swedish, Chapter 4 explores language play in the context of foreign languages used in Swedish comic strips. Examples included in this chapter illustrate language play in the form of creative depiction of Swedish, non-native usage of foreign languages such as Arabic, Danish, German, Italian, Norwegian, and Spanish. The analyses suggest that language play in the featured examples should be considered a form of self-disparagement humor (Zeigler-Hill and Besser 2011), due to the detailed deliberateness with which the speakers' incompetence in the language is depicted. The examples could also be argued to align with the superiority theory of humor (Hobbes (1996 [1651]), in Ferguson and Ford 2008) by virtue of the denigration of foreign languages and the people who speak them, which serves as an implicit evaluation of the 'other' as inferior to Swedish and Swedes. These competing interpretations are noteworthy. The ability and willingness to make fun of oneself, that is, to engage in self-disparaging or self-deprecatory humor, has been found to correlate culturally with generosity, as does imitation of others, which "can be highly insulting and derogatory" (Alford and Alford 1981: 159). Here, generosity should be understood as generosity of spirit or a form of selflessness (Alford and Alford 1981: 157); to be generous with insults, for example, is to extend them to all, including oneself, as opposed to reserving derogation for a select few. Language play in Swedish comic strips that trades on mockery of linguistic variation does not categorically target the 'other' but must be considered to indicate a measure of self-distance that, in turn, is associated with a cornerstone of Nordic culture, namely, the Law of Jante.[2] *Jantelagen*, as it is known in Swedish, refers to a general code of conduct that promotes a communal spirit, downplays individual worth, exceptionalism, and success, and calls into question any single individual's own superiority over others. Derogation of oneself as well as of others in equal measure, exemplified by imitation or mockery of linguistic variation in Swedish comic strips, can be considered one way of practicing *jantelagen*. The tension that is created between dualing interpretations of mockery as self-disparagement or mockery as an act of superiority enhances the humor, allowing the Swedish readers to recognize and laugh at their own foreign language incompetence while at

---

[2] The Law of Jante has its origins in the 1933 novel *En flykting korsar sitt spår* (*A Fugitive Crosses His Tracks*) by Aksel Sandemose.

the same time enjoying the humorous feeling of superiority to both the depicted Swedish speaker and the foreign 'other'.

Conspicuous in their absence from Chapter 4 are examples of the use of English in Swedish comic strips. This is due to the fact that English is so widespread in Swedish comic strips (as it is in Swedish society) as to warrant its own targeted treatment in the remaining chapters of the book. Chapter 5, "In English, please," provides a general outline of the historical and contemporary forces at work that have established English as Sweden's non-official second language. Selected comic strips illustrate how the prevalence of English in Sweden manifests most saliently as code-switching, running the gamut from lexical borrowings to intersentential switches to elaborate code-mixing. Continuing the discussion of eye-dialect and regiolectal spelling, Chapter 5 introduces the term 'interlanguage spelling' to denote respellings that impose the linguistic system of one language (e.g., Swedish) onto a target language (e.g., English), so as to represent a specific non-native variety. This chapter also includes a special focus on the use of English extracted from the media and analyzes the linguistic effects of English-language popular culture on modern Swedish. Finally, the frequent, cross-strip use of English in final-panel, final-utterance position illustrates the phenomenon of 'punchline English', serving to establish English as a language of play in Sweden.

Chapter 6, "Are you completely @#& fucking crazy?" considers the relationship between swearing and humor and targets the use of swear words and taboo language in Swedish comic strips. Examples of the use of Swedish swear words, English swear words, and the simultaneous use of both Swedish and English swear words in Swedish comic strips suggest that Swedish people share a general background knowledge with regards to native, Anglophone norms of the restricted use of English swear words and taboo language, but that their own, non-native use of English swear words and taboo language runs counter to such norms. English swear word usage characterized by playful irreverence in the comic strip context compromises the force of English swear words, while Swedish swear words invoked in earnestness or subjected to censorship serve to retain and re-affirm the strength of these native language forms. Recurring, cross-strip instances of English-language swearing in punchline position further confirms English as a language of play and establishes the pragmatic function of English-language swearing as indexing humor.

The book concludes with Chapter 7, "Face the facts." This chapter includes examples of the use of English in Swedish comic strips which depict conversations between Swedish, non-native speakers of English and other non-native speakers of English as well as native speakers of English. Building on previous examples of English-language play in the form of creatively invoking idioms, fixed phrases, or media quotations, the examples in Chapter 7 illustrate language play as free-form linguistic innovation. This chapter also examines how Swedes perceive other people's use of English, including native and non-native varieties, and how modern Swedish shows evidence of anglification. Finally, the future of English as the *de facto* language of play in Sweden is further explored via analyses that highlight Sweden's role in developing the ludic function of English as a *lingua franca* such that it can be reconceptualized as a *lingua ludica*.

While the Swedish comics artists represented by the comic strips featured in this book should all be celebrated as particularly talented word-smiths, writers, and humorists, their comics should be acknowledged for illustrating how language play and linguistic creativity characterize everyday, ordinary conversation. Indeed, it has been claimed that the practice of language play is not necessarily reserved for the talented (Pope 2005) but is a feature of everyone's discourse (Carter 2004; Cook 2000; Crystal 1998; Pennycook 2007; Swann and Maybin 2007). Even the performance of verbal art is likewise believed to be involved in all language use, in that both speech and writing are, essentially, forms of performance (Bauman 1975; Sherzer 2014).

As serial narratives enjoying regular, long-term publication in Sweden's broadsheet and tabloid newspapers, the Swedish comic strips presented in this book contribute to establishing language play as a common feature of everyday Swedish. Notably, they also capture the essence of language play and linguistic creativity as extraordinary social phenomena occuring in ordinary and even mundane social interactions. In other words, the comic strip texts constitute the "non-institutionalized, symmetrical, and informal talk" that marks precisely those social contexts in which language play "often signposts the nature of interpersonal relationships [and] plays an important role in the construction of identities" (Carter 2004: 62). The frequent and cross-strip instances of language play, linguistic creativity, and innovation in talk-in-interaction together constitute a national and unifying trait of Swedish comic strips. These comic strips in turn represent such practices as characteristic of everyday language use in Sweden, but also promote language play as essential to the performance and appreciation of Swedish linguistic humor. In focusing on the playful potential of everyday talk-in-interaction, contemporary Swedish comic strips highlight the meaningful space that text can inhabit within a comic strip while championing the central role of humor in comics. This book is an acknowledgement of the significance of this contribution to comic art as a whole.

2 Vällkamm to Sviden

Figure 1: Vällkamm to Sviden.   **Figure 2:** Tippikal Svedish kalltjör.

Many people around the world associate Sweden with sexually liberated, blond, and blue-eyed people driving their Volvos or Saabs to IKEA so as to furnish their red wooden houses, where they prepare meatballs and pickled herring and reap the benefits of a generous welfare system – albeit financed by extremely high taxes. The soundtrack to all this activity is, of course, provided by Abba. It is by reviewing these reigning stereotypes that we can acknowledge the outsider perspective of Sweden, which may be fraught with myths and misperceptions. Indulging in such clichéd presumptions thus allows us to orient ourselves to the Swedish context, so that we are fully prepared to embark on this exposition of language play and linguistic creativity in Swedish comics. We can then make an effort to move beyond stereotypes and get a deeper understanding of Sweden and the Swedish people through culture, comics, and language use.

Stereotypes are usually based on some kernel of truth, and those listed above are no exception, since they certainly ring true for some, but in no way apply to all of Sweden's ten million residents. Most Swedes are, however, aware of these stereotypes and can just as easily embrace as reject them. But considering that Sweden is a relatively remote and small nation, it works to the citizens' advantage to have an internationally recognizable brand. Thus, the general tendancy is not just to accept the stereotypes, but to lean into them. The panels in Figures 1 and 2 above, by Swedish creator Lena Ackebo, illustrate the awareness, on the one hand, of the overly-simplistic outsider perspective of Sweden and, on the other hand, the tongue-in-cheek advertisement of native popular culture. Titled "Let us show the world ... ", the two comics feature what one would assume to be Sweden's most admirable products or cultural artifacts, which are depicted in the illustrations and referenced in the accompanying texts. These texts, however, aren't entirely in (standard) English, and thus translations are in order. The comic on the left (Figure 1) reads, "Welcome to Sweden – the land of Björn Borg underwear and Dalecarlia horses!" and the comic on the right (Figure 2) states, "Typical Swedish culture is the Bingo Lottery with the Locomotive, a very popular show host!!"

The first comic acknowledges two symbols of Sweden: tennis great Björn Borg and the colorfully painted wooden horses of Dalecarlia. However, although Björn Borg made history as one of the best tennis players in the world, he is now better known for his eponymic underwear brand. Sweden is thus the land of branded boxer shorts and folksy, toy horses, presented here with an apparent enthusiasm that these products do not realistically warrant.

The second comic focuses on a popular cultural phenomenon probably known only among Swedes themselves: the long-running, nationally televised *BingoLotto*-gameshow and one of its former hosts, Leif Olsson (1981–1990), known by the nickname *Loket*, or "the locomotive". Despite the national success of this low-brow gameshow and its beloved host, it hardly qualifies as culture worth publicizing proudly as typical. It is also, apparently, of little to no relevance to the indigenous person being addressed or, by extension, to the rest of the world.

Indeed, these two comics' shared title, "Let us show the world ... ", appeals to the insider-group of native Swedes (denoted by "us"), demonstrating how to present their country to the non-Swedish world. The choice of aspects to symbolize Sweden, however, serves as self-aware mockery, recognizable mainly, if not exclusively, by Swedes themselves or others intimately familiar with Sweden and Swedish society. In this way, the comics illustrate the self-awareness necessary for self-deprecation.

Many Swedes may be able to appreciate the self-deprecatory humor inherent in the representation of Sweden as a land of celebrity underwear, wooden horses, and tacky gameshows, but it is, arguably, the texts of these comics that most aptly capture and mock the typical Swede. To understand this, we must consider yet another stereotype about Sweden – which, in fact, extends to the Scandinavian countries in general – namely, that its citizens are highly proficient in English. As discussed in further detail later in this book, learning and active use of the English language are promoted by Swedish educational, administrative, industrial, and cultural institutions, with the result that the extensive use of English in Sweden has rendered it, for all intents and purposes, a bilingual society (Fergusson 1994; Josephson 2004; Philipson 1992). It is objectively true that nearly all residents of Sweden who have completed a basic Swedish school education are competent in English; in fact, 89% of a 2006 sample population claimed proficiency in English (Parkvall 2009). However, it is also the case that Swedes may overestimate their abilities in English, or be unaware of their distinctly Swedish variety of English, characterized by nativizations, code-switching, code-mixing, basic grammatical errors, or accented pronunciation. In the *Låt oss visa världen*-comics above, the Swedish reader is playfully reminded of some of these typical features of Swedish English. Nativization (also called loan nativization) is exemplified by the word *kalsongs*, which reflects the application of English morphology, specifically the inflectional plural morpheme '-s', to the borrowed Swedish word (the plural of which is *kalsonger*). Code-mixing is illustrated by the form *poppis*, which is an unadultered Swedish word (Eng: "popular"), but even by *lockomotiv* and *dalahårsen*. These forms represent unsuccessful attempts at anglicizing the Swedish words *lokomotiv* and *dalahästen*. The spelling of the first word, with the addition of the letter 'c' in "lockomotiv", suggests an awareness of a difference between the Swedish and English words, both in orthograpy and pronunciation, the double consonants helping to produce a short vowel sound. The spelling of the second word, *dalahårsen*, indicates that the original Swedish compound and its morphology have been retained (including the Swedish definite article inflectional suffix *-en*), and only the lexical stem *häst* has been replaced by an English phonological approximant by way of non-standard spelling. Code-mixing at the level of orthography is an example of language play that is revisited in chapters 4, 5, and 6.

These examples thus bring us to the most salient aspect of the texts, namely, the misspellings of not only English words, but Swedish words as well. It is not uncommon for incorrect or non-standard spelling to be invoked in comics, prominently practiced in Richard F. Outcault's *The Yellow Kid* in the 1890s and George Herriman's *Krazy Kat* in the early 1900s. Such deliberate misspellings are reconceptualized as respellings, taking the form of eye-dialects (Krapp 1926; Preston 1982) when they are for the eye only but not the ear. In other words, the non-standard respellings of eye-dialects do not correspond to non-standard pronunciations. Respellings for the purpose of representing deviant pronunciations, on the other hand, are known as pronunciation respellings (Picone 2016), and those that represent regional accents and dialects are known as regiolectal spellings

(Androutsopoulus 2000) or dialect spellings (Honeybone and Watson 2013). In the case of the *Låt oss visa världen*-comics, however, it is not just a question of respelling to represent pronunciation, but of a deliberate mixture of Swedish and English orthography. The incongruity of the two spelling systems emphasizes the differences in phonologies, thereby making the typical aspects of Swedish-accented English all the more salient: the pronunciation of the letter 'w' as the voiced labio-fricative [v] in *vällkamm* /welcome, *Sviden*/Sweden, *Svedish*/Swedish; the devoicing of the final consonant in "is" (represented as *iss*); the shortening of vowels, effected by the double consonants in *vällkamm, tippikal, kalltjör,* and *värry* ("welcome", "typical", "culture", and "very"), and perhaps most eye-catching is the use of Swedish vowels *ä, å,* and *ö,* serving to monophthongize the pronunciation of the words *länd* and *änd* ("land", "and"), or to approximate English vowel quality in *ö* ("a"), *vällkamm, Bårg, Dalahårsen, kalltjör,* and *värry*. It is worth noting that the Swedish proper name (*Björn*) *Borg* and the English word "horse" are here both spelled with *å*, emphasizing Swedish-accented English by rendering the former incongruous with Swedish, and the latter incongruous with English. This particular variety of respelling (which also includes loan nativization) is discussed in greater depth in Chapter 5. While these comics orient to a Swedish, in-group target audience, they nevertheless illustrate that humor is largely a function of language play on many linguistic levels not only in Swedish but, significantly, also in English. The aim of this book is to explore the full scale of such multilingual language play and linguistic creativity in Swedish comics.

2.1 Highlighting Swedish humor

In general, Swedish people are not generally inclined to boasting,[3] but they are proud to point out that despite the country's population of only ten million people, Sweden is home to a large number of internationally renowned authors, athletes, artists, environmental activists, directors, designers, musicians, merchandisers, inventors, innovators, thespians, thinkers, and philanthropists – among a growing catalogue of other celebrated Swedes. Noticeably missing from this list, however, are internationally famous comedians. This begs the question: just how funny are Swedes? To be fair, humor is often anchored in culture and does not translate well, and for this reason, comedians may not achieve fame outside of their own national borders (unless they speak English or another world language). Nevertheless, the quality of being 'funny' is not

---

[3] See the discussion of the Law of Jante in Chapter 1.

one immediately associated with Swedes, as explored in Figure 3 below, from *Rocky*, by Martin Kellerman. In all examples following figures, transcriptions are provided. Swedish text (with the exception of proper names) is translated to English; original English text is underlined. Text in other languages is *italicized* or translated, according to necessity.

Figure 3: Swedish humor.

(3)   Swedish humor

    Rocky: Have you ever seen Italian TV? You've got everything that's wrong with the country in a shiny, tinfoil-wrapped package of poop with self-tanning lotion and a hairpiece.

    Horse: But what do you think Dansbandskampen[4] looks like to them?

    Rocky: At least we have humor! The only thing they laugh about in Italy is boobs and black soccer players. *Aahaha! Fotobolo chocolata! Prrsh!*

    Horse: Swedish humor probably isn't our biggest export either?

    Rocky: What? Nöjesmassakern[5] did win the *Prix Italia* for best European comedy program!

    Horse: Well there you go! Then the Italians must have the same sense of humor as we do?

    Rocky: They probably thought Rulle was a gypsy! *Ahaha! E Rollo Romani! E molto humoroso!*

---

4 A live "battle of the bands" program featuring audience voting which ran three seasons, 2008–2010.
5 A 1985 sketch comedy series.

In this comic, the two characters are comparing Swedish and Italian television, with Rocky's dismissal of the latter triggering Horse to question how much someone outside of Sweden could value, say, a Swedish battle-of-the-bands talent show. Rocky then claims that at least Swedes, using "we" to refer to the in-group, have a sense of humor; however, the global appeal of Swedish humor is similarly questioned by Horse. Rocky then claims that a Swedish sketch comedy series (*Nöjesmassakern*, "Massacre of enjoyment") was awarded the Prix Italia, as proof of an internationally appealing Swedish sense of humor. This claim is construed by Horse to mean that Italians and Swedes must share similar senses of humor. Rocky concludes the strip by counter-claiming that Italians must have mistaken the *Nöjesmassakern*-character Rulle, a forest troll, for a gypsy, a position which Rocky animates by mock-voicing an Italian, "Haha! And Rollo the Romani! And very funny!" Rocky thereby reasserts his own understanding of Italian humor, in a way which he thinks is funny: by mocking the Italian people in their own language (albeit imperfectly).

This comic strip thus thematizes the idea that what is entertaining or even humorous in one culture, may not be appreciated as such in another. It thereby acknowledges that Swedish humor, accordingly, may not exist beyond national borders. Significantly, however, this strip illustrates mockery of foreign cultures and foreign languages as a form of Swedish humor and, as the coming chapters demonstrate, it is one that is recurrent in Swedish comic strips.

2.2 Contemporary Swedish comic strips

The term 'comic strip' refers to one object within the medium of 'comics', which McCloud (1993: 9) defined as "juxtaposed pictorial and other images in deliberate sequence, intended to convey information and/or to produce an aesthetic response in the viewer." McCloud's focus is clearly on the image aspect of comic strips, to the detriment of the role that text plays. His position echoes Eisner (1985) who defines comics as "sequential art" and Kunzle (1973: 2), whose definition includes a "sequence of separate images" and a "preponderance of image over text." Meskin problemetizes the sequentiality of image (reasserted by Hayman and Pratt 2005), as essential to defining comics, citing as counter-evidence single-panel comics, which do not present a sequence of images. In fact, not all the comics featured in this book adhere to such definitions which hinge on sequentiality, since single-panel comics are also included among the examples. Furthermore, as many examples in this book illustrate, a sequence of images is sometimes nothing more than a mere repetition of one image, or slight variations thereof, and is thus comparable to a single panel. Carrier's (2000: 74) definition expands the essential features of comics to include "the speech balloon, the closely linked narrative, and the book-size scale." While the first two features apply to the comics in this book by acknowledging the textual aspect of comics, it is not the case that the included comic strips were originally written as part of a book-scale narrative. Instead, the comics reflect open-ended serial narratives that have simply been published at regular intervals as album collections. The contemporary Swedish comic strips included in this book are most aptly captured by Inge's (1990) appeal to a definition of comics that takes into account:

> a number of characteristics, such as its use of an open-ended dramatic narrative essentially without beginning or end about a recurring set of characters on whom the reader is always dropping in *in media res*. Relationships have been established before we arrive, and they continue with or without our attention [...]. The story is told or the joke is made through a balance of narrative text and visual action [...],dialogue is contained in seeming puffs of smoke called balloons [...], and the strips are published serially in daily newspapers [...]. (Inge 1990: 10)

This book explores language play in Sweden's most popular and commercially successful comic strips, all of which have in common the serial narrative format. In other words, they are continuous stories featuring recurring characters and unfolding in open-ended episodes. This serial narrative format is well suited to and greatly enabled by another common element among the featured strips, namely their original publication in daily newspapers. Each of Sweden's national broadsheet, tabloid, and even free newspapers promotes at least one featured comic strip by embedding it prominently within the newspaper, as opposed to relegating it, as tradition would dictate, to the back pages. This promotion of and deliberate alignment with a featured comic strip can be considered a result of the current commercial success and mainstream popularity of comic strips. The readership of contemporary Swedish newspaper comic strips has proven large enough not only to be considered a competitive advantage among newspapers, but also to warrant individual publication in collected volumes. The Swedish comic strip landscape is now populated by highly prolific and best-selling comic strip creators, each with their own series of album collections.

The comics included in this book represent the featured comic strips of Sweden's national broadsheet, tabloid, and free newspapers: *Dagens Nyheter*, *Svenska Dagbladet*, *Aftonbladet*, *Metro* as well as the now discontinued *City*. The comic *Rocky*, written by Martin Kellerman (born 1973), first appeared in 1998 in *Metro*,[6] a free tabloid newspaper distributed primarily throughout stations of public transportation. Between 2012–2018, however, *Rocky* was the

---

[6] Print circulation approximately 525,000 (2018).

featured comic strip of *Dagens Nyheter*,[7] Sweden's largest morning newspaper in terms of distribution. *Rocky* is an autobiographical comic strip, which chronicles Martin Kellerman's own life as a comic strip creator living in Stockholm, but also depicts experiences shared with or observed among his friends and family. Published primarily as a four-panel strip (but also as single, five- and six-panel strips), *Rocky*'s recurring themes include casual, social interactions, romantic (mostly failed) relationships with women, national and international travel adventures, professional successes and worries, and milestone events, following Rocky through his 20s, 30s, and 40s. In addition to appearing daily in *Metro* or *Dagens Nyheter* since 1998, *Rocky* has been published in a series of collected volumes (#34 was published in 2018), and in three multi-year albums, covering the ten-year period 1998–2008, and the five-year periods 2008–2013, and 2013–2018.

Sweden's second largest morning newspaper, *Svenska Dagbladet*,[8] boasts two featured comic strips, *Berglins* and *Stockholmsnatt*. *Berglins* premiered in *Svenska Dagbladet* in 1995, then titled simply *Berglin*, and created by Jan Berglin (born 1960). Since 2007, the comic strip as a collaboration between Jan Berglin and his wife, Maria Berglin (born 1960), is reflected in the current title, *Berglins*, an Anglophonic pluralization. In two-by-two thematically related single panels, the authors depict the mundane, everyday life and existential anxieties and absurdities experienced by middle-aged residents of a middle-class suburb of a medium-sized Swedish city. *Berglins* appears in *Svenska Dagbladet* Tuesdays, Thursdays and Saturdays; comic strip collections have been published in over 30 albums.

Stockholmsnatt ("Stockholm night"), which debuted in *Svenska Dagbladet* in 2005, is also a collaboration, written by Stefan Thungren (born 1973) and illustrated by Pelle Forshed (born 1974). The comic strip generally features one large panel beside two smaller, stacked panels. In contrast to *Berglins*' focus on married, middle-aged, suburban bourgeoisie, *Stockholmsnatt* chronicles the life of single hipsters navigating Stockholm's indie nightclub scene. *Stockholmsnatt* appears in Svenska Dagbladet's Friday edition, and has been published in four album collections.

Stockholm's free daily tabloid *Metro* has hosted a number of comic strips in addition to *Rocky*. From 2000–2010, Metro published *Elvis*, written by Tony Cronstam (born 1969). Like *Berglins*, *Elvis* became a husband-wife collaboration between Tony and Maria Cronstam (born 1970), with their first co-authored album collection appearing in 2006. In panels ranging from single to six across,

---

[7] Print circulation approximately 347,000 (2018).
[8] Print circulation approximately 193,000 (2018).

Elvis chronicled the authors' own lives, including marriage, parenthood, careers, friendships, and even their divorce in 2014. *Elvis* has been published in over 20 album collections.

Since 2013, *Metro*'s featured comic strip is *Lilla Berlin* ("Little Berlin"), by Ellen Ekman (born 1986). *Lilla Berlin* depicts the lives of a set of 20- and 30-something hipsters, exploring themes of equality, feminism, professional ambitions, and individuality vs. conformism in two-by-two stacked panels and, occasionally, single panels. Initially, the comic was set in Malmö, Sweden's third largest city, where Ekman attended the School of Comic Arts (*Serieskolan*); now the comic is not affiliated with any one Swedish city in particular but aims to depict an urban conglomerate. In addition to appearing daily in *Metro*, *Lilla Berlin* has so far been published in five album collections. As of 2020, it is the featured Saturday comic strip in *Dagens Nyheter*.

A contemporary to Ellen Ekman is Lina Neidestam (born 1984), the author of *Zelda*. Debuting in 2007, the *Zelda* comic strip (also in two-by-two stacked panel format) focuses on the eponymous main character, a young woman of the author's own age who tries, often unsuccessfully, to live as a feminist role model without perpetuating or herself falling victim to social stereotypes. Zelda appeared intermittently in *Metro* as well as regional newspapers before becoming the featured comic of one of Sweden's national tabloid newspapers, *Aftonbladet*[9] in 2012. To date, Zelda has been published in five album collections.

Lena Ackebo (born 1950), is one of Sweden's most well-known comics artists. Having begun publishing her strips in comic books in 1984, Ackebo soon received wider exposure beginning in 1987 with intermittent comic strips in *Dagens Nyheter* and *Aftonbladet*. Ackebo's most successful comic strip is *Fucking Sofo*, which was published as a serial narrative in the free daily newspaper *Stockholm City*,[10] during the paper's two-year distribution 2010–2011. In strips of two, three, and four panels (sometimes stacked), *Fucking Sofo* satirized the social interaction among a variety of characters in Stockholm's Södermalm district, specifically the trendy, New York City-wannabe area of Sofo: South of Folkungagatan. The entirety of the *Fucking Sofo* comic strip was published in an album collection, followed by a sequel, *Vi ses i Sofo* ("See you in Sofo"). Ackebo's various comics have been published in a total of ten album collections.

The comic strips of Martin Kellerman, Jan and Maria Berglin, Tony and Maria Cronstam, Stefan Thungren and Pelle Forshed, Ellen Ekman, Lina Neidestam, and Lena Ackebo that are featured in this book have all been first published as

---

9 Print circulation approximately 416,000 (2018).
10 Print circulation approximately 366,000 (2010).

newspaper comic strips in the serial narrative format and all chronicle the creators' own lives and personal observations, including the events of friends and family members as well as people in the authors' immediate vicinity. The range of characters represented in the comic strips includes people of different genders, ages, marital statuses, socio-economic backgrounds and geographical placements. *Zelda* and *Lilla Berlin* depict the lives of young singles in an urban environment, alternating between idealism and cynicism as they transition into adulthood and face the responsibilities that maturation entails. *Rocky* closely chronicles the life of Martin Kellerman, a Stockholm-based but jet-setting, successful, and wealthy member of the media elite, navigating his aging process as an increasingly introverted single male. *Fucking Sofo* and *Stockholmsnatt* satirize the absurd social rituals of a variety of city dwellers, including the homeless and working-class interacting with the middle- and upper-class as a result of gentrification. *Berglins* and *Elvis*, both of which are authored by husband and wife teams, center around the quotidian trials of rural, middle-class, middle-aged and married couples and parents.

2.3 A comic a day

The reigning popularity, prominence, and success of contemporary Swedish comic strips can rightly be considered a function of their newspaper affiliations. For a comic strip to be featured in a daily newspaper is an obvious contributor to establishing a wide readership, even if it is not a prerequisite for success. In other words, affiliation and daily publication alone do not guarantee a devoted audience, but these conditions enable comic strip writers themselves to cultivate a readership by developing story arcs that involve the reader and encourage a commitment to the narrative. One specific type of such serial comic strips is the 'serial story strip' or 'serial narrative', a form of comic strip that originated in the 1900s. According to Gardner (2012), the first serial story strip was:

> something decidedly new. This was not a series or a conventionally serialized narrative with a logical terminus. Neither was it a series with self-contained narratives around a recurring set of characters. [... T]here was no logical endpoint to the series [and], in fact, no reason it need ever end nor any economic incentive for the series' publishers to want it to do so. (Gardner 2012: 40)

Until the advent of the serial story strip/serial narrative, comic strips were characteristically self-contained or, as Gardner put it, they featured a logical endpoint. In fact, the origin of comic strips can be traced back to late 19th century illustrated books and stories, whereby a complete story was simply embellished with drawings. The first newspaper comic strips thus also featured fully developed, illustrated stories presented from start to finish either within multiple panels of one daily publication, or within a series of multiple panels over an extended publication period. Such self-contained comic strips are more accurately referred to as serialized narratives (Gardner 2012), to distinguish them from open-ended serial narratives. The extreme version of the self-contained comic strip is the so-called gag-a-day strip, in which the story is contained within one single panel (such as the *Låt oss visa världen* ... panels, above). Serial narratives, on the other hand, relate events that are on-going and open-ended. A common feature of serial narratives is the incorporation of current events into the story line, which serves to assert and emphasize the lack of a pre-conceived direction or termination to the story. In this specific regard, the serial narrative is "ideally suited" to the newspaper format (Gardner 2012: 40), since the "newspaper is the original serial form: appearing daily, open-ended, and with many recurring features" (Hilmes 1997: 82). Gardner points out, however, that not only do serial narratives align with the serial nature of the daily newspaper, but they could also satisfy readers with a continuity that may otherwise prove elusive in this publication form: "The newspaper story was by definition one that never ended; but it was also a form that could guarantee no continuity, as stories were regularly dropped, threads lost in the cacophony of events and political upheavals. The serial promised a way to bring to the newspaper the continuities and structures that the media intrinsically lacked" (Gardner 2012: 46).

Due to their own continuity, newspaper comic strips in the form of serial narratives have traditionally proven successful in captivating an audience. The result is a symbiotic relationship between newspaper and serial narrative: newspaper circulation benefits from the devoted readership cultivated by serial narratives, while serial narratives capitalize on the daily, continuous, open-ended format of the newspaper. It is for this reason that Hilmes (1997: 82) has claimed that "the role of newspapers [...] as important innovators in comic, film, and radio serials is an overlooked topic in media history."

The creators of the contemporary Swedish newspaper serial narratives analyzed in this book have collectively initiated, established, and further developed the genre of serial narratives firmly rooted in reality. The trend towards chronicling the everyday has in fact become so dominant as to have inspired a call for a revolution among Swedish comic strip creators. On March 3, 2011, *Dagens Nyheter*, published *"Manifest för en ny seriekonst"*, a manifesto for a new creative direction in comic strips. The text was authored by nine comic strip creators, who argued for a deliberate development away from the practice of realistically depicting the minutiae of the everyday and towards escapism and fantasy. The manifesto writers campaigned for an explicit abandonment of the comic strip content that has long dominated the contemporary comic strip scene, namely one that is grounded in realism and autobiography. The appeal had no apparent effect, as only more comic strips that chronicle the everyday have emerged since (such as *Zelda* and *Lilla Berlin*).

The newspaper comic strips that are included in this book are serial narratives that can be considered descendants of the groundbreaking autobiographical series *American Splendor*, by Harvey Pekar. As described by another pioneer of comic artistry and narrative, Robert Crumb, *American Splendor* is such an exact chronicle of the everyday that an identifiable plot becomes elusive: "Hardly anything actually happens ... mostly it's just people talking [...] There's not much in the way of heroic struggle, the triumph of good over evil, resolution of conflict, people overcoming great odds, stuff like that. It's kinda sorta more like real life ... as it lurches along from one day to the next" (Pekar and Crumb 1996: ii).

Works in the tradition of Pekar were inspired by everyday aspects of life, reflecting, according to Highmore (2002: 1), "the landscape closest to us, the world most immediately met." Venezia (2011) points out that such observational (and often autobiographical) comic strips are based precisely on 'quotidian-ness' and are appreciated by readers because of the recognizable themes of the everyday that are incorporated into the story. Schneider (2010: 37) has remarked that comic strips are increasingly developing into "a certain kind of work that privileges unexceptional everyday situations; stories that challenge any accurate plot description, often deprived of any special events and inhabited by characters doing nothing more than living out their own routines." Venezia (2011) asserts that serial narratives can and should be described as ordinary, common, banal or even trivial, and argues that it is precisely the aspect of the everyday that most captivates readers.

The *Rocky* comic strip in Figure 4 illustrates this focus on banal interaction, as the female Cat character complains about the inability of her conversation partners to talk about serious matters:

Figure 4: Of course we can talk seriously.

(4) Of course we can talk seriously

> Rocky: Of course we can talk seriously, but at four in the morning after four bottles of wine we're not exactly Aduktusson[11] in "Are You Smarter Than a Fifth Grader?"
>
> Cat: But you guys just goof around all day, too!
>
> Cat: You're so afraid of it turning serious it's pathetic.
>
> Rocky: Jesus, there were 30,000 serious fuckers who talked seriously in Copenhagen for three weeks, what did that amount to? Nothing!
>
> Rocky: Reinfeld[12] raised his hand and, like, uh, <u>we in Swiden tinks it's wery cold and wet all dö time, we plan to set up a gool for 2012 to ördj dö poor cantrys to let us cam dere in dö wintertime!</u>
>
> Rat: They were all, no, we're talking about lowing the temperature on Earth and all that...
>
> Rocky: Ookay, yeah, then nevermind. Is there anyone headed north?
>
> Rat: Share a jumbo-jet? I have room for 748 if anyone's going my way?

As exemplified in this comic, contemporary Swedish comic strips exhibit the hallmark features of serial narratives in reflecting a focus on the everyday, quotidian aspects of life – albeit with meticulous attention to linguistic detail. The depicted dialogues of contemporary comics are inspired by spoken modern Swedish and are themselves examples of current language usage. Journalist Gabrielle Håkansson (2007) predicted that, "In short, one hundred years from now [Swedes] will all talk like Martin Kellerman's Rocky and no one will find it odd at all." This explicit reference to the language of *Rocky*, currently one of Sweden's most commercially successful comic strips, confirms the central role of language and deliberate representation of conversational practices and phenomena in Swedish comics. The dialogues of *Rocky* and those of other comic strips equally devoted to depicting interaction are indeed inspired by and reflect real-life interaction (Spurgeon 2005), but according to Håkansson's prognosis, they can also be understood to influence, determine, and usher in new linguistic trends. The consumers of these comic strips, that is, the reading audience, are thus receptive to the comics creators' exploitation of the affordances

---

11 Gameshow host.
12 Sweden's Prime Minister at the time of publication.

of the comics medium to depict accurate representations of spoken Swedish in conversation.

An acute linguistic awareness is thus shared by both comic strip creator and comic strip reader. As in the portrayal of dialogue in film, television, literature, or other comparable sources, even though it might be manipulated or otherwise adapted to the medium, the consumer's confrontation with it is authentic and should be considered as dialogic interaction (Bakhtin 1984). If we adopt a Bakhtinian framework, then the language of comic strips can be considered a re-worked formulation of past, observed language use which in turn enables and encourages a response in the form of subsequent language use, thereby establishing a mutual feedback loop (Trotta 2010), such that the comic strip creators and their readers enter into a dialogue with each other. In this way, playing with language extends beyond the creators themselves and becomes interactive play.

An appreciation of attention to linguistic detail in Swedish comic strips is similarly suggested in additional journalistic sources, specifically highlighting Martin Kellerman's *Rocky* and Lena Ackebo's *Fucking Sofo*. Both series have been lauded for their realistic depictions of spoken interaction, signaling an appreciation by the audience of the creators' efforts to exploit the visual and written medium of the comic strip to convey oral, conversational features of language. Martin Kellerman has explicitly expressed dissatisfaction in the few instances that his comic strip may deviate from the norm of long, multiple conversational turns among his characters, stating that a lack of verbosity feels like "cheating" (Spurgeon 2005). Lena Ackebo's own insistence on realistic depictions of speech and interaction manifests itself in her practice of "saying the characters' lines aloud to herself to confirm that they actually sound like real speech" (Sköld 2010).

A further, significant feature shared among these comic strips is the fact that they are all reality-based chronicles of the daily lives of their creators, who depict their own experiences or personally observed events and interactions. As such, they can be considered autobiographical serial narratives, inhabiting a literary space somewhere between autobiography and autofiction, the former reflecting real-life inspiration and factual depiction, and the latter representing "a narrative mode that flags itself up as fictional whilst featuring a first-person narrator/protagonist possessed of a name and stock life-experiences identical to those of the author" (Hughes 1999: 111–112). Autobiographical serial narratives are thus comparable to visual diaries, documenting in word and image the creator's own interactions and observations, but also featuring fictional elements, for the sake of narrative, character development and/or humor.

2.4 The central role of language in Swedish comic strips

Contemporary Swedish comic strips exhibit the hallmark features of vérité serial narratives in reflecting a focus on the everyday, quotidian aspects of life – particularly on day-to-day conversations. The prominent and distinct focus on language, speech, and interaction is noteworthy. Actions are minimal and images static; it is not uncommon for illustrations to reveal only subtle manipulations or no changes at all from one panel to the next. The visual and written medium of comics strips is instead overtly exploited and manipulated for the purpose of accurately depicting the structure of spoken conversation as well as both oral and aural features of speech. On-going and structurally complex conversations among the comic strip characters are foregrounded, to the extent that multiple speech balloons can dominate the panel space, partially or totally obscuring the illustrations, and verbose dialogue can be maintained over several strips, as illustrated in Figure 5 from *Fucking Sofo*, and Figure 6 and Figure 7, from *Rocky*.

Figure 5: *Fucking Sofo*.

2.4 The central role of language in Swedish comic strips

Figure 5 (continued)

Figure 6: *Rocky* #2948.

Figure 7: *Rocky* #2949.

The overall purpose of the book is thus not only to explore language play and linguistic creativity in contemporary Swedish comic strips, but also to highlight Swedish comics as sites of innovative visual and verbal practice, as yet unobserved and unaccounted for in comics scholarship. Current theorists either seek to understand text only in relation to image (Bateman 2014; Cohn 2013; Magnussen 2000; Saraceni 2003; Varnum and Gibbons 2001), or outright privilege the image (Duncan 2012; Lefèvre 2009; Magnussen 2000), aligning with Groensteen's (2007: 8) assertion of its preeminence, since, "*except on rare occasions*, in comics it occupies a more important space than that which is reserved for writing" (emphasis added). Contemporary Swedish comic strips, however, are those rare occasions. The obvious images, i.e., the panel illustrations, are static and unchanging from panel to panel. It is the text, i.e., talk-in-interaction presented in speech balloons, which drives the narrative and dominates the panels. Rare as this notable deviation is on the international comics landscape, it is in fact common to Sweden's newspaper strips, as this book establishes.

Sweden's contemporary serial narratives are definitively episodic, open-ended dramatic narratives, unfolding on a daily basis on the pages of a newspaper. Particularly noteworthy, however, is their overt focus on language. As such, the Swedish comic strips included in this book defy easy categorization according to current comics scholarship. Namely, the reigning American, Asian, and Franco-Belgian traditions of comics studies do not adequately account for the text, image, and panel layouts that characterize Sweden's most commercially successful, contemporary comic strips. This is due to a singular phenomenon: the dominance of what McCloud (1993) refers to as moment-to-moment panel transitions. One of six categories of transitions identified by McCloud, moment-to-moment panel transitions (MMPTs) show only subtle manipulations in the panels or no changes at all between them, resulting in a deliberate marginalization of the depiction of physical action or changes in setting. The inclusion of MMPTs is rare or even non-existent in American, Asian, or other European comic strips (McCloud 1993), which instead make use of transitions highlighting variation in action, subjects, or scenes. The contrary is true for Swedish comics, where MMPTs are the norm, as illustrated in Figure 8 from *Stockholmsnatt*, Figure 9 from *Lilla Berlin*, Figure 10 from *Fucking Sofo*, and Figure 11 from *Rocky*.

Figure 8: *Stockholmsnatt.*

Figure 9: *Lilla Berlin.*

Figure 9 (continued)

Figure 10: *Fucking Sofo* trio.

2.4 The central role of language in Swedish comic strips

Figure 10 (continued)

Figure 11: *Rocky* at night.

Even more significant than this recurring practice across a number of comic strips is the fact that MPs are persistent, such that they can account for every panel transition in a strip, and often continue over several strips, as evidenced by the sequence of *Rocky* strips in Figure 12, Figure 13, and Figure 14.

Figure 12: *Rocky* #3436.

Figure 13: *Rocky* #3437.

Figure 14: *Rocky* #3438.

Contemporary Swedish newspaper comic strips are thus serial narratives, often autobiographical, that are dialogue-driven: they have in common the practice of depicting recurring characters based on real people and being textually dense. Specifically, it is through prolonged conversations such as the ones illustrated above that the comic strip creators depict and chronicle their own lives and/or the lives of those they closely observe, revealing an acute awareness of and fascination with micro and macro features of interpersonal communication. All of the featured comic strips exhibit tendencies towards or even salient use of the prolonged moment, which definitively establishes text as their most significant element. This is not to say that image is disregarded. On the contrary, the fact that illustrations reveal only subtle differences from panel to panel renders these differences all the more significant, as they serve to pace and punctuate the dense dialogues. This, in turn, directs attention to and highlights the comic strip's humor achieved through language play and linguistic creativity. The following chapters further explore how practices that are unique to the comic strip medium allow Swedish comics creators to foreground language play via the visual depiction of aural and oral features of talk-in-interaction.

3 Schwädu hupp jöördi hoo

By many of its inhabitants, Sweden is blithely described as remote and oblong. While the country is home to international celebrities, game-changing technology, and forward-thinking policies, it is perhaps these two simple qualities of geography that are most relevant with regards to Sweden's linguistic situation. In Chapter 4, we will consider the consequence of Sweden's location on language contact situations, and how these give rise to foreign language play. In this chapter, we make several stops along the length of Sweden, exploring stereotypes of regional dialects within a framework of dialect humor.

Almost four times as long as it is wide, Sweden stretches over 1,500 kilometers from north to south, resulting in a long expanse of land which is stratified by an array of regional dialects. As can be expected, linguistic and cultural stereotypes accompany each dialect and its speakers, and thus provide fodder for humor. Despite the many dialects of Swedish, however, an outsider could be forgiven for assuming there is only one variant, and it is quite incomprehensible. The reality of this assumption is personified by the "Swedish chef", an iconic muppet who enthusiastically sputters an unintelligble and non-sensical form of the Swedish language, a linguistic charicature that mocks its melodic intonation and the particularly non-Anglophonic lexicon and phonology. This perspective of Swedish is not unfamiliar to Swedes, as illustrated in Figure 15 below, from Martin Kellerman's *Rocky*, in which Rocky and two friends are seated at a Chinese restaurant when Rocky assumes the role of a child to pose a question to one of his friends.

Figure 15: Schwädu hupp jöördi hoo.

(15) Schwädu hupp jöördi hoo

> (Rocky): Dad, what does tjingtjong mean?
>
> (Dog 1): I don't know …
>
> Rocky: No, no one knows, but it's weird because it's the only word you know in Chinese but no one knows what it means!
>
> Dog 1: But is it a word? Isn't it just a racist imitation-word for how Chinese people sound to Western ears?
>
> Dog 1: Like the Swedish chef? There's probably a kid sitting around China now and asking his dad, "Do you know any Swedish? What does "schwädu hupp jöördi hoo"" mean?
> Rocky: No, what the heck! Didn't you hear the song? Tjing tjong tjing tjing tjong! That was the refrain, loud and clear!
>
> Dog 1: Now I've googled it, and there's no such word! With a little imagination it could be 'star bear' in Mandarin, but above all it's a racist term used by racists like you!
>
> Rocky: Okay, but what does it say about schwädu hupp jöördi hoo then?

In this strip, Kellerman provides both an insider and outsider perspective of language, using the trio's outsider perspective of Chinese ultimately to challenge and poke fun at Rocky's (and, by extension, the readers') insider perspective of Swedish. The nonsense phrase "schwädu hupp jöördi hoo" is as much a charicature of Swedish as "tjing tjong" is of Chinese, prompting the Swedish readers to acknowledge, question, and, ideally, laugh at the linguistic stereotypes they hold or may themselves be subject to. For the purpose of this chapter, example (15) initiates an exploration of language play to depict dialectal and even non-dialectal varieties of Swedish. Throughout the remainder of the chapter, language play and linguistic creativity are shown to enregister various linguistic forms as particular to Swedish dialects, especially from the perspective of an outgroup member. We begin the exploration of Swedish dialects by first establishing the Stockholm dialect as the norm (at least within comics) from which others notably deviate.

3.1 Sweden's linguistic capital

Before embarking on an investigation of the humorous depiction of regional dialects in contemporary, Swedish comic strips, it is necessary to establish a point of departure. The newspapers which carry the comics featured in this book are all Stockholm-based, as are several of the comics themselves, for example, *Stockholmsnatt* and *Fucking Sofo* explicitly reference the Stockholm setting in their titles. The comic strip *Rocky* is also notable for its connection to Stockholm, with Martin Kellerman having won the Bern award in 2009 for "his valuable contribution to the depiction of Stockholm's culture and nature, its institutions and its development, or other forms of Stockholm life" (Thorén 2009) and the Bellman award in 2010 for his efforts in highlighting the city of Stockholm in his art (*Göteborgs Posten* 2010).

With the exception of *Berglins*, which is loosely set in the creators' home of Gävle, the remaining comics are not tied to any one place, an aspect that is further established by the fact that none is written in any particular regional dialect. Instead, the characters of *Elvis*, *Lilla Berlin*, and *Zelda* inhabit larger, urban milieux (although size, here, is relative to Sweden's modest scale) and employ a *storstadsdialekt*, a big-city dialect, with few to no identifiable regional characteristics. The cross-comic strip predominance of standard variety usage allows for regional dialects (or other non-standard features) to appear all the more salient when they are indeed used, and further establishes the association of the standard variety with the capital city and its residents' style of speech. There is thus good reason for people to conflate 'Stockholmish' with standard Swedish, and contemporary newspaper comic strips can be said to facilitate this process. It is no wonder, then, that journalist Gabrielle Håkansson predicted a lasting effect of one example of comic-strip Swedish, namely, the language of *Rocky*, on the national standard in her 2007 article, claiming "*Rocky talar framtidens svenska*": Rocky speaks the Swedish language of the future.

Stockholm is not only Sweden's capital city, but Scandinavia's most populous as well, boasting a current population of over 1,500,000 people. Its status as the cultural, political, and economical center of Sweden is obvious, and it follows that the importance of this position awards the Stockholm dialect an undeniable element of prestige. Speakers of 'Stockholmish' or *stockholmska*, as the Stockholm dialect is known in Swedish, are considered modern, cool, urbane, and even haughty (Lindström and Hellberg 2006). Furthermore, language trends and linguistic change tend to originate in Stockholm, and from there, they eventually reach the rest of the country. Often, wide-spread adoption of features of the Stockholm dialect results in their inclusion in the national standard variety, *rikssvenska*.

While all of the featured comic strips tend to depict informal, face-to-face conversation and colloquialisms, Lena Ackebo's *Fucking Sofo* stands out as a singular exception to the general practice of using standard Swedish to do so. Throughout her comic art, Ackebo consistently employs non-standard spellings to depict the aural aspects of her characters' face-to-face interactions, as illustrated below in an excerpt from *Fucking Sofo*. Figure 16 features the first two panels of Figure 10 from Chapter 2, in which three young women interact. The transcription provides the original version, a standard Swedish version for comparison (italicized and in brackets, with differences underlined), as well as the English translation.

Figure 16: Who now?

(16) Who now?

>Speaker 1: Dom var ju där på missommar å de va ju på nån **ö** typ! [*De var ju där på midsommar och det var ju på nån **ö** typ!*]
>They were there on Mid-summer and it was on like some **island**!

>Speaker 2: Vicka då? [*Vilka då?*]
>Which ones now?

>Speaker 1: Pam å dom. De va jättemycke folk där som sov öv- [*Pam och dem. Det var jättemycket folk där som sov öv-*]
>Pam and them. There was a bunch of people there who slept ov-

>Speaker 2: Å va har **han** me **de** å göra?! [*och vad har **han** med det att göra?!*]
>And what does **he** have to do with **that**?

>Speaker 1: Vicken **han**? [*Vilken han?*]
>Which **he**?

>Speaker 2: Han me **båten**! [*Han med **båten**!*]
>The he with **the boat**!

Speaker 3: Vem då? [*Vem då?*]
Who now?

Speaker 1: Ja de va ju på hans båt å då kan han väl knappast bo i **Italien**! Pluss att han-
[*Ja det var ju på hans på och då kan han väl knappast bo i **Italien**! Plus att han-*]
Yeah it was his boat and so he can hardly live in **Italy**! Plus he-

Speaker 2: Amen är du **dum**! Man kan ja va ifrån Italien även fast man bor i Sverige!
[*Ah men är du **dum**! Man kan ja vara ifrån Italien även fast man bor i Sverige!*]
Oh man how **stupid** you are! Of course you can be from Italy even if you live in Sweden!

Speaker 1: Amen då pratar man väl knappast på svensk- [*Ah men då pratar man väl knappast på svensk-*]
Oh well then you hardly speak Swed-

Speaker 2: Amen gud han kan väl **lära** sej!! [*Ah men gud han kan väl **lära** sig!!*]
Oh my god you can **learn**!!

Speaker 1: Vadå? [*Vad då?*]
What?

Speaker 2: **Svenska**! [*Svenska!*]
Swedish!

Speaker 3: Är det nån man känner? [*Är det någon man känner?*]
Is this anyone I know?

Ackebo's efforts to accurately depict spoken dialogue can be favorably compared to conventions of linguistic transcription. For example, Kotsinas' (1994: 320) transcriptions in her study of youth speak in Stockholm include the following except, spoken by a female highschool student from a northern suburb of Stockholm:

Man e elegant strikt klädd å går omkring på stan å då, ja vet 'nte. Ja tycker de e kul å va lite, overclass på nå sätt, prata lite finare, inte stå å svära å så här. Ja har ingen lust å sätta på mej ett par pyjamasbyxer å gå omkring å svära på gatan å, dricka öl faktist, de e bara e så. Om man går omkring på stan me en kompis å så där så kanske man, typ tittar ner på dom som går omkring i pyjamasbyxer å tycker att "Vicke slödder!" på nåt sätt.[13]

---

[13] You're elegantly dressed and walking around town and then, I dunno. I think it's fun to be a little, overclass somehow, talk a little nicer, don't just stand and swear and all. I don't feel like putting on pajama pants and walking around swearing on the streets and drinking beer actually,

Particularly notable in the comparison between Ackebo's text and the transcript is the shared practice of writing *de* (nominative "they") as *dom*; *och* and *att* ("and" and infinitive "to") as *å*; *det* ("it") as *de*; *vilka, vilken/vilket* (plural and singular (masculine/neuter) adjectival "which") as *vicka* and *vicke*; *med* ("with") as *me*; and *mig/dig/sig* (1st, 2nd, 3rd person reflexive pronouns) as *mej/dej/sej*. While the first member of this list illustrates the pronunciation of subject-form *de* [de] as object form *dem* (pronounced [dom]), the remaining examples reflect the tendency towards final consonant deletion in colloquial pronunciation.

Both the *Fucking Sofo*-comic and the transcription extract illustrate eye-dialect, referring to the use of non-standard spelling that does not correspond to non-standard pronunciation (Honeybone and Watson 2013, Krapp 1926, Picone 2016, Preston 1982). Such spellings "make use of a language's accepted sound-spelling correspondences in an unconventional way, to represent a pronunciation which is widespread in the area where the text is produced" (Honeybone and Watson 2013: 313) and thus "look strange but [...] on closer inspection do not signal a pronunciation deviant from general norms [...]" (Schneider 2011: 93). Here, it is important to consider vernacular norms, as the eye-dialect corresponds to common colloquial pronunciations. At times, these nevertheless deviate somewhat from prescriptive, standard pronunciations. When non-standard spelling is used to represent such noticeable deviations from standard pronunciation, it is referred to as pronunciation respellings (Picone 2016); regiolectal spellings (Androutsopoulos 2000) or dialect spellings (Honeybone and Watson 2013) represent the systematic pronunciation patterns of regional accents and dialects.

Both the *Fucking Sofo*-comic and the transcription extract also include the discourse particle *typ*, which can be compared to the conversational use of English-language discourse particle "like". Yet another similarity between example (16) and Kotsinas' transcript is the sociodemographics of the featured speakers, namely young women from a northern suburb of Stockholm. While no explicit demographic background is provided for the three female characters depicted in example (16), the fact that they all have long blond hair, wear heavy make-up, follow a similar dress-code, and speak in precisely the same way that Kotsinas' subjects do triggers an upper-class, suburban stereotype that sets the women in stark contrast to the appearance and speech style of the stereotypical residents of the Södermalm Sofo-district. Figure 17 illustrates this contrast. In this strip, the characters Ullis and Lotta are seated at an outside table of a restaurant, when they are accosted by

---

that's just the way it is. If you go around town with a friend and like that then maybe someone, like, looks down on them walking around in pajama pants and thinks, "What trash!" somehow.

3.1 Sweden's linguistic capital — 41

Jörgen, a Sofo-fixture known for imploring other guests to treat him to beer. In the transcript below, the Swedish dialogue is translated, but the colloquial features are underlined.

Figure 17: Östermalm.

(17) Östermalm

> Ullis: Just go away
>
> Jörgen: What the hell one only wants to hang out a little <u>with</u> **mature** <u>women</u> a Friday night! <u>It</u>'s really only **14-year-olds** out and shaking their asses nowadays.
>
> Jörgen: Old hags in <u>your</u> age just sit the <u>hell</u> at home <u>with</u> curlers <u>and</u> corsets <u>and</u> guzzle box wine <u>and</u> suck on menthol cigarettes in some ugly fucking Ikea sofa that <u>they</u> bought on an installment pl-
>
> Lotta: Yeah the <u>ones</u> **you** know!
>
> Jörgen: Listen if you don't want to <u>mix it up</u> <u>with</u> people you shouldn't <u>sit yourselves down</u> at a joint like this!
>
> Jörgen: Go home to <u>Östermalm</u>! Fucking <u>upper</u>-class hags!

Throughout the *Fucking Sofo* comics, the Stockholm dialect is quite faithfully depicted via regiolectal spelling, with the most common examples including function words such as *me* instead of *med* ("with"), *de* instead of *det* ("it"), *å* instead of *och* ("and"), *mej/dej/sej* instead of *mig/dig/sig* (1st, 2nd, 3rd person reflexive pronouns), or *dom* instead of *de* or *dem* ("they", "them"). In the strip above, there are also lexical examples of the Stockholm dialect, such as the use of *fjortisar* (literally "14-year-olds", but corresponding to "teenyboppers"), which illustrates the tendency for speakers of *stockholmska* to clip words, such as *fjortonåring* and add the diminutive ending *-is*. This process of suffixation stems from Latin, and most commonly occurs in Swedish place names, although the productivity of the -*is* ending makes it overall one of the most frequent word formation processes in *stockholmska* and, consequently, in standard Swedish (Lindström and Hellberg 2006). The word for women, *kvinnor*, is written as *kvinner* in the comic strip, illustrating the tendency for the plural suffixes -*or* and -*ar* to both be neutralized and supplanted by a third plural suffix, -*er*.

Further examples of the Stockholm dialect are words or phrases such as *för fan*, *Östermalm*, and *överklass*, the spellings of which illustrate a consistent omission of the [r]-sound. This repeated phonological pattern combined with the mention of the Östermalm district and the upper class manages to emphasize the juxtaposition of two socioeconomically different regions of inner-city Stockholm. Sweden's capital city is namely divided into several districts which are north, south, east and west of city center: Norrmalm, Södermalm, Östermalm and Kungsholmen, respectively. Östermalm is the most affluent, exclusive, and conservative of the districts, traditionally housing the upper class. Södermalm, in contrast, is the most diverse of the districts with regards to the social class, ethnicity, profession, or political affiliations of its residents. *Stockholmska* is spoken throughout all the city districts, but the Östermalm dialect is known for its speakers' aspirations towards standard Swedish and its upper-class affectations, such as the slightly vibrating pronunciation of the long, high, front vowel [i]. Södermalm-resident Jörgen provides a contrast to the Östermalm dialect with his swear words (*föfan [för fan]*, *jävla*), slang (*fjortisar*), and non-standard accent, illustrated by the series of r-less pronunciations which further open the initial vowels, the low and back qualities of which stand in serendipitous contrast to Östermalm's upper-class [i].

Additional examples of *stockholmska* and the socioeconomic as well as linguistic tension between Östermalm and Södermalm are also illustrated in the *Rocky* comic strip below, Figure 18. Here, Rocky is at a café with a friend, who has stepped outside to smoke a cigarette while Rocky remains inside. They maintain their pre-cigarette break conversation, however, over the telephone:

Figure 18: Söööder!

(18) Sööööder!

> Rocky: Shouldn't you move back to Söder? You can't live up there in Östermalm all by yourself?
>
> Rocky: Everyone you know lives on Söööder. Are you ashamed of us?
> Rocky: Huuh? When you're hanging out at Café Opera on Stureplan with the yuppie-bears and stock market sharks?
>
> Rocky: Then you don't even want to acknowledge us common jokers, roight?
>
> Rocky: But you're a cat among stoats over there, I mean you and I both know that!
>
> Rocky: I don't even know what a stoat IS, but I know that you are not one!
>
> Bird: (reading from his phone): "A stoat is a mustelid, entirely white and oblong with thick fur ... mating is promiscuous, the males force themselves on the females, but do not take part later in the care of offspring ... "
>
> Rocky: (over the phone) You can hear for yourself!

In Rocky's second turn, he refers to Södermalm as "Söööder", drawing out and elongating the central vowel, thereby pronouncing the abbreviated name in a stereotypical way of residents of Södermalm. In Rocky's third turn (second panel), his reference to two exclusive Östermalm landmarks, *Café Opera* and *Stureplan*, is juxtaposed with the phrase *vanliga pajsare* ("common jokers") and an effected pronunciation of the tag question *eller hur* (literally, "or how") in his fourth turn. Finally, the sixth turn (third panel) includes a common, non-standard dialectal feature, the so-called broad [e]. This sound is often used to vocalize the letter *ä*, such that [e] is produced instead of the standard pronunciation [ɛ:], colloquially written as "e", as well. In this *Rocky* comic strip, the broad 'e' replaces the standard *är*, which is the present tense form of "to be" in both singular ("is") and plural ("are"). The broad 'e' is characteristic of colloquial Swedish, but has particular indexical value for the Södermalm dialect, also known as *Ekensnacket*. This term originates from 19th century nicknames for Stockholm, *Storhäcken* and *Stockhäcken* (literally "big hedge" or "stick hedge", although *häck* is also slang for rear-end), the *ä* of which was pronounced as [e] (Kotsinas 2002). So strongly is *Ekensnacket* and its broad 'e' associated with Södermalm that its explicit invocation here serves to contrast this demographically diverse district with the far more socially and linguistically conservative Östermalm. The fact that Rocky is not just talking about Södermalm, but indexes Södermalm via *Ekensnacket* further emphasizes the contrast.

Although the broad 'e' is arguably the most salient feature of *Ekensnacket* and colloquial Swedish (as illustrated by Kotsinas' transcripts), it is only rarely explicitly depicted, as it is here (and in example (19), below), in any of the featured newspaper comic strips. Indeed, it is conspicuously absent from the *Fucking Sofo* texts that otherwise provide a faithful record of spoken, colloquial Swedish. The fact that this singular feature that so reliably indexes non-standard Swedish is under-represented in the newspaper comic strip texts seems to confirm assertions that *e* is decreasingly substituting for *ä* in the Stockholm dialect (Lindström 2010), a development towards standard Swedish. This is evidence that the cross-comic strip use of the standard, i.e., *rikssvenska*, peppered with features of the *stockholmska* dialect serves to render depictions of other, non-standard ways of speaking all the more salient in comparison. The remainder of this chapter thus focuses on examples of non-standard Swedish, exploring the relationship between language play and sociolinguistic variation.

3.2 Sweden's Mark Twain?

With a 20-year (1998–2018) production period of the daily, serial narrative comic strip *Rocky*, Martin Kellerman's oeuvre represents a large corpus of conversations illustrating a number of national dialects, non-standard variations, and foreign languages. It is not only the fact that a wide range of linguistic varieties feature saliently in the *Rocky*-comics, but also that they are mined for humor that make them suitable for an analysis of language play. As illustrated above, language play and linguistic creativity are present first and foremost in the visual representation of the stereotypical aural and oral aspects of spoken language: the use of non-standard orthography in the form of eye-dialect, pronunciation respellings, and dialect spellings creates an incongruity that ultimately contributes to the humor of a comic strip. However, Martin Kellerman's pronounced engagement with language and linguistic variation in the *Rocky*-comics extends beyond mere representation to include overt observation of and commentary on linguistic cultures and language users. Kellerman's scrutinous depictions cover regional dialects as well as a range of non-dialectal variation, such as baby-talk, jibberish, foreign accents, or even speech by the hearing impaired. His ear for noticing aural distinctions and his talent for depicting them visually provide a fruitful foundation for language play, but it is Kellerman's combination of wonder and irreverence with regards to linguistic systems and language usage that establish him as a dialect humorist in the same vein as Mark Twain, according to Barrett's

(2000) linguistic analysis of Twain's dialect humor. By way of establishing Twain as a suitable target for dialect humor analysis, Barrett claims the following:

> While arguably the best humorist [the US] has to offer, Twain demonstrated a linguistic aptitude unsurpassed in American literature. Because of his keen awareness of the phenomenon of language, Twain's work serves to offer a wide corpus of a variety of dialects and linguistic variations, the majority of which are designed to elicit humor. [...] Twain's musings about language in general [...] are most valuable because of his talented ear and ability to transform the spoken elements of language to a written medium. It is this transformation which is of utmost importance because of Twain's admitted use of the oral storytelling tradition upon which he based much of his writing. Twain [...] was particularly conscious of the invaluable role of his acuity with language, whether it be English or other languages, and of the English vernacular. (Barrett 2000: 48)

With little to no qualification necessary, Barrett's characterization of Mark Twain can be applied to Martin Kellerman as the author of *Rocky*. The *Rocky*-comics showcase Kellerman's noteworthy ability to capture in the written medium, and thereby visually depict, the aural aspects of spoken language. While Kellerman is hardly alone among his contemporaries to possess this acuity with regards to language, he must be singled out for his practice of not just incorporating linguistic variation in his comics, but also writing explicitly about language and linguistic variation, a result, perhaps, of his own extensive domestic and international travel, which manifests itself in comic strip dialogues as insightful observations via humorous renderings of – as well as commentary on – different speakers and different ways of speaking. The content of the *Rocky*-comic strips is also reminiscent of oral story-telling. Indeed, similar to Twain's admission, Kellerman has admitted that his *Rocky*-comic strips serve as recordings of the stories told by Kellerman himself and his friends during informal, social interaction (Beers Fägersten 2017c). Because of the sheer range of linguistic variation the strip dialogues feature (from regional Swedish dialects to imagined languages), language play will be explored exclusively through the *Rocky*-comics in the remainder of this chapter.

3.3 Dialect humor

In Chapter 2, contemporary Swedish comic strips were shown to have in common the recurrent use of prolonged moment-to-moment panel transitions (MMPTs). The over-representation of MMPTs, it is argued, is due to the cross-comic strip focus on text in the form of talk-in-interaction. Image is of secondary importance, but the tendency for illustrations to remain static and generally unchanged throughout all panels of a strip renders salient the most minimal of changes, and, significantly, highlights the preponderance of text in the form of dialogue. Contemporary Swedish comic strips are thus dialogue-driven and as such, it is not only the content of the dialogue but also its form which provides a strip's plot and punchline. In the remainder of this chapter, humor in *Rocky* is explored as a function of both the depiction and mockery of non-standard language and its users. Specifically, depictions of regional dialects, foreign languages, and non-standard usages are proposed as forms of dialect humor, referring to:

> a way of creating humor by using language in a way that highlights non-standardized aspects of ways of speaking that are associated with particular groups of people. Selected features from all aspects of the linguistic system, ranging from accent to word choice to grammar to discourse patterns, can be assembled in an imitation of a speaker of a particular dialect.
> (Davies 2014: 201–202)

In this definition, it is important to note the phrase "selected features from all aspects of *the* linguistic system" (emphasis added), suggesting that dialect humor is monolingual in nature. Davies notes that the phenomenon of dialect humor is "widespread" and "probably universal"; nevertheless, most of the existing academic research on dialect humor focuses on varieties and dialects of English. Barrett's (2000) study on dialect humor in American English is no exception, but in this chapter, her framework for linguistic analysis of dialect humor is applied to the use of Swedish dialects and non-standard varieties in the context of serial narrative comic strips.

Barrett's use of the term 'dialect' refers to both social and regional varieties of a single language, which in her study is American English. Her definition of dialect humor is similar to Davies', in that non-standardized aspects of language are highlighted, but the demographic aspect of dialect humor is emergent only through the merging of linguistic and/or literary aspects of dialect, which comprise a taxonomy of five components: comic narrative, dialect joke, dialect mixing, dialect clash, and dialect mimicry. Comic narrative is a literary representation of dialect humor based on traditions of oral story-telling; the dialect joke is a linguistic and literary representation of dialect humor based on language play, homophones, and puns; dialect mixing is a mostly linguistic representation of dialect humor that exploits contrasts in varieties of a single language or of two or more different languages; dialect clash is not attributed any explicit linguistic or literary representation, but refers to dialect humor resulting from miscommunication caused by differences in dialects or varieties of a single language; finally, dialect mimicry is a strictly linguistic representation of dialect humor that trades on stereotypes.

As on-going, daily, serial narratives with a focus on depicting face-to-face interaction, the *Rocky*-comics do present characteristics of oral story-telling. However, because *Rocky* qualifies as, in Inge's words, an "open-ended dramatic narrative essentially without beginning or end about a recurring set of characters on whom the reader is always dropping in *in media res*" (Inge 1990: 10), it is not an example of literary oral story-telling, as Barrett (2000) envisions. And while the *Rocky*-comics consistently culminate in a humorous punchline, the strips are not exploited as contexts for the telling of jokes that follow a conventional joking script. As such, neither comic narrative nor the dialect joke is applicable to the dialect humor of *Rocky*. Furthermore, dialect clash, which trades on humor resulting from miscommunication due to monolingual dialectal differences, is not represented in the *Rocky*-comics, although miscommunication due to contrasts in different languages does occur within the component of dialect mixing. Indeed, the remaining components of dialect humor that involve linguistic representations, namely dialect mixing and dialect mimicry, are those in which language play and linguistic creativity can be expected to occur. Dialect humor in *Rocky* is exclusively in the form of dialect mixing and dialect mimicry. Both apply to dialectal variation within one linguistic system (i.e., one language), but an exploration of dialect mixing is reserved for the context of foreign language usage in Swedish comics (the subject of Chapter 4), while dialect mimicry is applied to the depiction of domestic and regional varieties in comics as examined in the next section, as well as non-dialectal, non-standard varieties, as examined further on.

3.4 The sounds of Sweden: West, south, and north

Stockholm, situated on the eastern coast of Sweden, is easily put into geographic contrast with Sweden's second biggest city, Gothenburg (population circa 500,000) in the west, the third biggest city, Malmö (population circa 300,000) in the south, and Umeå, the largest city of Sweden's northern expanse, Norrland (Sweden's 13th largest city; population circa 84,000). These coastal cities boast dialects so readily recognizable that each easily lends itself to stereotyping, mimicry and, especially in the context of comic strips, mockery.

In the *Rocky*-comics, the recurring practice of naming places serves to orient readers to the corresponding regional dialect, such as in the *Fucking Sofo* and *Rocky* strips in examples (17) and (18) above, in which both Östermalm and Södermalm are named and aspects of their dialects are subsequently invoked. Place-naming often triggers meta-language in the form of talk about the dialect or language associated with the place, followed by dialect humor in the form of dialect mimicry, showcasing both linguistic and cultural stereotypes. The following series of examples (Figures 19–23) illustrate how explicit naming of the cities of Gothenburg, Malmö, and Umeå, respectively, prime their reader for a forthcoming depiction of a regional dialect and both trigger and trade on associated stereotypes.

Figure 19: E du go ellör?

(19) E du go ellör?

    Rat: Do you find any flea market bargains on your car trips?

    Monkey: No, it's just crap at flea markets nowadays. Bait to lure in people to have coffee with.

    Monkey: This one is probably worth a hundred, but I burned through fifteen-hundred on a rental car and gas before I found it in Flen ...

    Rat: What, have you been to Gothenburg and back today?

    Monkey: No, Flen is just outside of Stockholm.

    Rat: **What**?! I've always thought it was like near Gothenburg? It sounds that way – "Flyyn? Are you crazy?" [*Flen? Är du knäpp eller?*]

    Monkey: Yeah, if you say it in broad Gothenburgish then it does actually sound like it could be in Gothenburg ...

    Rat: Yeah, that's surely what I'm saying! Is there going to be coffee or what? [*Ja, det är väl det jag säger! Blir det nån fika eller?*]

In this strip, two places in addition to Stockholm are named: Flen and Gothenburg. As Rat's comments perhaps make clear, Flen is the lesser known of these cities and as such, not as readily associated as Gothenburg is with a particular dialect. The mention of Gothenburg in contrast to Flen and Stockholm in panels two and three thus primes the readers for potential mimicry, but also prompts them to draw from their own knowledge of Gothenburg as well as familiarity with its dialect, especially in the form of linguistic stereotypes. The texts of the third and fourth panels deliver on these stereotypes, as the rat mimics *göteborgska* by rounding the vowels in his pronunciations of *Flen*, *eller*, *säger*, and *ja* (aptly illustrated with protruded, rounded lips); using the broad *e* instead of standard *är*; invoking the famously Gothenburgian phrase "*E du go eller?*"; and using the assertive adverbial *la* instead of standard *väl* ("surely, certainly"). This comic strip thus illustrates dialect humor in the form of dialect mimicry, but the humor is also a function of the strip's meta-language, whereby the characters not only draw from linguistic stereotypes (e.g., *e du go ellör?*) but saliently acknowledge the fact that they do so (e.g., "broad Gothenburgish"). Dialect mimicry thus functions as dialect humor not simply at the expense of the target, that is, those who speak the dialect being mimicked, but also at the expense of the perpetrators, that is, those who perform the actual mimicry. Furthermore, by exposing the characters' gullibility and complicity with regards to stereotypes, dialect mimicry in the *Rocky*-comics can also, as shown in the next example, reveal a vulnerability to stereotype that leads to self-sabotage.

Figure 20: Ångörreeed!

(20) Ångörreeed!

> Rocky: What's annoying about going to Gothenburg is that it's so hard to not mimic Gothenburgish!

Rocky: It's the corniest non-humor there is, bellowing Avenyyyn and carrying on!

Rocky: But as soon as you get close and see a sign for the Angered exit your throat starts to spasm! Try saying Angered in Stockholmish, it's physically impossible!

Frog: Eh! "Kenta and I wot, we're crashing in a totally cool pad over in Ångörreeed!"

Frog: Damn it!

Rocky: But in Gothenburg maybe they don't notice that they're being ridiculous, since everyone talks like that? It's more embarrassing when you're in Stockholm and hanging out with Jepson who's from Gothenburg, and automatically switch to Gothenburgish to say something stupid or corny for fun!

Rocky: But mimicking Gothenburgish has become such a huge and natural part of speaking Stockholmish that in the end we'll have switched entirely to Gothenburgish!

Frog: Lasse Kronér will come to the city and be all, "I don't get what these losers are saying any more!"

This comic opens with the naming of Gothenburg, followed by an explicit mention of mimicry, priming readers for examples to come. Unlike the previous example, this comic strip mentions features of Gothenburg in addition to just invoking the place name, including the main boulevard of Gothenburg, called *Avenyn* ("The Avenue"); Angered, a suburb of the city; and Lasse Kronér, a well-known television host and musician, who hails from Gothenburg. With regards to Gothenburgish, or *göteborgska*, readers may recognize the non-standard pronunciation of *Angered* as *Ångöreeed*, illustrating the characteristic *a-å* substitution (Lindström 2019: 117), as well as lexical items specific to the dialect such as *kinesa, störtskön,* and *barre*, and the expression *att haja klyket* (Lindström and Hellberg 2006). But while this strip includes dialect mimicry in panels two and four, dialect humor is also a function of meta-language. Rocky admits a propensity towards mimicry with regards to Gothenburgish and the urge to switch to this dialect to invoke stupidity or silliness. He also acknowledges that one can go so far with mimicry as to, ultimately, wholly appropriate a particular way of speaking, such that the original speakers no longer understand the appropriated form.

In examples (19) and (20), dialect mimicry trades on stereotypes, to which it is assumed that readers have access. Barrett (2000: 66) claims that, "without some knowledge of the stereotypes and the scripts inherent in humor, many will not be equipped to appreciate the intended joke or humor event." Barrett criticizes theories of humor (such as Raskin 1985) that are unable to account for dialect humor outside of the script of a joke, but while she herself purports to deal with the "wider phenomenon of laughing at a dialect or the use of dialect in discourse" (Barret 2000: 66) she only considers the targets of dialect humor. Examples (19) and (20), however, rely on access to two dimensions of stereotypes in order for the dialect humor to be successful: the linguistic stereotypes of the target: Gothenburgish; and the cultural stereotypes of the perpetrator: Stockholmers, whose knowledge of Gothenburg, Gothenburgians, and Gothenburgish is apparently limited to stereotypes. Kellerman's dialect humor is thus a double-edged sword, and as such, it provides an argument for considering dialect humor from the perspective of the relationship between the mimicked and the mimicker.

The next set of examples considers Barrett's (2000: 61) claim that dialect humor via dialect mimicry "makes use of linguistic stereotypes more than of accurate representations of dialects and/or varieties." Examples (21) and (22) challenge this claim, as they illustrate how humor can be achieved via language play in the form of non-standard orthography precisely for the purpose of achieving accurate representations. Similar to examples (18), (19), and (20), dialect humor in the examples below is initiated via place naming, specifically the city of Malmö, the capital city of Skåne (also known as 'Scania' in English), a region in which the dialect *skånska* is spoken. In these examples, Rocky and two friends are on a trip to Buenos Aires. In the example transcripts, all Swedish is translated to English; the standard Swedish translation of the Scanian dialect, *skånska*, is provided in brackets.

Figure 21: Sån läjvnadsgläjdje!

(21) Sån läjvnadsgläjdje!

> Rocky: Did you bring your video-camera? Are you going to make a documentary about the favelas in Buenos Aires?
>
> Dog: No, I thought I'd just record a little from vacation...

Rocky: If you were from Malmö you would have made a documentary about the favelas! Everyone who lives in Skåne has made at least one! Film themselves in tank-tops and hats when they're bonding with poor people and dissing the welfare system, that's powerful!

Rocky: You just have to take the tourist bus and film the poor people through the window, then add voice-over narration in Skånish! "How many Zlatans are there here who have never gotten a chance?" [*Hur många Zlatans finns här som aldrig fått nån chans?*]

Rocky: "But they're happy even though they're poor!" [*Men de är lyckliga fast de är fattiga!*]

Rocky: "Such a love of life! Not like at home where people work and consume so that the state shall be able to pay for healthcare and other crap!" [*Sån levnadsglädje! Inte som hemma där folk jobbar och konsumerar så att staten ska kunna betala för sjukvård och annan skit!*]

Rocky: "They take care of themselves here!" [*Här klarar de sig själva!*]

Dog: How do you delete?

Figure 22: Precis sum i Möllan!

(22) Precis sum i Möllan!

Dog: Seems like a nice city this Buenos Aires! Do you think we'll want to move here after we've been here a month?

Rocky: Yeah, so fucking cool here! Exactly like in Möllan! [*Ja, så jävla fett här! Precis som i Möllan!*]

Rocky: I'm going to buy a house when I've sold my documentary about the favelas! Or I'm going to ask Timbuk to buy a house here, he's a friend of mine! Jason! [*Jag ska köpa ett hus här när jag sålt min dokumentär om favelan! Eller jag ska be Timbuk köpa ett hus här, han är en polare till mig! Jason!*]

Rocky: Jesus, Timbuktu must be the only one who has a job in Malmö! Everyone else works with him in some way, plays maracas in his band or makes videos …

Rocky: He's like Scania for Malmö! If he gets shut down it'll be a crisis for the municipality.

Dog: Will be? It is a crisis in the whole country, I was given notice last week! Do you think he needs a finance reporter in the band?

Rocky: If you don't play maracas it's tough in today's market.

Similar to example (20), in which Lasse Kronér is mockingly offered as a celebrity representative of Gothenburg, examples (21) and (22) include references to professional soccer player Zlatan Ibrahimovic and musician Timbuktu (né Jason Diakité) as Malmö's cultural pillars. The cultural references continue with the naming of "Möllan", a nickname for the ethnically diverse neighborhood of Möllevången which, due to gentrification, has become a center for arts, shopping, and dining. The repeated references to *favelas*, however, in conjunction with the naming of Malmö, conjure up the city's infamous Rosengård district, with a high immigrant population, high crime rates, and frequent violence. The comic strip texts thus plunge the reader into the most basic of Malmö's stereotypes.

Rocky's explicit mentions of Malmö (and references to *skånska* in example (21) and *Möllan* in example (22)) trigger linguistic stereotypes and prime the reader for language play. It is widely held in Sweden that *skånska* is the "ugliest" and "most incomprehensible" of the nation's regional dialects (Lindström and Hellberg 2006). This negative stance can be blamed on the fact that *skånska* deviates markedly from standard Swedish, especially with regards to vowel quality and diphthongization (Lindström 2019).[14] The former applies to a systematic replacement of the standard Swedish /o/ with /ʊ/, illustrated by "dum" (*dom*), "fulk" (*folk*), "jubbar" (*jobbar*), or "futt" (*fått*), and /e/ with /i/, in "himma" (*hemma*), "sjilva" (*själva*) or "fitt" (*fett*). The latter primarily targets the sound [ɑː], here rendered as "jao" (*jag*), "skao" (*ska*), "betaola" (*betala*), or "klaorar" (*klarar*). In the comic text, however, diphthongization is rampant, applying to nearly all of the represented vowel sounds, such as "höur" (*hur*), "häur" (*här*), "däjr" (*där*), "läjvnadsglädje" (*levnadsglädje*), "sjöukvåord" (*sjukvård*), or "peoolare" (*polare*).

---

14 https://www.grundskoleboken.se/wiki/Svenska_dialekter

As seen in previous examples, non-standard orthography in the form of regiolectal spelling (or dialect spelling) is used to depict the aural aspects of spoken dialect features. This creates a two-tiered incongruity: one between standard and non-standard spelling and one between standard and non-standard varieties. The incongruity is able to be resolved (and consequently understood as humorous) when a reader recognizes the dialectal features and the linguistic stereotype. The dialect humor, thus, is a function of the accuracy of representation. However, in the *Rocky*-comics, it is not a question of accurate representation of a legitimate speaker of the targeted dialect, but an accurate representation of the actual, depicted speaker who is mimicking the target: Rocky. For example, the comic strip texts reveal some inconsistencies with regards to representing *skånska*, such as the writing of *här* as *häör* (example (21), panel 1), *häur* and *häjr* (example (22), panel 2). Kellerman's representation of *skånska* is accurate enough for readers to recognize the dialect, but the inconsistencies serve to mock Rocky's ability to reproduce it. The linguistic stereotypes the comic strips trigger thus apply not just to the targeted speaker but to the perpetrator: the comic exploits the idea that while most Swedes share an ability to recognize *skånska*, varying success by outsiders attempting to imitate it accurately is a reliable source of humor.

The examples presented so far illustrate the recurring practice of place naming prior to depicting the associated regional dialects. Linguistic stereotypes have been shown to be invoked primarily phonetically, but also lexically and discursively. Nevertheless, the comics have so far illustrated more of an effort towards mimicry at the expense of the mimickers as opposed to derision of the regional dialect or its speakers. In example (23), place naming continues to signal the coming use of a regional dialect that is similarly subjected to mimicry by Rocky who, however, derides its speakers in a way that evokes a negative linguistic stereotype.

(23) Varför int'?

>Dog: Could you live here in Umeå?
>
>Rocky: Why not? [*Varför inte?*]
>
>Waitress: There's a coat-check right by the entrance...
>
>Rocky: Okay, thanks!
>
>Bouncer: There's a coat-check where you can hang up your jackets... [*Det finns en garderob där ni kan hänga̲ av er jackorna*]

3.4 The sounds of Sweden: West, south, and north — 55

Figure 23: Varför int'?

Rocky: Oh, it's straight-jacket off here? We didn't see that, but can't we drink the beer we bought and then we'll go?

Bouncer: First check your coats and pay, then pay the entrance fee ... It's like that at all nightclubs ... It'll get too crowded here with all the jackets ... [*Först häng av er och betala, sen betala inträde ... Så är det på alla nattklubbar ... Det blir för trångt med alla jackor ...*]

Rocky: But there's no one here! And noone said anything about any entrance fee when we we made our entrance!

Bouncer: It's like that at all nightclubs.

Dog: So you want our clothes and 240 crowns extra so that we can drink the beer we've paid for?

Rocky: Let's go. It's no use making sense. [*Vi går ... det är inte lönt att begripa ...*]

Dog: Could you live here in Umeå?

Rocky: The stupid thing about answering "Why not?" is that you sometimes get your answer right away!

As the largest city of the northern expanse of Sweden known as Norrland, the mention of Umeå suffices to evoke the linguistic and cultural stereotypes of the Norrland regional dialect. Speakers of this dialect are known as socially reticent and emotionally cool (Lindström 2019), but when they do communicate, it is, according to stereotype, mimimalistic, monosyllabic, and no-nonsense (Lindström and Hellberg 2006). The linguistic manifestations of these cultural features include, most saliently, omitted word endings in "bätal" (*betala*) or "bägrip" (*begripa*) (also illustrated in example (23) by the underlinings in the translations to standard Swedish in brackets), the rending of /e/ as /æ/, and the use of *hä* for *det*, "it" (Lindström 2019). The bouncer also twice uses the phrase *sån är det* ("that's the way it is"), which is reminiscent of *så är ne*, which Lindström (2019) identifies as a particular Umeå-ism (Lindström 2019: 271).

The strip's text not only portrays the northern dialect but also presents dialect speakers, according to stereotype, as on-message and no-nonsense, unconcerned with non-essential politeness or niceties (Lindström and Hellberg 2006). Rocky's own, accurate use of the dialect indicates an awareness of both the northern way of speaking and thinking and serves to deride the dialect and its speakers. The final panel cancels out any good-will towards Norrland that was established in the first panel.

Language play in the context of depicting linguistic variation provides, as a general rule, an opportunity for self-deprecation with regards to Rocky's linguistic limitations and/or cultural naiveté, even if the explicit derision illustrated in example (23) is not unusual in the Rocky repertoire. As the examples presented so far illustrate, the dialect humor in the form of mimicry of regional dialects in *Rocky* applies to both the targeted and the targeter, invoking linguistic and cultural stereotypes and showcasing linguistic acuity via non-standard orthography in the form of pronunciation respellings and dialect spellings. Significantly, language play in the form of dialect humor is a function of framing: dialect humor is consistently prefaced by place-naming, serving to prime the reader for mimicry. In the next section, additional examples of mimicry are proposed as further examples of dialect humor, drawing less from established dialects and stereotypes and instead engage readers more actively in language play.

3.5 Visualizing variation

It was shown in the examples presented so far that place naming in *Rocky* tends to precede depictions of regional dialects. In a similar way, non-dialectal variation is introduced by meta-language, such that comic strip characters begin talking about linguistic variation before mimicking it. In the examples presented in this section, meta-language primes the comic strip readers for language play, focussing now solely on accent, again in the form of non-standard orthography. But while invocations of regional dialects relied on Swedish readers' assumed familiarity with linguistic stereotypes of regional variation to decode the non-standard spelling, the following depictions of non-regional, non-dialectal variation require active and participatory reading to decipher the language play. In Figure 24, the strip opens with Rocky recounting information about how cavemen may have spoken in a higher register than what most people believe.

Figure 24: Titti! In mimmit!

(24) Titti! In mimmit!

> Rocky: Evidently they've now found that cavemen didn't sound that way we have believed, with low, grunting voices, but rather they spoke super high-pitched!
>
> Bird: "Look! A mammoth! Let's chase it over a cliff!" ["*Titta! En mammut! Vi jagar den utför en stup!*"]
>
> Bird: Maybe they didn't have their scrotum hanging free back then? Thus the pitch?
>
> Bird: They had to put up with sounding like the Bee Gees in exchange for not getting their sack ripped off by a saber-toothed tiger.
>
> Rocky: When I hear the Bee Gees I always wonder if he coughs like crazy after every song?
>
> Rocky: Just like stay'n aliiiiiiiiiiiiiiiiiiiiiiiiiiiiiiiiiive! Cough cough!
>
> Rocky: Or if he just talks like that all the time?
>
> Bird: "Thanks guys, that one'll be a hit! Now something to eat would be nice!" ["*Tack grabbar, det där blir en hit! Nu ska det smaka med en bit mat!*"]

Much like the examples depicting regional dialects, example (24) can also be understood as encouraging its readers to sound out the non-standard text so as to decode the message. In this example, Bird aims to reproduce (and mimic) the imagined, high-pitched voice of cavemen by replacing all vowel sounds with the high, front, unrounded vowel [i]; the spread 'lips' of the beak and bared teeth provide a visual complement to the aural rendition. The high pitch is achieved textually in panels 1 and 4 through systematic replacement of all vowels with the letter 'i'. While this surely becomes obvious to the readers, this language play nevertheless requires active reading so as to decipher the non-standard Swedish pronunciation and reveal the actual content.

The next example similarly appeals to *Rocky*'s Swedish-speaking readership, demanding an even greater effort to interpret the text. The focus remains on capturing in writing the aural aspects of spoken language, but draws from a linguistic stereotype that may be considered taboo, namely, deaf-accented speech. In Figure 25, Rocky's friend does not want to watch television with subtitles for the hearing impaired.

Figure 25: Nill mattobinen!!!

(25) Nill mattobinen!!!

> Frog: Don't turn on sub-titles for the hearing impaired like you usually do!
>
> Rocky: But I think it's so nice when it says what's making noise in the background, so that you understand!
>
> Rocky: There should be dubbing for the deaf, where everyone talks like the deaf! Batman crashes in through a door and is all, Robin! I'm going to rescue you from the stupid Joker, to the Batmobile!!! [*Robin! Jag ska rädda dig från den dumma Jokern, till batmobilen!!!*]
>
> Frog: Ha ha!

Rocky: Are you talking to me? There's no one else here! Are you talking to me? [*Pratar du med mig? Är ingen annan här! Pratar du med mig?*]

Frog: That there is good stand-up material! You should sell it to a stand-up comedian!

Rocky: I usually draw it in a comic so they can steal it and tell it in Parliament[15]...

Frog: (attempting the accent) I usually draw it in strip so they steal it and tell in Parlament [*Jag brukar rita serie så sno de det och dra i Parliament!*]

While this strip is a particularly good example of how Martin Kellerman actively engages his readers in language play, its lighthearted façade does not diminish the fact that Kellerman nevertheless takes great risks with the content. Not only does the comic strip demand more cognitive effort from its readers than typical Rocky strips, but its content also seems to make the readers complicit in mocking the deaf. The language play so engages the readers in figuring out what is being said that the target of the mimicry is momentarily forgotten, overshadowed by Rocky's talent for accurate imitation. It is not until the final panel when confronted with the frog's casually discriminatory, less successful mimicry that the target of the humor resurfaces. Despite its taboo nature, the language play in this particular example of dialect humor via mimicry allows the readers to take offense at the content, while still appreciating the form. In other words, while not condoning the mimicry, readers may experience that the strip is so funny they had to laugh. Indeed, according to Davies (2014: 203), "[g]iven that an aspect of some kinds of humor is that it violates prohibitions, dialect humor in everyday interaction can be tricky. The humor mechanism can be valued at the same time that the content can be disapproved."

This chapter's final example does not concern any kind of recognizable linguistic variation based on regional background or even a speaker's physiological features, and in that sense does not technically qualify as mimicry. However, similar to example (24), it is an imagined way of speaking, which the text represents an effort to reproduce. Rocky announces that he will start speaking only in vowels.

---

[15] A Swedish satirical news program.

Figure 26: Tired of consonants.

(26) Tired of consonants

> Rocky: I'm going to start talking only with vowels. A-a-ö-a-a-a-e-a-a-o-a-e! Did you understand what I said?
>
> Rat: No ...
>
> Rocky: Yeah, I said, I'm going to start talking only with vowels. A a ö-a a-a e a-a o-a-e! A e ö å o-o-a-e!
>
> Rocky: "I am tired of consonants!" A e ö å o-o-a-e!
>
> Rat: Are you stupid or what? Consonants are much cooler! Vowels are for fucking wimps! Shit. [*Är du dum eller? Konsonanter är mycket tuffare! Vokaler är för jävla mjukisar! Fy fan ...*]
>
> Rocky: No! You're the stupid one! You can't talk with only consonants, that's idiotic! [*Nä! Du är ju dum! Man kan inte prata med bara konsonanter, det är idiotisk!*]
>
> Rat: It's surely not any more fucking idiotic than only using vowels? No one understands what you're yammering about! [*Det är för fan inte mer idiotiskt än att bara använda vokaler? Man fattar ju inte vad du gaggar om!*]
>
> Rocky: What about you! You sound like a fucking idiot! [*Du då! Du låter som en jävla idiot!*]

Perhaps even more than the previous examples, Figure 26 illustrates how the comics medium can be exploited for language play that may otherwise not be possible in a spoken language context. While one may be able to pronounce and even understand the strings of vowels that Rocky produces, Rat's consonant-only utterances would be more likely to defy comprehensible production and reception in a face-to-face setting. The visuality of the comic strip, however, provides the reader with a written form and, crucially, the time to decode it.

Since Rocky is a humor comic, it can be assumed that its artist, Martin Kellerman, aims to amuse his readers. When engaging in language play, Kellerman can be said to be playing not only with language, but also with his readers. The examples presented in this chapter show that Kellerman does so by drawing on his readers' knowledge of and experience with regional dialects, with humor as a reward for recognizing the shared cultural and linguistic stereotypes encased in the language play. Examples (24), (25), and (26), on the other hand, represent greater challenges to the readers in that the language play concerns non-dialectal variation that is not as immediately recognizable (if at all) as regional dialects. Example (24) does not include any hints or assistance for decoding the 'caveman speech', but relies on the reader's ability to recognize the systematic replacement of vowels. In examples (25) and (26), on the other hand, Kellerman does help the reader by providing standard speech 'translations' of some of the language play. The lack of a complete answer key, however, serves to increase the reader's involvement, and thus these strips along with example (24) can be understood as language as an object of play or language games which, if won, inrease the pleasure and enjoyment of the comic strip reading activity. In the next chapter, language games continue, moving on from Swedish to consider language play in a variety of foreign languages.

4 Gracias de nada!

The Swedish language as represented in comic strips comprised the focus of the previous chapter, with the longitudinal expanse of Sweden serving as the impetus for exploring language play and humor related to regional, dialectal variation. Using as its point of departure another geographical feature of Sweden, namely its remote location in relation to the more populated parts of the world, this chapter considers the presence of foreign languages in Swedish comics. The use of languages other than Swedish in contemporary Swedish comic strips serves as a testimony to general linguistic awareness among Swedish people, as well as a manifestation of language contact, especially contact brought about by globalization, digital media, immigration, as well as increased travel and mobility. Although an effort to adopt more sustainable forms of travel is currently being embraced, Swedes have been initiators of social contact via extensive travel to other countries and interaction with speakers of native languages other than Swedish. Indeed, while Sweden can claim only a low annual influx of tourists compared to other European countries (6 million international arrivals to Sweden in 2016, compared to France's 82 million, Spain's 75 million, or Germany's 35 million[16]), a rather large percentage of Swedes participate in tourism and travel: over 80% of the population participated in a tourism trip for personal reasons, and over half the population logged at least one overnight stay in a destination abroad in 2017.[17] One effect of these travel patterns is that few non-Swedes may receive any meaningful or prolonged exposure to Swedish in such transient contexts, as most often another language, typically English, is used in communication with Swedes. However, another outcome of the dedication among Swedish people to travelling abroad is encounters with foreign languages other than English.

In the present the chapter, examples of language play and linguistic creativity in comic strips serve to illustrate the linguistic situation of Sweden, reflecting modern developments and historical remnants of language contact and cultural and linguistic stereotypes. While Chapter 3 considered play and creativity in the context of dialectal variation solely within the Swedish language, this chapter focuses on foreign languages. Continuing the focus of Chapter 3, this chapter's examples are drawn primarily from the substantial *Rocky*-repertoire, in which language play targets a variety of languages, including Arabic, Norwegian, Danish,

---

16 https://data.worldbank.org/indicator/ST.INT.ARVL?year_high_desc=true
17 http://ec.europa.eu/eurostat/statistics-explained/index.php?title=Tourism_statistics_-_participation_in_tourism

https://doi.org/10.1515/9781501505119-004

French, German, and Spanish. Conspicuous in its absence from this list is English. Language play in the context of English usage, however, is so widespread in a range of Swedish comic strips that it warrants its own series of investigations, and is therefore the subject of the remaining chapters.

The application of the framework of dialect humor is also maintained, at least to the extent that the comics are explored in terms of dialect mixing, so as to account for the inclusion of another language for the purpose of mockery. In dialect mixing, humor is a function of incorporating contrastive elements of language varieties, such as differences between two languages, often with the goal of mocking one of them (Barrett 2000). Dialect mixing in *Rocky* thus has the potential to create humor via both incongruity and the disparagement of foreign languages. However, whereas the dialect mimicry explored in Chapter 3 showcased Martin Kellerman's linguistic acuity in the depiction of Rocky's mastery of Swedish dialects, the analysis of dialect mixing in the present chapter highlights Rocky's linguistic incompetence. The examples illustrate how Rocky's incompetence does not manifest as no competence whatsoever (which indeed would prevent foreign language use), but as enough competence to communicate in flawed ways, such that errors create incongruity. The subsequent analyses highlight how Rocky's incompetence in its turn reflects Martin Kellerman's multilingual capabilities, which may prove challenging to the strips' readers.

In the *Rocky*-strips featured in this chapter, the use of foreign languages immediately establishes a contrast with the Swedish language and introduces potential targets for disparagement: the foreign language itself, its speakers, or its associated nation(s) or culture(s). Indeed, in the examples featured, the representation of foreign languages plays into and exploits linguistic and cultural stereotypes that are conducive to broad disparagement. Disparagement humor "refers to communication that is intended to elicit amusement through the denigration, derogation, or belittlement of a given target" (Ford 2015: 163) and is commonly analyzed according to one of two psychological theories: psychoanalytic theory or superiority theory. According to the former, the underlying goal of disparagement humor is to attack an adversary, but the act of managing unacceptable impulses via expressive means that belittle the target both reduces the need for (hostile) alternatives, and results in cathartic pleasure (Ferguson and Ford 2008: 285). Superiority theory is based on Hobbes' (1996 [1651]), in Ferguson and Ford 2008) hypothesis that people enjoy the misfortune of others, which makes them feel good about themselves. The observation of defects in others allows us to feel superior to them which, quite simply, is amusing or humorous. We can also similarly enjoy someone else's observation or mockery of defects in others if we feel affiliation with the observer (Wolff et al. 1934, in Ford 2015).

Foreign language usage (or meta-language about foreign languages) is not invoked in *Rocky* for the primary purpose of target-language denigration. Instead, foreign languages in the *Rocky*-comics operationalize the disparagement of the Swedish speaker of the language, most often Rocky himself. The set-up thus aligns with the psychoanalytic theory of disparagement humor in that a foreign language (or its speakers, etc.) appears to be targeted, but the subsequent depiction of the incompetent Swedish speaker reflects a type of bait-and-switch, ultimately shifting the readers' focus from the foreign language to the weaknesses and foibles of another. The comic strip thus invites the readers to feel amused by and enjoy their own superiority to Rocky, the incompetent speaker of the foreign language. The readers may even recognize themselves in Rocky, at which point the humor can be appreciated as affiliative (Martin 2007), in-group disparagement humor (Martineau 1972), whereby social relationships are enhanced and in-group membership is affirmed. Examples of foreign language usage are presented in the following sections, after which I return to a further discussion of affiliative, disparagement humor.

4.1 The other languages of Sweden

While it should come as no surprise that Swedish is the official language of Sweden, it may be a lesser known fact that this status was awarded as late as 2009. Already a decade earlier, the following five minority languages of Sweden were recognized: Finnish, Meänkieli (also known as Tornedalian), Sami, Romani, and Yiddish. The first three of these languages are spoken by people indigenous to particular geographic regions, while the last two are supported and preserved for historical reasons. With an estimated 200,000 native speakers in Sweden (Parkvall 2015), Finnish is by far the largest of these minority languages and, after Swedish, has long outranked all other natively spoken languages within Sweden.[18] Since completing his survey of Sweden's languages in 2015, Parkvall now estimates, however, that the number of native speakers of Arabic in Sweden is more than those of Finnish. Parkvall explains the shift as a function of an aging and non-reproducing population of Finnish speakers, and a young, multiplying population of speakers of Arabic, who have increased in number in Sweden since

---

[18] Compared to 11000, 6000, and 3000 native speakers of Romani, Sami and Yiddish, respectively (Parkvall 2016). Figures for Meänkieli are more difficult to determine (Parkvall 2015), but one source claims 30000 speakers in Finland, https://www.ethnologue.com/18/language/fit/

2015 and the European migrant crisis. The wave of migration of Muslims to Sweden has contributed to a greater awareness of the ever-increasing presence of Arabic and of followers of Islam, but accurate knowledge about the language or culture may require more time to acquire. As a result, linguistic and cultural stereotypes abound, as evidenced by the *Rocky* strips in Figure 27 and Figure 28.

Figure 27: Hu-alllah mu-hackbar.

(27) Hu-allah mu-hackbar

> Rocky: One thing I've been thinking about: Christians? How do they imagine it really is in heaven?
>
> Rat: Probably fat babies sitting around and playing harp on a cloud?
>
> Rocky: Yeah, but I mean ... modern Christians? They don't see themselves bouncing around on a puff of cloud all day long for eternity?
>
> Rocky: And if they do, where do they think they're going to sleep?
>
> Rat: They probably imagine paradise, a beach with palm trees and hula-girls ...
>
> Rocky: There can't be any hula-girls in heaven? Then you'd have to go to Islam's paradise, there it's 70 virgins for every guy!
>
> Rocky: Christian heaven is just a bunch of grandmothers and dead dogs that you get to be reunited with. Yyyyaaaayyyy ...
>
> Rat: I just say hu-allla mu-hackbar!

4 Gracias de nada!

Figure 28: Alhadr moqtadrrr al-sadrrr!

(28) Alhadr moqtadrrr al-sadrrr!

> Rocky: As always when I'm single, I feel unsure about monogamous relationships!
>
> Rocky: Then when I'm in one myself I immediately get all alhadr moqtadrrr al-sadrrr!
>
> Rocky: But it just doesn't make sense to expect two people to keep the passion alive for years, it's impossible!
>
> Rocky: Should you take out passion-insurance and start passion-saving one erection a month until you're sixty-five?!
>
> Rocky: Nah, that won't work, so what do you do? Yep, you let the passion in a relationship turn into friendship!
>
> Rocky: But now the question is, why not just keep all relationships in the friendship phase?
>
> Rocky: You're friends with a girl, have a kid with her, but then she can be with whomever she wants, for the passion!
>
> Dog: You would go crazy with jealousy!
>
> Rocky: No, because of course you only have kids with friends you hate!

The use of 'pretend' Arabic serves first and foremost to establish both Rat and Rocky as able only to produce stereotypical approximations of Arabic, positioning their lack of knowledge (one that Swedish readers may recognize in themselves) as central to both strips' self-disparaging humor. The use of Arabic also serves to associate the language with Islam (in example (27)) and terrorism (in example (28)). In example (27), Rat's preference for the Islamic version of paradise and his apparent readiness to convert are undermined by the incorrect invocation of

"Allahu Akbar"; in example (28), Rocky's extreme intolerance for a potential partner's infidelity is conveyed by a loose approximation of an Arabic exclamation, conjuring images of radical terrorism.

Following Simpson (2003: 95), these comic strips can be classified as satirical discursive acts in that there is both an imitation (Arabic) and an opposition (mocked vs real Muslim/Arabic), each of which contribute to incongruity. At the same time as the strips manage to poke fun at the Swedish characters' reliance on broad linguistic and cultural stereotypes, they also parody the Arabic language and Islamic culture. In so doing, they testify to the increased presence of Arabic and Muslims in Sweden (as well as in the national and international media) which entails being an ever-more expected subject of conversation, not to mention target of humor.[19] These strips thus continue the pattern identified in the *Rocky* examples presented in Chapter 3, namely recurring depictions of imperfect mimicry which allow Kellerman to position himself (or his friends or even the Swedish readership) as the target of humor due to linguistic incompetence, while at the same time disparaging linguistic varieties and their speakers.

4.2 Neighboring languages

Parkvall's (2015) list of the 20 largest languages in Sweden (according to number of resident native speakers) can be divided into two categories. First, there are languages whose representation is a function of modern migration, such as Arabic, Bosnian, Croatian, Serbian, Kurdish, among others. A second category is one of historical immigration, represented by Finnish, Norwegian, Danish, and German. While Arabic dominates the first category and is now the second-largest language in Sweden spoken by resident native speakers, it is not spoken natively in any of the countries neighboring Sweden, nor is it similar to Swedish or, as a Central Semitic language, in the same Indo-European family of languages. In other words, Arabic is both geographically and linguistically distant, and the number of its non-native speakers in Sweden has been duly affected, compounded by xenophobic and racist attitudes towards migrants (Mella, Ahmadi, and Palm 2013), especially since 2015.

Spoken in Sweden's neighbor to the east, Finland, the language of Finnish would be a good candidate for a large number of Swedish, non-native speakers.

---

19 These strips should also be read in the context of their time, published between 2008–2013, after the publication of Lars Vilks' drawings of Muhammed, but before the Charlie Hebdo shooting.

However, not only is Finnish, as a Uralic language, substantially different from Swedish, the history of Sweden's presence in Finland has resulted in the institutionalization of Swedish in Finland and a much greater number of Finns who know Swedish than Swedes who know Finnish. Instead, as a Scandinavian language, Swedish is very similar to the languages of Sweden's closest neighboring countries, the Germanic languages of Norwegian, Danish, and German. In fact, so alike are Swedish, Norwegian, and Danish that they can be considered dialects of the same language. Each can be traced back to a Proto-Nordic (or Proto North-Germanic) language spoken in Scandinavia between the 2nd and 8th centuries (Hellquist 1948). This language evolved into modern-day Swedish, Danish, and Norwegian, which are now nearly mutually intelligible. Written Norwegian and Danish share many commonalities, while spoken Norwegian is more similar to spoken Swedish. Danes and Swedes tend to find communication with each other the most difficult (Sandelin 2013).[20] The varying degrees of mutual intelligibility between Swedish and both Norwegian and Danish are nicely represented in the *Rocky*-strips featured in Figure 29 and Figure 30.

Figure 29: Ett nei er ett nei!

(29) Ett nei er ett nei!

> Female: Rocky? Don't you want to party a little with me?
>
> Rocky: (thinking) Go away, damn it! Don't you understand that just because the girl I want doesn't want me doesn't mean that I want a girl I don't want?
>
> Rocky: (thinking) But I should do probably, considering that she's surely lying around at home in Stockholm and happily sexing it up! And with laws and rights and morals and ethics on her side, yeah it's fucking awful.

---

20 https://svenskaspraket.si.se/skandinaviska-for-nyborjare/

Rocky: (thinking) But what the hell! You can't get revenge on someone who doesn't care by hooking up with someone you don't want to hook up with, with a dick that just wants to sleep!

Rocky: No thank you! A no is a no! Don't you understand Norwegian?

Rocky: (Just think what a good and morally superior person one has become after all! Ah, love!)

Female: Hey! Grandma! Are you going home already?

Rocky's outburst in Norwegian, in which he rejects the female's advances, implies a simplicity of both content and form: a no is a no. That Rocky then questions the female's grasp of Norwegian conveys to the reader Rocky's own evaluation of the language as simplistic, a position of superiority from which he soon is to tumble. Having briefly lived in Norway during his youth, Martin Kellerman is perhaps not representative of the average Swede with regards to knowledge of Norwegian. In fact, this residency should entail better than average skills in the language, which this comic seems to confirm, with three turns spoken in Norwegian. However, Kellerman's depiction of Norwegian includes specific minor inaccuracies[21] (Swedish *ett* instead of Norwegian *et*, *bäste-mor* instead of *bestemor*) that exploit the similarities with Swedish so as to stir empathy for Rocky as an imperfect speaker. It should be noted that these errors would, in all likelihood, not be noticed in speech, since the orthography hardly (if at all) corresponds to any non-standard pronunciation. In the comics medium, however, where spoken language is rendered in written form, such features must be attributed meaning. As the examples presented throughout this chapter ultimately establish, there is a pattern of language play with foreign languages that serves both to ridicule the language in question and trade on Rocky's flawed proficiency – one that the *Rocky*-reader will recognize and empathize with, and thus be better positioned to appreciate the humor.

In contrast to the facility of Norwegian suggested in example (29), Danish is presented in example (30) as a more difficult language for Swedes.

---

21 Martin Kellerman's Norwegian agent has stated (via personal communication) that, in his experience, Kellerman does not make inadvertent errors.

Figure 30: Ö and consonants.

(30) Ö and consonants

>Rocky: Have you done anything fun since last time?

>Rat: No, but I was in Copenhagen last weekend, what a shithole!

>Rat: Everyone's heads are the size of tombstones, have you thought about that?

>Frog: It's probably because they're Vallonians.

>Rat: Melons are what they are! And you can understand zilch of what they're saying, just ö and consonants.

>Frog: That's because it's another country, Klas …

>Frog: It's funny how you can be bothered more by a language where you understand a little, than by one where you don't understand a thing.

>Rat: Their alphabet is ö, b, c, d, ö, f, g, h, ö, j, k, l, m, n, ö, p, q, r, s, t, ö, v, x, ö, z, ö, ö, center öö!

While Rat issues a series of disparagements of Copenhagen, Danes, and Danish, it is the latter (i.e., the language) which seems to cause the most disgruntlement. Even though it is a question of a foreign language, as Frog points out, spoken in another country, this does not alleviate the frustration that Danish causes Rat as a speaker of Swedish, a language so closely related to Danish that mutual intelligibility should be a matter of fact. Rat's constrastive perspective of Danish is illustrated by his recital of what he imagines is the Danish version of the Swedish alphabet, with the vowels *a, e, i, o, u, y* as well as *ä* and *å* (the third- and second-to-last letters of the alphabet) replaced by *ö*, while *ö* (the last letter of the Swedish alphabet) is replaced by an emphatic *center öö*.

Indeed, the quality of vowels in Danish has been identified as a significant contributing factor to the general unintelligibility claimed by Swedes (Sandelin 2013) for whom, similar to Rat, the dominance of one vowel sound may compromise the ability to register any others.

Examples (29) and (30) highlight linguistic incompetence in the form of Rocky and his friends as imperfect communicators in Norwegian and Danish. At the same time, it is both implied and explicitly stated that these languages are simplistic or unintelligible, respectively, thereby positioning Swedish as the superior language, and Sweden as the superior nation.

4.3 Visualizing the struggle

As established by the *Rocky* comics presented in Chapter 3, language play in the context of regional dialects co-occurs with place-naming, while non-dialectal play is framed by meta-language, both of which serve to trigger the reader's linguistic and/or cultural stereotypes. An appeal to stereotypes is equally essential to the appreciation of the foreign language play in the comics presented in this chapter. However, whereas the examples presented in Chapter 3 highlighted Martin Kellerman's linguistic acuity via non-standard orthography in the form of dialect spelling deployed to accurately depict varieties of Swedish, the examples in this chapter showcase linguistic limitations, inabilities, or difficulties in using foreign languages. Figure 31 and Figure 32 feature Italian.

Figure 31: Al dente.

(31) Al dente

Girl: The spaghetti is too hard!

Rocky: That's called *al dente*! It's Italian and means "to the tooth", or in your case, "to the milk tooth"!

Girl: Do you speak Italian?

Rocky: *Si, prego! Ciao ciao Angelo's cicciolina questa con dicci solstrålen pizzeria e solario, tuttifrutti labero gelato di aglio e olio benito* ...

Girl: That wasn't Italian, you're just pretending!

Rocky: You can't know that, you're just a kid and kids can be tricked all sorts of ways! I could have said I was an astronaut and you wouldn't even have batted an eye!

Girl: What's an astonat?

Rocky: An astronaut is a person who collects empty soda cans and sticks them in a machine that makes chocolate milk!

Girl: No way! You're not an astornat because you have lots of soda cans but no chocolate milk!

Figure 32: Katastrofani idioto!

(32) Katastrofani idioto!

Rocky: A terrible thing has happen in Norway! Do you know?

Rabbit: Are you rapping?

Rocky: No, I'm speaking English so the children cannot understand and be afraid!

Rabbit: But our dad is from Australia, they understand English better than you do!

Rocky: Uhh ... *questa tutti giorno ... Norvegiese mafioso coco bello ratata di isla bonita katastrofani idioto*!

Rabbit: But now neither you nor I understand what you're saying!

Baby: (babbles)

Rocky: *Isch habe nicht allen fakten auf der borden aber das rapport zu siegen das eine vahnzinnisch händels haber ... hänt.*

Examples (31) and (32) illustrate phenomena familiar to many people, namely, the reciting of known Italian words – or words that sound Italian – as an attempt to speak the language. In example (31), the long string of words contained in Rocky's second turn gives the impression of fluency and proficiency, even though some of the words are Swedish (*solstrålen*) or simply Italian (-sounding) names (*Angelo, Labero, Benito*). The utterance is generally void of any meaningful proposition at all. In effect, it is not Rocky's goal to say anything in particular; rather, the recitation is an act performed only to convince the children that Rocky speaks Italian. When, as in example (32), Rocky does want to communicate meaningfully in Italian, it proves to be much more difficult. This particular comic strip was published following the attacks in Oslo and Utøya, Norway on July 22, 2011, in which 77 people were killed. Rocky has apparently heard news of the attack and wants to share it with Rabbit, but because of the scale of the tragedy, Rocky would prefer to encode the discussion in a foreign language in the presence of her young siblings. His first attempt to do so is in English, committing one grammatical error (*"has happen") followed by the non-idiomatic "so the children cannot understand and be afraid." Rocky's foreign language struggles have thus begun, and continue in Italian. Whereas in example (31) when Rocky had no particular message to convey and was free to string together any combination of Italian words, in example (32) the propositional content takes precedence. Rocky's filled pause and subsequent hesitations indicate that he must make an effort to produce a meaningful utterance. Ultimately, however, he resorts to his previous strategy of stringing together noun phrases which fail to deliver the message.

Rocky's third attempt to relay the news entails yet another code-switch, this time to German. Compared to the previous turn in Italian, the German utterance is relatively lucid and allows for a rough translation: "I don't have all the facts on the table but the report shows that a crazy event has happened." A reader versed in German will notice, however, a number of errors in the text, notably misspellings: *isch / *ich*, *su / *zu*, *siegen / *zeigen*, *vahnzinnisch /

wahnsinnig, *das / *dass*; and the inclusion of Swedish lexemes and morphology: borden (Sw. *bord*="table", Ger. plural inflection), händels (Sw. *händelse*="event"), haber (Ger. *haben*="to have", Sw. verbal inflection) and hänt (*hänt*=Sw. past participle "happened"). Had this text been spoken, most of the misspellings would likely go unnoticed, since they in fact correspond to standard pronunciation, e.g *ich* and the suffix *-ig*, both of which can be pronounced [ɪʃ] corresponding to the written "isch" and "-isch". The orthographic manipulation suggests that Martin Kellerman's intention is to make visible these otherwise inaudible foreign language deficiencies, something the comics medium allows him to do.

In contrast to example (31), the filled pauses and hesitations in the third and fourth panels of example (32) give the impression of cognitive processing. The fact that Rocky has sat down and diverted his gaze in panel 4 further suggests that the urgency of recounting the news has been tempered by deliberations about linguistic form. While it is possible that the shock of the Utøya event is the cause of Rocky's disfluencies and difficulties, we must also consider that the act of using a foreign language is experienced as so cognitively demanding as to cause Rocky to lose sight of his original communicative goal. In this example, Martin Kellerman manages humor by addressing an unfamiliar and difficult event with unfamiliar and difficult communication: "Jokes are forms par excellence that deal with situations of unspeakability, because they may conjoin an unspeakable, and hence incongruous, universe of discourse to a speakable one" (Oring 1987: 282). The unspeakability of the massacre is conveyed by Rocky's own literal inability to find the words to recount it. In this way, the character of Rocky is positioned as the butt of the joke, and this self-disparaging humor serves to absorb the reader's own anxiety by providing comic relief.

In examples (31) and (32), Rocky's use of Italian is at home as opposed to using the language abroad, in Italy. In the next two sections, examples illustrate how being abroad in countries where German and Spanish, respectively, are spoken serves to trigger language play. Rocky's more meaningful engagement with these languages thus warrants an examination of their status in Sweden.

4.4 German-language play

Because of Germany's industrial, political, and cultural ties with Sweden dating back to the Middle Ages, the German language was long promoted in Sweden. It enjoyed the status of main foreign language in the Swedish school system from 1807 until it was decided in 1939 that English would take on that distinction, completely replacing German in the Swedish curricula in 1946 (Dahlberg 1999). German remains, however, a popular choice at school as an additional foreign language (generally offered at least from grade 7), and interest in Germany among Swedes is seemingly high: since 2015, it is second only to Spain as the most favored travel destination (Andersson 2017). A renewed interest in Germany is due in part to its proximity, such that for Sweden's southern population, Germany is closer and can be more quickly reached than Stockholm. Another reason for the resurgence is the popularity of the capital city, Berlin, which has emerged in recent years as a tolerant, free-thinking, cultural, artistic, and intellectual metropolis. Ease of travel, attractive destination cities, and even mutually beneficial industrial, cultural, political, and educational exchanges have increased interaction between Swedes and Germans. Still, Germany's role in the Second World War remains ever-present, as illustrated in Figure 33 below.

Figure 33: Sieg heil!

(33) Sieg heil!

Rocky: Klasse and I are going to Berlin tomorrow! We're going to be there a month!

Frog: What are you going to do there?

Rocky: Drink beer and get loud I guess, that must be what you do there? *Ölin'* and *brölin'*[22] in Berlin!

Rocky: It's going to be damn fun, but I'm worried about how we'll manage to avoid telling Nazi jokes for a whole month!

Rocky: Linda managed to say Arbeit macht frei to the whole office the first fifteen minutes of the first meeting on her first day when she was there working!

---

22 Roughly translates to "beerin' and bellowin' in Berlin!"

Frog: *Scheize*.

Frog: I'm sure it'll go well, you're going to have a great time! How do you say cheers in German?

Rocky: *Sieg heil!*

The mention of Berlin in the first panel should prime the reader for a code-switch to come, according to convention established thus far by examples in Chapter 3. However, the reader first encounters a mixing of English and Swedish ("*Ölin'* and *brölin'* in Berlin") in panel 2 before the anticipated code-switch to German materializes in panels 3 and 4. The first two panels thus serve to present Berlin as a destination of pleasure and leisure, not immediately associated with the German language, and removed from its Nazi history as well. This respite is nevertheless short-lived, as Rocky invokes the Second World War in panels 3 and 4. At this point, Rocky's own trepidation about his ability to avoid making Nazi jokes is reminiscent of the *Fawlty Towers* (a BBC sitcom airing 1975–1979) episode "The Germans", which memorialized the phrase, "Don't mention the war." In this episode, the main character Basil Fawlty is advised not to mention the war to a group of German guests at his hotel, but ultimately Basil can do nothing but. Similarly, this seems to be the fate of Rocky's named acquaintance Linda, who failed to last more than fifteen minutes at her German workplace without inappropriately referencing concentration camps, which thus gives Rocky further cause to be anxious.

Nazism, the leadership of Adolf Hitler, and the atrocities committed in World War II are established targets of humor (Bryant 2006; Dundes 1983; Dundes and Hauschild 1988; Hillenbrand 1995; Lipman 1991; Raskin 1992). The act of joking can allow those particularly sensitive to or affected by such trauma, tragedy, or disaster to cope with their anxiety, distance themselves from the event (Smyth 1986), or even exercise resistance (as illustrated by Jewish humor during the Holocaust, Hillenbrand 1995; Lipman 1991). Joking can also serve to disparage those suffering disaster or those responsible for it. However, upon closer inspection of example (33) and the use of Italian and German in example (32), it becomes clear that the overt target of humor is not the trauma of World War II or the tragedy of Utøya; indeed, neither victims nor perpetrators are positioned as the butt of any joke. Instead, it is insufficient competence in a foreign language that ultimately delivers the humor in both examples.

The subject matter of example (32), the attacks in Norway and particularly the massacre of almost 70 youth on the island of Utøya, cannot (as yet) be understood as joking material that is as similarly accessible as Nazism, at least in contemporary Swedish society, despite the claim that "nothing is so sacred, so taboo, or so disgusting that it cannot be the subject of humor" (Dundes and Hauschild 1988: 249). Nevertheless, example (32) does not feature jokes about the trauma or the crimes of World War II; neither the war nor Germans are explicitly disparaged. Instead, the humor of the comic strip derives from the mockery of Swedes who lack communicative competence in German. In addition to the acquaintance who inappropriately invoked concentration camps, Frog exhibits a reaction to the anecdote that is not only a potentially offensive swearing expression, *Scheiße*, but also in an incorrect form (**Scheize*), while Rocky foreshadows his own grave social faux pas by claiming that the German version of "cheers" is the Nazi greeting, *Sieg heil!* Due to the inclusion of the German phrases, the strip gives the initial impression of joking about German history. Ultimately, however, all instances of German usage are recognized as flawed, thwarting any expectations of conventional disparagement of Germany's past, and establishing the Swedish speakers' foreign language usage as the target of mockery, the humor of which is further asserted by the use of German in punch-line position, as much in panel 3 as in panel 4.

The final examples of German spoken as a foreign language focus on aspects of the language that may pose difficulties for the foreign speaker, namely, the system of counting and pronunciation. In Figure 34, Rocky and Rat are seated at a café in Berlin, when Rocky decides to review how to count in German. In Figure 35, Rocky recounts his troubles pronouncing a street name.

Figure 34: Ten ...

(34) Ten...

   Rocky: Let's see now... *ein, zwei, drei, fier, fünf, zex, zieben, acht, nein*... What's ten?

   Rat: *Zehn*...

   Rocky: *Zehn, einzehn, zweizehn, dreizehn, fierzehn, fünfzehn, zexzehn, ziebzehn, achtzehn, neinzehn, zwanzich!*

   Rocky: *Ein unt zwanzich, zwei unt zwanzich, drei unt zwanzich...*

   Rocky: *...acht unt neinzich, nein unt neinzich, hundren! Ein unt hundren, zwei unt hundren, drei unt hundren, fier unt hundren, fünf unt hundren, zex unt hundren, zieben unt hundren, acht unt hundren, nein unt hundren...*

   Rocky: What's ten again?

   Rat: *Zehn*...

   Rocky: *Einhundren unt zehn, ein hundren unt einzehn, ein hundren unt zweizehn...*

Figure 35: They're like vhat?

(35) They're like vhat?

   Rocky: Welcome Gonzo! Was it hard to find?

   Crocodile: No, I took a taxi. But it was hard to pronounce the address so that he could understand...

   Rocky: I know, it's really irritating! You're all, *Paul-Heyse Schtrasse* bitte! They're like vhat? *Paul-**Hayse** Strasse* then? No, no reaction. *Paul-**Hööyse** Strasse*? No... *Paul-HAJTZE* then damnit?

Rocky: He's like huh?

Rocky: Then you show it on your phone, and he's all, aahaa! *Paul-Heyse Strasse*, ookey!

Rocky: I've quit taking taxis to *Sschlesschisscheschh Tor* because of that! I ride to Görlitzer and walk the rest of the way!

Rocky: The Germans are just as anal about pronunciation as the French! Stockholm is great, if a tourist gets into a taxi and says Dröttninggatan, tack! The driver surely wouldn't say "*Dröttninggatan*? Noo, I've never heard of that ... "

Crocodile: No, they say "It's my first day, can you show me the way?"

In example (34), there are several indicators that the German counting system poses some difficulty for Rocky. First, he establishes his incomplete mastery of counting by verbalizing the initiation of his review ("Let's see now ... "). Second, he uses his fingers to assist in the counting process, an action associated with poor mathematical skills (Gersten et al. 2005). Third, he gazes up and to the right, a gesture indicative of mental processing (McCarthy et al. 2008), and one depicted earlier in example (32) in a comparable situation of linguistic difficulty. Rat's own slight variations in facial expression convey an evaluation of Rocky as inept, progressing from disinterest in panel 1, to bemusement, fatigue, and irritation in panels 2, 3, and 4, respectively. Definitively establishing Rocky's ineptitude is the counting itself, and as an additional, key resource of the comics medium, orthography is exploited to this end. As early as the first panel, five of the nine numbers counted (one, four, six, seven, and nine) are spelled incorrectly: *ein (*eins*), *fier (*vier*), *zex (*sex*), *zieben (*sieben*), and *nein (*neun*). These misspellings indicate possible confusion of form (*ein* corresponds to indefinite article "a/an"), language interference (Swedish *en* or English *one*; German *nein* ("no") vs. English *nine*), or the use of the native orthographic system (the letter *z* instead of *s* when pronounced [z], the letter *f* instead of *v* when pronounced [f]). The misspellings persist throughout the strip, joined in the second panel by additional errors in the form of *einzehn (*elf*), *zweizehn (*zwölf*), *zwanzich (*zwanzig*), and *ein unt zwanzich (*einundzwanzig*) and so on, and in the third panel by *hundren (*(ein)hundert*), *ein unt hundren (*(ein)hunderteins*), and so on. The forms *einzehn and *zweizehn suggest that Rocky is counting according to a regular system and based on analogy with subsequent (correct) numbers *dreizehn, vierzehn*, etc. However, the irregularity of the German number system with regards to 'eleven' (*elf*) and 'twelve' (*zwölf*) mirrors that of Swedish (and English) in that Swedish *elva* ("eleven") and *tolv* ("twelve") similarly deviate from the subsequent numbers of the '-teen' format (Sw: *tretton, fjorton, femton* ... ;

"thirteen", "fourteen", "fifteen" ...). In this case, counting in German should be facilitated by positive transfer, and Rocky's failure to realize the similarities provides more evidence of his incompetence. The forms "zwanzich" and "ein unt zwanzich" ("twenty" and "twenty-one") serve as further examples of misspellings which depict correct pronunciation, corresponding to German ending *-ig* realized as post-alveolar fricative [ɪʃ] and the devoicing of word-final d in *und*.

Panel three reveals a noteworthy deviation from the prolonged moment-to-moment panel transition. It is in this panel that the reader realizes that an unusually large amount of time has elapsed, namely, the time required for Rocky to count from 23 to 89. We understand this counting to have taken place due to the ellipses concluding the text of panel two and beginning the text of panel three, and by the conventions of closure (McCloud 1993: 67), which entails conjecture as to the action that transpires in the space between the panels (known as the 'gutter'). Furthermore, with Rocky having arrived at the double digits, we also understand that the counting has been time-consuming, since German numbers are relatively long, thanks to the fronting of the second digit in two-digit numbers and the insertion of "and", such that, e.g., 'twenty-one' is realized as *einundzwanzig*, literally "one-and-twenty". The writing of the numbers as separate words in the comic (**ein unt zwanzich*, **ein unt hundert*) fortifies the impression of the recitation as drawn out and tedious, especially in the fourth panel, where Rocky's perpetuated errors result in ever longer forms, such as "*ein hundren unt einzehn*" for German *hundertelf*. Considering the repetitive nature of the counting system, it should strike the reader as absurd that Rocky would need to count every single number. In so doing, however, not only is the reader convinced of Rocky's incompetence as he commits the same errors over and over, but through this repetition Martin Kellerman also manages to poke fun at the German language, highlighting the potential absurdity of its counting system.

This disparagement of the German language is subtle, and perhaps only appreciated as humorous by those sufficiently familiar with German. In example (35), mockery of German and Germans is more explicit and draws from stereotypes, making it more accessible to the non-Germanophone reader. First, as Rocky recounts his many attempts to pronounce his own street name correctly, Martin Kellerman provides the reader with a series of alternative renditions, once again playing with orthography to capture the aural aspects of spoken language. Kellerman then takes fuller advantage of the material affordances of the comics medium, drawing water drops to indicate the spittle that is produced when pronouncing the [ʃ] sound, occurring in *Schlessisches Tor*. When Rocky admits that his quite close approximations are dismissed as unintelligible and he is forced to either show the address on his cell phone or alter his route to avoid problematic pronunciations altogether, he appears once again to be the target of disparagement, playing the role of incompetent speaker. By the fourth panel, however, the disparagement is redirected, as Rocky's compares the Germans to Frenchmen, drawing from the stereotype of the latter of being persnickety about correct pronunciation. This comparison invites the reader to reinterpret Rocky's pronunciation attempts rather as evidence of the strangeness of the German language and as failures by the Germans (whom we understand are strange by analogy) to comprehend or to listen sympathetically. The disparagement is made further explicit by the subsequent contrast with Stockholm, where taxi drivers would be neither genuinely nor affectatiously challenged by a tourist's pronunciation of *Drottninggatan* as "*Dröttninggatan*".

The readers' full appreciation of the strips featured in this section depends on their familiarity with the German language, German history, or in example (33), perhaps even the German capital. Martin Kellerman can thus be understood as taking a risk with the extent to which he plays with the form and idiomaticity of the German language in such a way that may alienate his non-Germanophone readers (Ezell 2012: 25). The fact that Kellerman provides no 'answer keys' in the form of translations or explanations suggests that he operates under the assumption that his readers are sufficiently familiar with the German language and culture to fully appreciate the humor resulting from the foreign language play. Indeed, according to the Special Eurobarometer 386 (2012: 21), 26% of Swedish respondents claimed to be proficient enough in German to hold a conversation, putting this language after English (86%) but before French (9%) as the most widely known foreign languages among Swedes. Spanish, on the other hand, was not among the top three, and only 4% of Swedes claimed to understand Spanish well enough to follow news or radio programs (Special Eurobarometer 386 2012: 31). The difference in comprehension and use is reflected in the Spanish-language examples presented in the next section.

4.5 Spanish-language play

Spanish ranks among the top ten largest languages in Sweden with regards to number of native speakers, estimated at 75,000 in 2012. Despite its current position as prominent among the foreign languages represented within the country, Spanish cannot lay claim to the same historical foundation in Sweden as German, initial contact with which dates back to the Middle Ages. Furthermore, while German has been a staple of the Swedish school curriculum since 1807 (as has French), Spanish was not officially included as a modern language elective until 1994.[23] From the 2000s onward, Spain has consistently ranked among the most popular tourist destinations among Swedes, topping the list since 2012.[24] This development entails ever more language contact with Spanish. However, despite the number of native speakers of Spanish in Sweden and the popularity of Spain among Swedes, the relative novelty of Spanish in contemporary Swedish society and in the school curriculum may entail less familiarity with it than with German, which in turn may be compounded by the dissimilarities between Spanish (a Romance language) and Swedish (a Germanic language). In the examples featured in the previous section, Rocky was portrayed as having a basic knowledge of the German language, culture, and history. His readers were assumed to be similarly familiar, since no translations or contextualizations were provided, and essential to appreciating Rocky's self-disparaging humor was the readers' own ability to recognize Rocky's language usage as flawed. In the examples of Spanish foreign language usage presented in this section (Figures 36–38), it is Rocky's incompetence that once again operationalizes the humor, but metalanguage now explicitly constructs Rocky as a non-speaker of Spanish.

Figure 36: Spray it don't say it!

(36) Spray it don't say it!

> Rocky: Klasse taught me a little Spanish before we left! *Qualsa de la pappileria? Deme hambörgesa!*
>
> Rocky: *E so si!*
>
> Frog: Where's the stationery store? Give me hamburger! That's it!

---

23 Survey of "Modern languages" for Swedish National Agency for Education, 2010, p. 6.
24 According to the Vagabond Travel Barometer for the years 2012–2017, available at http://www.vagabond.se

Crocodile: I went around the whole day yesterday and said *pablo español*! I mixed up Italian and Spanish and total idiocy!

Crocodile: *Pablo inglés? No pablo español!*

Rocky: Are you Pablo Inglés? I am Pablo Español! Give me hamburger!

Rocky: Spain should be like Israel for all lispers, because you're **supposed** to lisp here! *Thiente-thinco-theith! Ethtathion!*

Crocodile: Spray it, don't say it!

Example (36) is characterized by metalanguage throughout the panels, initiated by Rocky, whose claim in panel 1 to have learned "a little Spanish" from a more competent peer establishes him as a novice. This status is further confirmed by Rocky's exhibition of his newly acquired knowledge in the form of an interrogative and an imperative – the paradigmatic simplicity of which is typical of learner language – as well as a formulaic exclamation. None of the constructions are grammatically or even orthographically correct: "qualsa" does not exist (but may be derived from the question-word *cuál*), *papelería* is misspelled, as are *hamburguese* and *eso sí*. In the event that the reader would be unable to decipher the imperfect foreign language usage, Frog inhabits the role of expert and provides a translation, which helps the reader understand Rocky's utterances as flawed and incoherent. This is a service absent in other-language examples presented thus far, which suggests that Martin Kellerman does not assume as much knowledge of Spanish among his readers.

Explicit discussion about the Spanish language continues with Crocodile adopting Rocky's playful key in recounting his own foibles in foreign language usage. At this point, it is Rocky who takes on the role of expert by attempting a translation, and he maintains the playfulness by incorporating the ungrammatical non-sequitor "give me hamburger." Although Rocky and Crocodile have thus far been portrayed as novices, by the fourth panel, their meta-language reveals them as astute observers of linguistic phenomena. Rocky specifically addresses a well-known characteristic of Castillian Spanish, namely the pronunciation of the alveolar fricative /s/ as dental fricative [θ], resulting in a lisp that is known as *ceceo*. Rocky exemplifies *ceceo* in his pronunciation of *ciento-cinco-seis* ("one hundred-five-six"[25]) as "thiente-thinco-theith", whereby the

---

[25] Perhaps Rocky is attempting to produce *"ciento cincuenta y seis"* (Eng: "one hundred-fifty-six")

letters "th" are used to represent the sound [θ]. Similar to example (33), this final panel shows Martin Kellerman once again taking advantage of the affordances provided by the comics medium to embellish Rocky's turn with droplets of water, so to convey spittle as the by-product of the pronunciation in question. The punchline of the strip is in the form of a code-switch to English, invoking a rhyming phrase normally directed at someone who inadvertently spits while talking, "Say it, don't spray it." While Crocodile's inversion of the phrase serves as a useful rule of thumb for Spanish pronunciation, it is most noteworthy for establishing the humor of the strip as a function of multilingual word play. The code-switch to English – particularly in punchline position – reflects a recurring practice in contemporary Swedish comics, further explored in the remaining chapters. In this comic strip, however, the invocation of the English phrase highlights the fact that play is not limited to usage of the target language, but extends even to the interlocutors' meta-discourse: their talk about language play itself incorporates language play.

Meta-discourse continues in examples (37) and (38), but Rocky's progression in his Spanish language skills is evidenced by an appropriation of salient linguistic attributes.

Figure 37: El Robocopo!

(37) El Robocopo!

    Rocky: How do you say "where's the toilet" in Spanish?

    Frog: *Donda esta la chokolateria?*

    Rocky: I have to learn Spanish! The next time we come here I'm going to take a class!

    Frog: You said that last time too...

Rocky: And you always say you're going to start jogging when you're abroad, but when you get home you've forgotten all about it!

Frog: I am going to start when we get home! I really want to run, my legs are already moving!

Rocky: And I'm going to learn Spanish! My tongue is already moving! *Yo soy una pappileria con des pantalones Maiquel Yason! Chiki Chiki!*

Rocky: (snapping his fingers) *El Robocopo!*

Frog: I really want to run now actually ...

In example (37), Rocky's initial question positions Frog as a speaker of Spanish, establishing their roles as novice and expert, respectively. The reader's own familiarity with Spanish is not crucial to the first instance of language play, where Frog's blithe translation of "toilet" as "chocolate factory" is fairly obvious scatological humor. Rocky's subsequent statement can be interpreted as an acceptance of Frog's translation as factual, which, along with the explicit admission of a need to learn Spanish, reinforces his novice status. Rocky is not completely without skills, however, as evidenced by the fourth panel, although his limitations are evident in light of the propositional content of the utterance, roughly, "I am a stationery store (Sp: *papelería*) with Michael Jackson pants!" Rocky's performance in Spanish can be compared to his use of Italian in example (31), which also resembled fluent incoherence. The persistence of pappileria (Sp: *papelería*) suggests Rocky's fondness for this word that is not anchored in complete comprehension, as it once again is both misspelled and used in a fatuous context. In Rocky's final turn, he illustrates a common strategy among foreign language users, namely, the adaptation of words to the target language by applying what Barrett (2012: 59) refers to as "morphemic stereotypes", that is, typical grammatical, lexical, or phonological attributes. With his arms raised, fingers snapping, and legs moving, Rocky is depicted here as performing the dance "The Robocop", which he adapts to the target language by using the Spanish masculine definite article *el* and the derivational suffix [-o], producing "*El Robocopo*".

Examples (36) and (37) have established Rocky as a novice foreign language user via meta-discourse ("Klasse taught me a little Spanish ... "; "How do you say ... ") and foreign-language utterances characterized by mispronunciations, grammatical errors, and incoherence. At the same time, Rocky has shown progression in his acquisition of Spanish, identifying and producing typical phonological, morphological, and syntactic attributes, such as *ceceo* ("ethtathion"), [-o]-suffixation ("robocopo"), and post-modification ("des pantalones Maiquel Yason"). Example (38) provides additional evidence of proficiency, with Rocky employing formulaic expressions and showing awareness of target-language phonology and morphology.

Figure 38: Gracias de nada!

(38) Gracias de nada!

    Rocky: What's he saying? Es complicado or what?

    Frog: It's broken yeah ... That's information we already knew about, it's a bit of the reason we called you guys actually!

    Frog: Oh thanks! A number to a fourth Team Supermario & Luigi who can come over and point and tell us it's broken.

    Frog: Perfect! He'll come some time between Wednesday and Sunday, so we need to stay put in the apartment five more days!

    Rocky: Gracias de nada!

    Frog: Spain ... I'm having a brain haemorrhage.

    Rocky: Then two emergency care technicians will come and point at you. He sicko, you eshould call someo[ne].

The practice of using meta-discourse to initiate a comic strip that includes foreign language content continues, as Rocky asks Frog what the Spanish-speaking plumber is saying. He ends this first turn by code-switching, employing the formulaic "*Es complicado*". In his next turn in panel 3, Rocky combines two formulaic expressions "*gracias*" and "*de nada*". While the first formulaic expression is properly formed and appropriately invoked, the second must be considered an instance of language play. *Gracias*, an expression of gratitude ("Thanks"), constitutes the first part of a conventional adjacency pair, triggering an acknowledgement such as *de nada*, meaning "of nothing" or the more idiomatic response to gratitude, "Not at all." It could be the case that Rocky, as a language learner, has internalized the adjacency pair as a single unit. In the context of unwelcome news from the plumber, however, it is more likely that Rocky is deliberately playing with the language, exploiting his novice, non-native speaker status to convey a sarcasm, "Thanks for nothing." The absence of any sense of urgency or professional competence among a series of repairmen and the long period as well as conditions of waiting for service to the water heater cause Frog to disparage Spain in general. In response, Rocky does not speak Spanish in his final turn, but rather plays the role of a novice Spaniard speaking Swedish, complete with ungrammaticalities ("he sicko"), and stereotypical phonological and morphological features, such as the epenthetic [e] in "eringa" (Sw: *ringa*) and the suffix [-o] in "sjuko" (Sw: *sjuk*). In this way, Rocky can align with Frog's negative stance towards Spain by mocking both the language and speakers of the country. Significantly, Rocky can shed his own novice status by asserting superiority via mimicry and disparagement humor.

4.6 The multicompetence underlying incompetence

In Chapter 3, dialect mimicry as a foundation of dialect humor (Barrett 2000) was explored in *Rocky* comics, focusing in particular on Martin Kellerman's noteworthy ability to visually depict in the comic strip medium the distinct phonology and aural qualities of regional Swedish dialects. The analyses revealed that a defining characteristic of episodes of dialect mimicry was the instigating practice of place-naming, serving to activate the readers' linguistic and cultural stereotypes, thereby priming them for dialect humor. In the present chapter, foreign language usage in the *Rocky* comics can also be considered an example of dialect humor, now in the form of dialect mixing, whereby the use of two (or more) languages allows for "contrasting elements of language variation [to be] mixed in an effort to elicit humor." (Barrett 2000: 58) Similar to the instances of dialect mimicry, dialect humor in the form of dialect mixing is characteristically preceded by a particular linguistic practice; in this case, it is in the form of language-naming or other meta-language that triggers stereotypes and prepares the reader for foreign language usage.

Invoking stereotypes via foreign language usage and cross-linguistic contrasts sets the scene for disparagement humor: readers expect the foreign language or the foreign language speaker to be mocked or denigrated. Indeed,

Barrett (2000: 67) has claimed that, in much of dialect humor, "the speaker of a targeted dialect is considered the target of that humor." According to the analyses above, however, that which saliently characterizes the *Rocky*-comic strips featuring foreign language usage is not attacks on the target foreign language, its speakers, or affiliated culture, but rather directs the readers' attention to Rocky's own incompetence. Indeed, it is Rocky who tends to make himself and his own mistakes the butt of the joke. As such, the examples can be considered to align with the superiority theory of disparagement humor, such that Rocky's self-disparagement allows the readers to feel superior.

The examples should also be considered from the perspective of humor style, since self-disparagement can be interpreted as either adaptive or maladaptive humor (Martin 2007), that is, humor that is either beneficial or detrimental to one's own and others' well-being. With regards to maladaptive humor, self-defeating humor "is a form of injurious humor that is used to enhance relationships at cost to the self through acts such as self-disparagement" (Zeigler-Hill and Besser 2011: 1197). In contrast, adaptive humor in the form of an affiliative humor style "refers to benign humor that is used to enhance relationships by saying funny things or engaging in witty banter to amuse others" (Zeigler-Hill and Besser 2011: 1197), and may include self-deprecating humor (Beermann 2014: 364). Self-enhancing humor describes another adaptive humor style in which an individual maintains "a humorous perspective in the face of adversity" (Zeigler-Hill and Besser 2011: 1197) or "a humorous point of view on life and its incongruities" (Beermann 2014: 364). In the context of a daily humor comic strip, Rocky's foreign language incompetence as a form of self-disparagement should be viewed through the lens of adaptive humor, illustrating via language play a distinct strategy for dealing with the adversity and incongruities that foreign language usage entails, but aiming, primarily, at amusing the readers. The analyses reveal that Rocky does not simply perform poorly in a foreign language, but that Martin Kellerman quite purposefully manipulates the foreign language as an object of play, in other words, playing with the language as understood by Lantolf (1997), Cook (2000), and Bell (2012). Considering that the comic strip medium affords Kellerman the opportunity to confirm the linguistic accuracy of his foreign language texts, the inclusion of errors can be nothing other than a deliberate act of performance of foreign language incompetence.

The extent to which Kellerman plays with foreign languages as various as Arabic, Norwegian, Danish, Italian, German, and Spanish entails a substantial risk: readers may not be familiar enough with the featured languages to recognize the manipulation as language play. There is evidence that Kellerman on occasion helps his readers decode the language play, but more often than not the readers are left to their own devices. On the one hand, this may result in alienation of readers with little to know foreign language knowledge. On the other hand, it may create what Ezell calls an "imaginative space", whereby readers who do not understand the foreign language (and thus cannot decode the foreign language play) would fill in their own blanks. Providing readers with agency in this way enhances the readers' "intellectual connection" to the artist (Ezell 2008: 25).

Readers who are proficient enough in foreign languages to recognize Rocky's incompetence will also appreciate its disingenuousness. The examples featured in this chapter suggest that foreign language play in the form of a variety of linguistic errors constitutes a performance of an incompetent speaker, enacted in a "self-aware fashion that makes a joke out of the poor quality" of the foreign language usage (Davies 2014: 203). It is only thanks to Martin Kellerman's own broad knowledge of correct forms and linguistic conventions in foreign languages that he is able to play with them (Cook 2000). In other words, it takes a high degree of competence to perform incompetence.

Rocky's struggles with various foreign languages are exploited for the sake of humor. Rocky's ability to engage in language play suggests, however, that he is not a deficient but instead a multicompetent language user. Multicompetence refers to "the compound state of mind with two grammars" (Cook 1991: 112); accordingly, a multicompetent speaker may be mistaken as incompetent. Belz (2002: 21), however, argues that language play among language learners is evidence of a "new state of mind that has been mediated by foreign language study and use." Of significance to the analysis of foreign language play as multicompetence is the written medium of texts in comic strips. Writing in a foreign language, and especially playing with or in a foreign language in writing "exemplify episodes of carefully crafted language" (Belz 2002: 21). Language play in the *Rocky*-comics featured in the present chapter reflects a collaboration between the written form and the spoken version it represents: the care taken in crafting foreign language play is evident in the orthographical, phonological, morphological, and syntactic manipulations, as well as in punctuation, lettering, and visualization of paralinguistic details.

Ultimately, the use of foreign languages in *Rocky*-comics establishes linguistic contrasts that are amenable to disparagement, whereby either the foreign language itself and, by extension, its native speakers are disparaged, or the novice, non-native speaker (Rocky) is. The examples presented in this chapter provide evidence, however, that humor is a function not solely of disparagement, but also of multifaceted language play that showcases Martin Kellerman's (and Rocky's) multicompetence and, crucially, intellectually rewards the multicompetent readers.

5 In English, please

Despite a relatively small population of just over ten million people, the country of Sweden boasts a multilingual society, with an estimated 200 different languages spoken.[26] Not unsurprisingly, the majority of residents – at least 85% according to Josephson (2014) and Parkvall (2015) – speak Swedish, which was awarded the status of official language of Sweden in 2009. As reviewed in Chapter 4, a further five languages have official minority language status, including Finnish, Meänkieli, Sami, Yiddish, and Romani. Additionally, Sweden is inhabited by native speakers of languages other than Swedish, the top ten of which include Arabic, Finnish, Serbo-Croatian languages, Kurdish, Polish, Spanish, Persian, German, Danish, and Norwegian (in decreasing order according to current extrapolations on calculations from 2012; Parkvall 2015). In terms of its native-speaker representation in Sweden, English just fails to clear the top-ten threshold. However, the number of English native-speaker residents in Sweden does not have bearing on the national status of English, which occupies a position of explicit prestige on par with that of Swedish itself (Hult 2012: 243; Josephson 2014: 108).

Scandinavians have been recognized as having a high level of English proficiency (Ferguson 1994), and Sweden, similar to Denmark, Norway, and The Netherlands, is often identified as an exemplary nation in terms of the general population's success in achieving a high level of proficiency in English (Haugen 1987; Labrie and Quell 1997; Phillipson 1992). According to the Special Eurobarometer 243 report published in 2006, 39% of the Swedish survey respondents reported using English on an almost daily basis, with half of the respondents using English either often (20%) or occasionally (30%); only 11% claimed to not use English at all (Special Eurobarometer 243 2006: 155). In other words, English, via either active use or passive exposure, has been established as a daily reality within Swedish society. Parkvall (2009: 119) has estimated that 89% of Sweden's population know English. What this means in practical terms can be gleaned from the Special Eurobarometer 243, which revealed that "89% of [survey] respondents in Sweden indicated that they know

---

[26] https://www.sprakochfolkminnen.se/om-oss/for-dig-i-skolan/sprak-for-dig-i-skolan/spraken-i-sverige/manga-modersmal.html

Note: Parts of this chapter are adapted from Beers Fägersten (2017b).

https://doi.org/10.1515/9781501505119-005

English well enough to have a conversation. Of these, 35% had a very good knowledge of the language, 42% had a good knowledge and 23% had basic English skills" (Special Eurobarometer 243 2006: 153). Andersson (2016) suggests that while many Swedes may over-estimate their own skills in English, this positive orientation towards English proficiency should be considered evidence of how important it is for one's own identity as a Swede to be considered a good speaker of English.

There are both historical and contemporary reasons for the fact that English figures so saliently and occupies a rather privileged position in Sweden. The nation has long had a policy of including English in the school curriculum beginning at the elementary levels, and of promoting the use of English in the domains of trade and industry. Mandatory English instruction was introduced as early as 1849. In 1946, the "English for all" educational movement proposed an even more proactive language planning policy, arguing for nation-wide instruction in English as "a vital tool for democratization" (Hult 2012: 232). By 1962, the inclusion of English in the national school curriculum was a *fait accompli*, "framed as integral to Swedish society as a tool for gaining socioeconomic opportunities" (Hult 2012: 232, citing Cabau-Lampa 1999, 2005; Teleman 2003). Thus, the promotion of English as a required school subject was explicitly related to the use of English in business, industry, or trade in order to target international markets and to maximize Sweden's global reach. In effect, the use of English has been institutionalized in Sweden, with the goal of facilitating mutual communication with and contact between external parties. Indeed, the number of domains where English is becoming indispensable throughout Swedish society is constantly increasing (Haberland 2005; Josephson 2014; Phillipson 1992; Teleman 1992). Due to the prominence – and pre-eminence – of English in Sweden, it can be said to have attained the status of a second language rather than a foreign language (Andersson 2016; Josephson 2014), a distinction that is not without significance, as discussed below. However, despite the privileged status of English in Sweden, its co-existence with Swedish is not entirely uncomplicated, as the *Berglins* comic strip in Figure 39 illustrates.

Figure 39: In English, please.

(39) In English, please.

> Caption: Where does this idea come from that we of all people should be especially good in English?
>
> Speaker 1: Damn, every day you sure get praised here for your English!
>
> Speaker 2: Yeah, you notice how much you really do know after chatting a while.
>
> Caption: Businesses and schools are quick to abandon Swedish for a more international flare ... but how does it actually <u>sound</u>?
>
> Priest: Dear parishioners ... just in time for our Christmas morning service, our fine old Cahman organ has frozen, but Cantor Bladmyr will try to lead the psalm on a kazoo ...
>
> Caption: If by language skills we mean breadth, depth, and a feeling for nuances and stylistics, then the stages actually look like this:
>
> first step: fairly good English
>
> second step: good

third step: wrote his dissertation in English!

Speaker 1: Exquisite sherry, I say!

fourth step: real Anglophile!

fifth step: somewhat talented 12-year-old English schoolgirl

Caption: Ok, I'm of course worthless in English, but I'll challenge anyone at all who thinks they're good to a synonym-duel!

Speaker 1: Tail   Ass   Arse
          End   Backside   Seat
          Rump   Bottom   Behind Backend
          Stern-side

Speaker 2: Um ... Bottom
          Arse ...
          Read end
          Wait ...

In this strip, the reader must initially confront both the stereotype of Swedes being particularly proficient in English and the possibility that a Swede may over-estimate his own skills if the object of comparison is an average inhabitant of a rather remote part of the world. The second panel of the strip acknowledges the eagerness of using English to foster internationalism, but it implies that the result is auditorily displeasing: substituting Swedish with English is likened to the result of replacing an elaborate organ with a kazoo. The third panel provides a critical perspective of the realities of proficiency in English among even the most linguistically advanced Swedes when compared to basic native-speaker ability, and by the fourth panel, the narrator acknowledges his own deficiencies in English, but defends himself with an implication of the superiority of his own native-speaker proficiency in Swedish. This comic strip thus touches on a range of issues concerning the role and use of English in Sweden, hinting at an underlying discomfort with an ever-more pronounced embrace of English. Indeed, the increasing usage and dominance of English in Sweden is well documented and has been a source of both national pride and cultural panic (Holm 2006; Josephson 2004; Sharp 2001, 2007; Teleman 1992; Westman 1996). Claims that English has precluded Swedish in certain domains of communication and interaction are countered by arguments that English does not pose a total threat to Swedish, but rather serves as a linguistic resource for lending nuances to communication. Considering the deliberate and even aggressive integration of

English in Swedish society, it is not surprising that the co-existence of two languages can create tension with regards to the languages' respective positions and purposes. A one-panel extract from another *Berglins* comic strip illustrates confusion as a side-effect of this multilingualism, as seen in Figure 40.

Figure 40: Laxpink ... ?

(40) Laxpink ... ?

> Caption: The shopping must be done ...
>
> Thought bubble: Salmon pee ... ?

In this example, the sign in the grocery store includes information written in both Swedish and English: Swedish *lax* (Eng: "salmon") and English "pink". In other words, the sign is advertising "pink salmon." There are clear contextual cues that would help the reader decipher the second word as English: the words are separated, whereas in Swedish they would constitute a compound (*laxpink*), and the word "pink" is highlighted with shading. Nevertheless, the depicted shopper makes an effort to understand both words as Swedish (*pink* means "pee"), suggesting not just a resistance to the infiltration of English, but also a subversion of it. The similarity in form of the English and Swedish words enables language play, which mines an inter-linguistic tension for humor, namely, that which is created by a seemingly unmotivated usage of English. By playing with the word "pink", comics artists Jan and Maria Berglin encourage the reader to question the sensibility of using English not only in this specific context, but in any other. In effect, the panel seems to question the very necessity of using English at all, illustrating how it can have unintentionally silly results. The Berglins seem to be in the minority in this regard, however, since the incorporation of English is a quite common feature of both written and spoken interaction among Swedes, for which comic strips provide ample evidence. Language play in the form of Swedish-English code-switching sequences ranging from the simple to elaborate are exemplified in various contemporary Swedish comic strips, showcasing linguistic creativity and dexterity, as explored in the next section.

5.1 English code-switching in Swedish comics

Höglin (2002: 56) notes that while Swedish has been completely replaced by English in certain domains, the dominance of English is actually best understood as extensive code-switching, which, in informal conversation among youths, for example, is estimated to be as often as once per minute. The prominent role of English in Sweden and its consequent spread from high-status to low-status domains has helped encourage an ideological shift in the view of English as a foreign language to English as a second language. This shift is meaningful, as it reflects both the ever-increasing use of English across domains, and the progression beyond the approach to the language as merely a source for lexical borrowing to the use of English as a valid, viable code for native communication. Indeed, code-switching predictability and predominantly occurs among bilingual speakers sharing the same or over-lapping linguistic repertoires (Grosjean 1982; Li Wei 2005). The shared linguistic background of interlocutors automatically establishes them as members of an in-group, which code-switching can either serve to confirm or help to establish. Thus, code-switching frequently functions as a communicative strategy for achieving social goals, including to signal interpersonal relationships (Blom and Gumperz 1972), to redefine social roles (Myers-Scotton 1988) or to manage social relations (Auer 1988). While there are many terms and over-lapping concepts in the bilingualism and language contact literature, code-switching can for simplicity's sake be considered the umbrella term for the phenomenon of the simultaneous use of two languages in one conversational exchange. Code-switching can furthermore be distinguished as intra-sentential or inter-sentential, depending on where the switch occurs, that is, within a clause or between clauses. The more syntactically compatible languages are, the more conducive they are to intra-sentential code-switching, which is illustrated in the *Stockholmsnatt* strip in Figure 41, where code-switches to English are underlined in example (41).

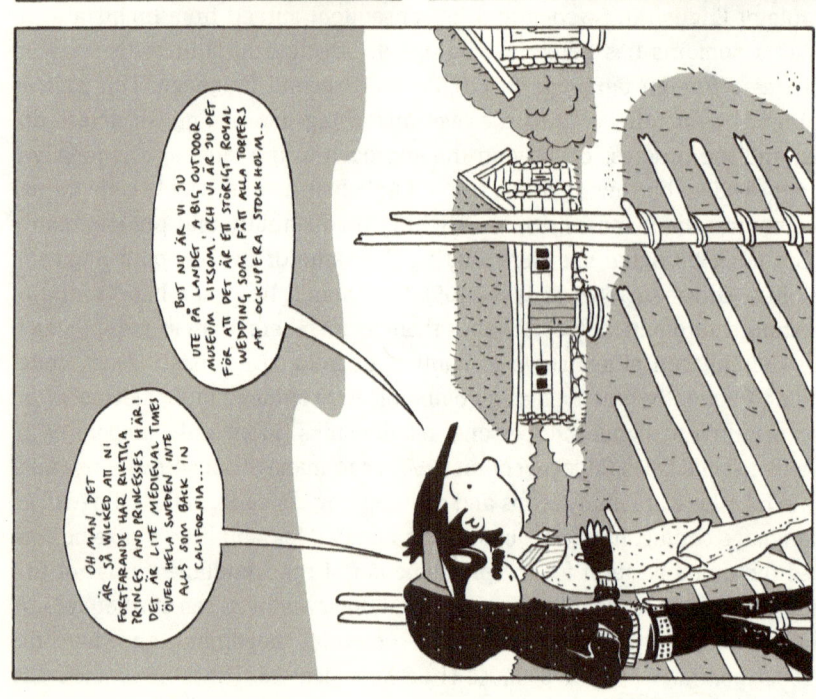

Figure 41: How primitive ...

5.1 English code-switching in Swedish comics — 97

(41) How primitive ...

> Speaker 1: Oh man, it's so wicked that you still have real princes and princesses here! It's a little medieval times over all of Sweden, not at all like back in California ...
>
> Speaker 2: But now we're out in the country, like a big outdoor museum! And that's because of a bothersome royal wedding that's got all the cottage-dwellers occupying Stockholm ...
>
> Speaker 1: But look, that farmer there has an Iphone! So you at least got a little future here too!
>
> Speaker 2: That's probably not a farmer, in Sweden we call it a Bombi-Bitt[27] hipster on summer holiday.
>
> Speaker 1: Oh god, Europeans are so left behind ...
>
> Speaker 1: Is that a toilet? How primitive ... When did you say it was built?
>
> Speaker 2: Well, about the same time as Columbus discovered America ...

According to contextual cues such as Speaker 1's reference to "back in California" and his use of second-person plural pronoun *ni* (Eng: "you (all)") to address Speaker 2, the dialogue seems to be between an American and a Swede. As such, the code-switching in this bilingual conversation may be a strategy to deal with linguistic deficiencies, such as lexical gaps. Yet there is other evidence to suggest, rather, that deliberate language play is at hand, as both speakers reveal an underlying target language proficiency. For example, Speaker 1's first turn includes the correct Swedish adjectival inflection for plural in the word *riktiga* (Eng: "real"), while Speaker 2's first-turn usage of "torpers" (Swe: *torpare*; Eng: "cottage-dweller(s)") reflects an appropriation of English morphology via substitution of Swedish derivative suffix *-are* (indicating occupation or activity) with English "-er" and of the zero-morpheme plural with the English inflectional suffix, "-s". In panel 2, Speaker 1 inflects English "farmer" with Swedish definite article suffix *-n*: "den där farmer**n**", while Speaker 2 shows awareness of English SVO-word order conventions: "In

---

[27] Bombi Bitt is a Tom Sawyer-like character from Fritiof Nilsson Piraten's 1932 novel *Bombi Bitt och jag* ("Bombi Bitt and I"), which was later developed into a film (1936) and television mini-series (1968).

Sweden vi call it [...]" instead of Swedish VSO word order after adverbials, *I Sverige kallar vi det [...]*.

Even though code-switching is a common feature of Swedish interaction (Höglin 2002; Sharp 2001, 2007), the great extent of intra-sentential code-switching depicted in example (39) should not be considered representative of conventional communication between Swedes. In her spoken-language data, Sharp (2007) observed that code-switches to English can be broadly categorized as mixed and unmixed utterances (roughly corresponding to intra- and inter-sentential switches), which can be identified in the following ways:

- English elements forming parts of mixed utterances conform to the morphosyntactic framework of Swedish, and the English words may or may not display signs of adaptation to Swedish in the form of Swedish inflectional suffixes
- The words making up unmixed utterances constitute *embedded language islands* [citing Myers-Scotton 1993], i.e. isolated utterances entirely in the transferred language and thus totally unconstrained by the Swedish matrix (Sharp 2007: 226; original italics).

Code-switching among Swedes thus tends to be "asymmetrical" and "unidirectional" (Muysken 2000: 75–81), meaning English is inserted into Swedish, which acts as the "matrix language" (Myers-Scotton 1993: 166, as cited in Sharp 2007: 226) such that, "Swedish governs the semantic and syntactic structure of the discourse" (Sharp 2007: 226). In example (41), the governing language is not so simply identified, nor are there any isolated strings of English that are saliently in contrast to a predominantly Swedish discourse. The inclusion of intra-sentential or mixed utterance code-switching of this degree in a comic strip should therefore be considered a form of language play that Swedish readers, versed in Swedish-English code-switching practice, should be able not only to process, but also to appreciate.

Switches to English are instead predominantly characterized by two phenomena: (1) the incorporation of idioms, formulaic language, or other simple phrases, and (2) the citation of media sources. Figure 42 from Ellen Ekman's *Lilla Berlin* illustrates code-switches of the first type (code-switches to English are underlined in example (42)).

Figure 42: Here we go again …

(42) Here we go again...

> Speaker 1: Let me guess... You're a Cancer right?
>
> Speaker 2: <u>Here we go again</u>...
> Speaker 1: Don't know if you've read your horoscope today, but it said that you would meet a tall and handsome man tonight...
>
> Speaker 2: Ah, how weird! Which horoscope did you read? It can't be the same one that I read?
>
> Speaker 2: That one said namely that I would go to the bar and meet a bunch of idiots as usual, give up on the male species and go home to my five cats instead. I would end the evening there with a Game of Thrones-marathon, an evening jack-off and then fall asleep in front of the TV with a pizza on my belly. A perfect evening if you ask me.
>
> Speaker 2: I mean... what does he want me to do? The universe has spoken.
>
> Speaker 3: <u>You don't mess with universe</u>...
>
> Speaker 2: Exactly.

Höglin (2002: 56) found Swedish-English code-switching in informal conversation among youths to be characterized by the use of such fixed phrases "That's not my business", "No problems", "Shit happens", and "Back to basics." Similarly, Sharp (2007: 231) noted that, within her study population of young adults, unmixed utterances of longer strings of English or complete clauses were common and included such idioms as "Check it out!" or formulaic phrases as "I don't know." In example (42), the use of "Here we go again" further illustrates this phenomenon. Among the contemporary Swedish comics featured in this book, *Lilla Berlin* and Lina Neidestam's *Zelda* represent the young adult generation. *Lilla Berlin* is particularly characterized by code-switches to English in the form of formulaic phrases or idioms, such as:
– wear it with pride
– make it count
– rub it in
– never let go
– amen to that

- don't bite the hand that feeds you
- don't get your hopes up
- I rest my case
- I don't think so
- I think not
- you can't argue with that
- always good to have you on the show
- let's get the hell out of here
- thanks but no thanks
- that's what I'm talking about
- still got the looks
- in it to win it

The formulaic nature of such code-switches renders them multi-word composites which, as Sharp (2007: 232) explains, "have been practised over and over again at school and [. . .] probably require very little cognitive effort by the speakers, as little actual 'putting together' is necessary." This conclusion is supported by the second code-switch in example (42), occurring in the final panel: "Don't mess with universe." While there is some degree of fixedness in "don't mess with", it is not a complete idiom but requires some "putting together." Specifically, the final slot must be filled with a noun phrase (e.g., "me", "Texas", or "the best"), which in example (42) was done in a non-idiomatic way with regards to an omission of the definite article. Such minor errors may or may not be accidental; they may or may not be recognized by the reader. Above all, they serve as a reminder that English is an auxiliary language in Sweden, and as such its usage often has more indexical significance than propositional value. A switch to English often indexes playfulness, which is established and continuously reinforced by the comic strip context. This is particularly substantiated by the recurrent, cross-strip practice of code-switching to English in punchline position, which is illustrated in Figures 43–45, featuring a collection of final-panel code-switches in *Lilla Berlin*, in Figure 46 from *Zelda*, and in Figure 47 from *Stockholmsnatt*.

Figures 43–45: Punchline English in *Lilla Berlin*.

Figure 46: Take me now.

(46) Take me now

> Male: You are so beautiful! I've never liked the anorectic silicon-ideal. You don't need to be blond and porno-waxed!
>
> Male: I love natural women! No make-up, peach-like cheeks, soft curves in the morning light. No additives, just 100% woman!
>
> Zelda: Excuse me, I just need to go pee a little bit of rose water
>
> Zelda: Take me now or lose me forever.

Figure 47: That's how we scroll…

(47) That's how we scroll…

> Speaker 1: To be on a genuine **obsessive-compulsive paternity leave** is like so much bigger than just being on paternity leave… Most are just superficially on leave and then when the child goes to daycare they go back to their old ways…
>
> Speaker 2: You shave off the soft-edgy beard, put away the stroller, stop scrolling at playgrounds, and listen to Deportees.[28] Abandon the four elements…
>
> Speaker 1: But getting shut out of open pre-school is a hard blow that makes many throw in the towel too… That was like where you went to scroll together…
>
> Speaker 2: Yeah and to talk about vomit stains and other style tips…
>
> Speaker 1: Although I actually think it's good that some stop their paternity leave when they start working. The fake ones get like sifted out from the genuine ones…
>
> Speaker 2: **OCP for life**, like, that's how we scroll…

---

28 A Swedish indie-band.

5.1 English code-switching in Swedish comics

Due to the sheer ubiquity of code-switches to English in interaction among Swedes and as represented copiously in comic strips, to claim that every occasion is an example of language play is a dubious endeavor. For this reason, code-switches in punchline position are particularly interesting, because they are imbued with a comical subtext. Ultimately, the punchline serves two purposes: delivering the humor of the comic strip and establishing English as a language of play, as seen in Figure 48 and Figure 49.

Figure 48: No further questions your honor!

(48) No further questions your honor!

Rocky: My New Year's resolution is to ask more questions and follow-up questions, so hold on because here come some!

Rocky: What do you do?

Horse: I work with children and youth who have Asperger's ...

Rocky: Yeah Asperger's! That's the cool variety of autism, isn't it? They're geniuses but don't like to do the dishes?

Horse: They're not automatically geniuses. But often they're really focused on one thing or another ...

Rocky: That's like me! I can sit all day looking at pictures of pretty Facebook-girls without thinking that I should go to work.

Horse: Yeah but that disease has a whole other name ...

Rocky: No further questions your honor!

Figure 49: I have no further questions your honor...

(49) I have no further questions your honor...

Speaker 1: So nice that you could come! What did you think?

Speaker 2: To be honest, that was one of the most naïve things I've seen in a long time. "Exploring family conflicts", isn't that just **so** done? And then we haven't even mentioned the technique... It feels a little like a teenaged girl has randomly cut and pasted in her diary... What were you thinking actually?

Speaker 3: What the hell Mira... was that really necessary? Couldn't you have just said, "Good"?

Speaker 2: Hey, if there's something I always am then it's honest.
Speaker 3: No, you're not honest, you're **rude**.

Speaker 2: Pssh, okay "Magdalena Ribbing",[29] I myself believe in being candid. The truth maybe hurts, but they deserve to hear it!

Speaker 3: Oh please, the Idol jury called and wondered how your schedule looks... Why would it be good to *always* tell the truth? What do you have to lose by sugar-coating the truth and being a little friendly?

Speaker 2: It... isn't as fun?

Speaker 3: I have no further questions your honor...

Examples (48) and (49) illustrate not only how "punchline English" is invoked similarly in different contemporary Swedish comic strips, but they also provide evidence of the second type of phenomenon that characterizes code-switches to English, namely that longer strings of English or even fixed phrases and idioms can be traced to media sources. Neither switch to English in examples (48) and (49) is entirely necessary; each punchline could have been delivered in Swedish while retaining much of the humor. The switch reflects therefore a stylistic choice, one triggered by the questioning performed in each strip, which seems to evoke comparisons to litigation of the type that is often dramatized in television and films (especially US-American productions). Humor in the form of language play is thus the result of three intersecting features of discourse: (1) a code-switch to English that (2) occurs in punchline position and (3) references media sources. This latter feature is explored further in the next section.

---

29 A Swedish author and columnist (1940–2017) who was an expert in etiquette.

5.2 The impact of media

While English has been explicitly promoted in Swedish society in the domains of education, industry, and trade, it is perhaps most saliently present in popular culture media such as television, film, radio, Internet, video games, printed press, and music. It is important to note that, like many Scandinavian and Northern European countries, Sweden's imported television programs and films, the majority of which are in English, are not dubbed; English-language music – both imported and nationally produced – dominates the airwaves; and the Swedish linguistic landscape is riddled with English (Hult 2003). Thus, equally represented in Sweden is what Preisler (1999a, 1999b, 2003) refers to as "English from above" and "English from below", with the former serving pragmatic purposes of communication and the latter allowing expression of identity and style. English from above vs. English from below acknowledges that the linguistic practices that characterize a speech community, such as the extensive use of English among Swedes, may be less imposed upon them from institutions and more autonomously appropriated as an active construction of discursive identity. In other words, the language used in channels of popular culture, such as broadcast, print, and digital media, can be considered the result of a process in which linguistic practices are appropriated from below as opposed to imposed from the top down. Indeed, according to Phillipson (2001: 25), instead of dictating language change, the language of the media reflects changes that have occurred or are in progress:

Language change is less determined by the way establishment values are propagated top-down, via the obligatory learning of English as foreign language [...] and much more by bottom-up, identity-driven choice of language to indicate group values, as in choice of style, communicative activities, and language, signaling membership of internationally oriented sub-groups.

In Sweden, there is ample evidence that language usage in Sweden is evolving in the form of frequent code-switches to English, which itself is more and more a function of consumption of English-language popular culture. The use of English on television or in films, music, or advertisements serves as input, often handily packaged, that consumers may easily appropriate and ultimately re-purpose. Figure 50, which features Rocky and a friend watching television in a hotel room while on vacation in the United States, illustrates the process.

Figure 50: Now that's what I want!

(50) Now that's what I want!

> Television: Switch to Geico and cut your cellphone bills in half!
>
> Television: Now that's what I want!
>
> Rocky: These eight-dollar nuts taste like Sami-scrotum, do you think I can seal up the bag so they don't notice anything?
>
> Chicken: Try twelve-dollar gummy bears, pork fat has never tasted so good!
>
> Rocky: Now that's what I want!
>
> Chicken: This is the good life, Stimpy!
>
> Rocky: You said it! That's what people don't get, you don't go away to run around sightseeing or go to The Lion King! The deal with traveling is taking it easy and doing stuff like this!
>
> Rocky: Home in Stockholm you'd be too stressed to lie around chilling in front of Beauty and the Geek the whole day and then walk around checking out loonies a couple of hours before going home and falling asleep to downloaded South Park!

Rocky: Change to channel forty-seven, I think that show with hairdressers from the sticks changing places with hairdressers from L.A. is on after the commercials.

Chicken: Pass me the Sami-nuts!

In this example, familiarity with and consumption of English-language television – particularly as a valued pastime – are made explicit with a depiction of television viewing and references to the series *Beauty and the Geek*, *South Park*, and *Split Ends*. Significantly, the process of appropriating and re-purposing media language as an effect of media consumption is twice depicted: first, when Rocky repeats the commercial slogan "Now that's what I want!" directly after viewing it, and second, when Chicken quotes a line from the cartoon series *Ren and Stimpy*.[30] The act of quoting from television, films, music, etc. is not unique to Swedish code-switches to English; rather, it is a wide-spread and predictable consequence of media consumption (Harris et al. 2008; Smyers 2016). However, so frequently are code-switches to English among Swedes in the form of quotations from televisual media, that Sharp (2007) identified it as a phenomenon she calls "the quoting game." In Sharp's data, the quoting game would begin when one interlocutor's code-switch to English referenced a specific media source, thereby triggering quoting behavior from another interlocutor. Example (48) can be considered an illustration of the quoting game in that Rocky initially quotes the television commercial, and Chicken subsequently quotes *Ren & Stimpy*. Figure 51, from *Lilla Berlin*, illustrates the quoting game in its purest form, where a media quote is recognized and acknowledged with an additional quote from the same source.

(51) One cat to rule them all ...

> Speaker 1: I heard on the radio that IS has begun using cute cats in its propaganda on social media. It's apparently a strategy to appear more like common folk and less like a terrorist organization that eats babies for breakfast.
>
> Speaker 2: What? That's the evilest thing I've ever heard.
>
> Speaker 1: Isn't it! Do you see how far this cat phenomenon has gone when even the cruelest terrorist organization in the world uses it! I mean, how effective can it be really?
>
> Speaker 2: Do not underestimate the power of the cat! I'll tell you what, the first country to swap out propaganda posters of old man dictators for iconic pictures of cute kittens is going to accomplish world domination.

---

30 Season 1, Episode 5: Space Madness.

Speaker 1: "One cat to rule them all ... "

Speaker 2: "One cat to bring them all in the darkness ... and **bind them**!"

Speaker 1: Oh no, it's all over ...

Figure 51: One cat to rule them all ...

Sharp (2007: 233) noticed among her study population of young adults explicit expressions of waning appreciation of the quoting game. In other words, interlocutors developed a sensitivity to over-engagement in the game, reaching what Sharp termed a "tolerance threshold." So widespread is the practice of English-language media quoting that it runs the risk of becoming void of any humorous effect. This possibility is illustrated in Figure 52 from *Elvis*.

Figure 52: Nobody puts Mattias in a corner!

(52)   Nobody puts Mattias in a corner!

> Speaker 1: I **hate** people who push and cut in line! When we were going to see Bruce Springsteen we ended up in the world's fattest line. I mean suuuuuuuuper long!
>
> Speaker 1: And it wasn't moving either! Then on the right there must have been some VIP-line or something, because suddenly Blossom Tainton slides on by past the whole line with her entourage! What the hell!
>
> Elvis: Oh! Beastly!
>
> Speaker 1: I was all: "**Nobody** puts Mattias in a corner!"
>
> Elvis: Because you thought a little line-dropping from Dirty Dancing would help you get in?

In this example, it is not the switch to media-English that provides the punchline, but rather the switch is used as fodder for the punchline, setting up the quoting itself to be mocked. Also noteworthy in this example is the adaptation of the quote to fit the situation, in this case simply a change of name to the speaker's own (Mattias) from the original, "Baby": "Nobody puts Baby in a corner." Such alterations to English-media quotations may offer a way to continue playing the quoting game while retaining an aspect of novelty. Figure 53 and

Figure 54 illustrate how Rocky makes references to a lyric from the acoustic version of Neil Young's song *Hey hey, my my*: "It's better to burn out than to fade away."[31] In example (53), Rocky plays with the order of the constituents; in example (54) (a single panel comic), he plays with the wording.

Figure 53: It's better to fade away.

(53) It's better to fade away

> Rocky: It has been a while since anyone we know has gotten burned out, huh? For a time it seemed like there was one a week!
>
> Rat: Well isn't everyone unemployed now? It's tough to get burned out from sitting in comfy pants and crying in front of A-Ekonomi[32] ...
>
> Rocky: Yeah, that's probably a positive consequence of the crisis ...
>
> Rat: What do you mean? Both alternatives entail going on sick-leave for depression!
>
> Rocky: But it's surely better to get fired than to work yourself ragged for some other fucker and get sick!
>
> Rat: It can't be better than working yourself ragged for someone else and getting fired and then getting sick?
>
> Rocky: No, the best thing must be to totally laze about at work, get fired and not care, and then spend the rest of your life in your parents' basement in a narcotics cloud!
>
> Rocky: <u>It's better to fade away than to burn out</u>, Neil Young can say whatever the hell he likes ...

---

[31] Nirvana-member Kurt Cobain perhaps helped this lyric become salient in popular culture when he cited it at the end of his suicide letter.

[32] A news program about economics and financial events, broadcast on SVT 1990–2011.

Figure 54: It's better to sell out.

(54) It's better to sell out

> Rocky: It's better to sell out than to fade away, I suppose …

The examples of code-switching so far have established a progression along a scale of increasing intricacy, starting with single words ("*lax* pink"), increasing to simple phrases and formulaic expressions ("here we go again"), then to media-sourced English ("Nobody puts Mattias in a corner") and finally to adapted quotations ("It's better to sell out … "). The *Rocky*-strip in Figure 55 takes the progression one step further, illustrating media-inspired code-switching.

Figure 55: Jack Shit! ATF!

(55) Jack Shit! ATF!

> Dog: <u>Jack Shit</u>, that's a good name!
>
> Rocky: <u>Special agent Jack Shit, Federal Bureau of Alcohol, Tobacco and Firearms!</u>
>
> Rocky: Why are alcohol and tobacco included? Firearms are understandable, that's highly dangerous, but how much do they work with cigs and booze?
>
> Rocky: We've never seen that on tv …
>
> Rocky: They rush in with their weapons drawn because some drunk is smoking in the outdoor eating area, <u>freeze mother!</u>
>
> Rocky: <u>Jack Shit! ATF!</u>
>
> Rocky: <u>Listen shitbird! We don't give a rats ass about you! Tell us who is your supplier and we'll plea your bargain!</u>
>
> Dog: ICA-Aptiten![33]

Much of the content of *Rocky*-comics centers on Rocky's own media consumption, and he is frequently depicted watching television. The dialogue in example (55) suggests that Rocky is more than passingly familiar with the genre of police drama, as he is able not only to repeat conventional lines but also to improvise accordingly. Minor errors ("rats ass", "who is your supplier") and non-idiomaticities ("we'll plea your bargain") characterize the use of English as non-native and inject an element of playfulness. Indeed, this instance of code-switching must be regarded as role-playing: Rocky's use of English is less for bona fide communication and more for performance purposes. Essentially, he is not using English to speak for himself, but rather to speak as an envisioned 'other'. Thus, another category of code-switching to English is established, whereby the use of English indicates the voice of another. Significantly, this voicing may also serve as mockery, as illustrated in Figure 56.

---

33 ICA is a Swedish grocery store chain; ICA-Aptiten is located in the Södermalm district of Stockholm.

Figure 56: Cops!

(56) Cops!

Rocky: Cops! All black suspects will be concidered guilty until proven to be white!

Frog: Hi! No, I'm in the country with Rocky … we're just taking it easy, working a bit … I don't know, on Sunday maybe …

Rocky: Yeah, I've been patrolling this neighborhood since -98, a lot of crack whores, babies on angel dust, naked rednecks with aids, and I've got hemorrhoids! I love it!

Phone: Beepbeep!

Phone: Bidobidobido

Frog: Hey! I'm in the country with a friend … yeah, shit that would be fun, but the last ferry has gone …

Frog: Sorry, I'll set it so it doesn't make so much noise …

Rocky: I'm going to set mine so it makes more noise …

Television: Freeze nigg … öh … asshole!

Due to the misspelling of 'considered', Rocky's first turn must be interpreted as being delivered in his own voice, with the use of English reflecting an accommodation to the language of the media currently being consumed, presumably the series *Cops*. The idiomaticity and lack of any errors (not even in the spelling of "hemorrhoids") in Rocky's second turn, however, clearly indicate that he is voicing the English-speaking police officer shown on the television screen. As such, this episode of code-switching can be likened to what Reyes (2004) calls imitation quoting, whereby a change in voice signals that the code-switcher is playing a character and to what Lee (2000, cited in Belz 2002) has called voice-quoting, that is "the re-uttering of a previously encountered word or phrase" (Belz 2002: 67) commonly practiced among language learners. There is no evident modulation of voice quality depicted in the comic; however, Rocky's shift in register and attention to accuracy establish the role-playing mode enabled by previous experience. At this point, Martin Kellerman's own proficiency in English must be recognized, as he is able to depict two styles of English, one non-native (Rocky), and one native (police officer). The contrast between the two styles is significant: it is the accuracy of the native style that serves to highlight the non-native style, which ultimately appeals to the readers as similarly non-native. Such playful awareness of a distinct Swedish, non-native variety of English is explored in the next section.

5.3 The Swedish variety of English

Since Swedish is the dominant language of Swedish comic strips, code-switches to English are discursively significant. Not only do code-switches reflect the in-group linguistic norms shared by the depicted characters (and, presumably, by their real-life counterparts) but can also reflect (or even introduce) a similar linguistic behavior among the wider Swedish reading public. When code-switches are limited to single words, simple phrases, or idiomatic expressions, they can be experienced as significant but nevertheless unobtrusive. It is when code-switches are stylized that extra attention must be paid to their symbolic potential and indexical value. Specifically, code-switches to English that overtly establish a native/non-native speaker opposition can be exploited as sources of humor by capitalizing on linguistic incongruities in group-member identities.

Chapter 2 included examples of eye-dialect and pronunciation respelling via the use of the Swedish alphabet and additional non-standard orthography to represent the Swedish variety of English. Further examples of this practice are presented here, so as to investigate more fully English language play and linguistic creativity as humor in Swedish comic strips. First, two examples are presented that relate to the theme of media-sourced English, namely the depiction of singing English-language pop songs. In the panel featured in Figure 57, extracted from *Fucking Sofo*, a group of young women celebrating a cheerleading competition victory are featured singing the Britney Spears song, *Oops! ... I did it again*. In Figure 58 from *Lilla Berlin*, a young girl is shown singing the Ace Wilder song, *Busy doin' nothin'*, made popular by the annual Swedish song contest, *Melodifestivalen*.

Figure 57: Oops.

(57) Oops

> **Women: <u>OOPS WE DID IT AGAIN! CHEERS! HAHAHAHAHAHAHAHA</u>**
>
> Speaker 1: UUUUHHH!

(58) Ajm bissi bissi bissi

> Child 1: <u>I'm busy busy busy doin' nothin' at all, I'm stressin' over nothin' don't bother to call</u> …
>
> Child 2: WAAHHH!!!
>
> Child 1: (in background) <u>Don't wanna work, just wanna make money while I sl-</u>
>
> Man: It's crazy what awful taste in music kids have … when I have kids I'm going to make sure they listen to a little *quality music* at home!
>
> Woman: Hey, they pick that up at pre-school so it wouldn't make any big difference.
>
> Man: Then there's no other solution than to start an indie-pre-school! No fucking Song

Festival-shit, just Morrissey, Stone Roses and Velvet Underground, and all the parents need to take an entry exam where their taste in music is tested! Only the best are let in, the rest are sorted out.

Woman: Oh lord ... poor kids!

Man: Yeah, the other kids ... I know. But you can't save them all!

Figure 58: Ajm bissi bissi bissi.

Like television or film dialogue, songs provide a linguistic model: word choice, word order, pronunciation, tempo, and other qualities of speech are recorded and serve as a permanent target for potential performers. Examples (57) and (58) show attempts to approach the respective featured targets with what must be, from the perspective of the Swedish speaker of English, results that are comical not only in form, but also in their recognizability. In example (57), the English-original lyric "oops, I did it again" is acceptably edited to include the plural, first-person pronoun 'we' instead of "I", but the spelling of every single word is altered to such an extent that it is nearly unrecognizable at first glance. Only upon sounding out the words does it become clear. This is the case in example (58) as well. However, although both examples highlight the distinct Swedish accent of English, the use of non-standard orthography serves different purposes. In example (57), the song is meaningfully performed, but the delivery is compromised by a state of intoxication. In example (58), in addition to the Swedish pronunciation, the forced lexical reanalysis (that is, the flawed parsing of words resulting in pseudo-words (Honeybone and Watson 2013: 313), for example, 'stressin' over' as "stressin nover") render the performance of the song an approximate recitation without apparent comprehension. These examples also illustrate the bottom-up influence of English-language popular culture on the use of English in Sweden, particularly with regards to the use of English among young people.

In the final two examples of this chapter, the Swedish variety of English is illustrated in contexts where Swedish speakers use English to communicate with non-Swedish speakers. In Figure 59 (previously featured as Figure 4 in Chapter 2), English is used as a *lingua franca* with speakers of other languages; in Figure 60 English use represents communication with US-American, native-speakers.

Figure 59: It's wery cold and wet.

5.3 The Swedish variety of English

(59) It's wery cold and wet

> Rocky: We can certainly talk seriously, but at four in the morning after four bottles of wine, we're not exactly Adaktusson[34] in "Are You Smarter than a Fifth-Grader!"
>
> Cat: But you guys babble all day long, too! You're so afraid of things turning serious that it's pathetic!
>
> Rocky: Jeez, there were 30,000 serious assholes talking seriously in Copenhagen for three weeks, what'd we get out of that? Nothing! Reinfeldt raised his hand and was all, ööh, we in Swiden tink it's wery cold and wet all dö [the] time. We plan to set up a gool [goal] for 2012 to ördj dö poor cantrys [urge the poor countries] to let us cam dere in dö wintertime [to let us come there in the wintertime]!
>
> Rat: They're all, 'No, we're talking about lowering the temperature on Earth and that …'
>
> Rocky: Ookay, right. Then never mind … Is anyone headed north?
>
> Rat: Share a jumbo-jet? I've got room for 748 if anyone's going my way?

Figure 60: Aj dånt tink så!

(60) Aj dånt tink så!

> Elvis: By the way, have I told you what it was like to go to the movies in Harlem?
>
> Money: No?
>
> Elvis: Totally crazy! Towards the end of the movie people who just finished seeing another movie next door would always come tumbling in, ha ha.

---

34 Lars Aduktusson is a Swedish television journalist.

Elvis: And forget the candy. People sat and ate FOOD at the movies. And SMOKED! And you know how in Sweden we think it's bothersome when people don't turn off their cell-phones?

Monkey: Yeah?

Elvis: Foggedaboudit. [Forget about it]. There it's all about cell-phone conversations, playing music, and "the-using-phone display-as-a-flashlight-and-shining-at-people-behind-you-game".

Elvis: And you know how you can get really bothered by nuts who sit and whisper during the whole movie here in Sweden?

Elvis: You can compare that to a whole theater shouting things like, "Run, Bitch!!" or "Don't go there, man!!" as soon as it gets exciting.

Monkey: Did you say anything?

Elvis: Are you crazy? "Hellå evribåådi, ajm de little nuuw wajt gaj datt moved in heer ä kappel åff månths agåå. Kän you pliis shatt de fakk app? Jor destrojing de moovi!" [Hello everybody, I'm the little new white guy that moved in here a couple of months ago. Can you please shut the fuck up? You're destroying the movie!]

Elvis: "Ooh, wääjt! Pliis dånt brejk maj arms!! Jår höörting mii!" [Ooh wait! Please don't break my arms! You're hurting me!]

Elvis: Aj dånt tink så!! [I don't think so!!]

In example (59), it is Sweden's then-Prime Minister Fredrik Reinfeldt who is targeted by Rocky as a speaker of Swedish, non-native English; in example (60), the main character, Elvis, self-identifies as such. Again, the aspect of non-nativeness is represented primarily by the use of Swedish spelling to approximate a non-native accent; the transcripts above include a standardized spelling of the English utterance. Additionally, the use of English in example (59) includes an error in subject-verb agreement ('we ... think' as "we in Swiden tinks"), and example (60) features a non-idiomatic string of adjectives ("new little white"[35]).

Similar to example (57) and example (58), these strips can be said to wield non-standard orthography and non-idiomaticity as a means to highlight

---

[35] The phrase "little new white" does adhere to the conventions of adjective ordering in English, that put 'size' (e.g., "little") before 'age' (e.g., "new"). However, Google searches show that "new, little COLOR" is ten to twenty times as frequent as "little, new COLOR" for the colors white, black, red, blue, yellow, orange, and purple, and twice as frequent for the color green.

incongruities between native and non-native varieties. The use of the Swedish alphabet in particular creates salient contrasts and subsequent incongruities in both language use and linguistic representation. Here, it is not a question of eye-dialect or pronunciation respellings, nor can these examples be considered regiolectal or dialectal spellings. Instead, they illustrate a phenomenon that can be called interlanguage spelling. An interlanguage is the idiolect of a foreign or second language speaker which shows evidence of having features of the speaker's first language and the target language (Selinker 1972). The term 'interlanguage spelling' thus refers to the imposition of features of the native language system onto the target language so as to depict and represent a distinct non-native variety. The juxtaposition of two linguistic systems that is inherent in interlanguage spelling results in salient incongruity and is conducive to language play.

Examples (59) and (60) illustrate code-switching for the purpose of communicating with non-Swedish speakers. For this reason, the switches can be further categorized as situational (Blom and Gumperz 1972), since they are direct responses to a situation requiring the use of a specific language, i.e., English. The source of humor in these code-switches to English can be attributed to incongruity resulting from a native/non-native opposition. Such incongruity is generally acknowledged as a basic prerequisite for linguistic humor:

> At the basis of much linguistic humor are the various types of linguistic units and their interrelationship. The notion of incongruity is crucial to such humor. It involves the disarray of phonological and grammatical elements, the twisting of the relationship between form and meaning, the reinterpretation of familiar words and phrases, and the overall misuse of language. (Apte 1985: 179)

Critical to the recognition of this incongruity and thus the appreciation of humor is the status of the featured characters as members of an in-group, one based on a shared national, cultural, and linguistic background, which the distinct use of English can both help to establish and serve to confirm. Indeed, the "misuse" of English depicted in the examples above serves two purposes: it delivers the comic strip's humor and it appeals to the reader as similarly capable of such transgressions. The mockery resulting from the exploitation of the native/non-native opposition is acceptable, and ideally even humorous, precisely because it is restricted to other in-group members with regards to its source and target. In this way, it can be considered a form of self-deprecating humor capitalizing on a personal quality that may characterize other in-group members: Swedes may either recognize themselves or their compatriots in young children or drunken partiers singing in English; they may take pleasure in the idea that the prime minister speaks just like (or worse than!) them; and they may relate to the experience of representing the Swedish, out-group member in native English contexts.

Compared to the earlier examples of the use of fixed phrases and idioms as well as participation in the quoting game, the examples of situational code-switches to English suggest a degree of distance to the language on the part of the speaker. In other words, the code-switches depicted in examples (42)–(54) provide evidence of English being used as a second language, invoked proficiently and idiomatically among bilinguals to add communicative nuance. The code-switches in examples (55)–(60), however, suggest that English is experienced as a foreign language in the depicted contexts: English is presented as a language of the 'other', such that its usage by Swedes can be likened to a performance. The "disarray" and "misuse of language" noted by Apte (1985: 179) which also characterize these examples further highlight the foreignness of English and allow for a Swedish variety of English – distinctly lacking idiomaticity or proficiency – to be identified.

The widespread use of English in contemporary Swedish comic strips reflects both the ubiquity of English but also its dual nature in Swedish society. Significantly, the differences in the depicted code-switching practices suggest that comics artists' language play reflects a shared symbolic competence (Kramsch and Whitehead 2008: 667), defined as "the ability to shape the multilingual game in which one invests – the ability to manipulate the conventional categories and societal norms of truthfulness, legitimacy, seriousness, originality-and to reframe human thought and action." Whereas in some instances proficiency in English and a familiarity with English-language culture are highlighted, at other times linguistic skills and cultural knowledge are suppressed in favor of presenting a saliently Swedish, non-native speaker identity. Language play in the comic strip medium allows for the distinction to be visualized, such that standard English is contrasted with Swedish English via incongruities in orthography, grammar, lexicon, and idiomaticity. Despite the dominance of Swedish in the multilingual society that Sweden has become, it is the English language that is consistently and reliably mined as a source of humor and an essential aspect of Swedish identity. The next chapter takes a more detailed examination of the Swedish variety of English, focusing specifically on the use of English swear words.

6 Are you completely @#☠ fucking crazy?

In Chapter 5, the widespread presence and usage of the English language in Sweden was explained as the result of English having entered the Swedish speech community from two directions: from above, via a process of institutionalization as a result of language planning policy, and from below, most noticeably through the global spread of English-language popular culture (Preisler 1999a). The result of these combined forces is that nearly everyone in Swedish society can be assumed to come into sporadic if not regular contact with English, in the form of learning, actively using, or simply being exposed to English. Thus, similar linguistic experiences collectively constitute a common, society-wide background knowledge, which can be exploited for various communicative goals. For example, their shared background knowledge allows Swedish people to capitalize on English as a linguistic resource for pragmatic purposes, one of which is to convey humor. In this respect, the context of comic strips is key to both constructing and reinforcing this particular pragmatic function via language play.

Having considered the role of English in Sweden by exploring the indexical value of code-switches to English as a source of humor in comics, Chapter 5 has also laid the foundation for an attempt, in the current chapter, to understand why specifically English-language swearing occurs in Swedish discourse, and why English-language swearing in Swedish would elicit a humorous reaction. The aim of this chapter is thus to consider the potential humor of English swear word usage in a Swedish discourse context, taking into account Swedish shared background knowledge of and familiarity with swearing practices in Anglophone contexts. In so doing, a mutual feedback loop (Trotta 1998: 104, 2010: 47) can be affirmed: while the comic strip context serves to frame English swear words as funny, the use of English swear words, which draws on shared background knowledge with regards to intercultural contrasts, encourages a humorous reading of the comic.

While different sociolinguistic and pragmatic variables can prompt swear word usage or be conducive to a communicative exchange involving swearing, one desired goal or even unintentional outcome of swearing can be humor. Swear word usage has also been shown to have humorous effects even when swearing utterances are not delivered in a humorous tone or joking context (Beers Fägersten 2012a). The relationship between swearing and humor has

---

Note: Parts of this chapter are adapted from Beers Fägersten (2017c).

https://doi.org/10.1515/9781501505119-006

been further established in studies that show that people use swear words to elicit humor and mask aggression (Jay 1999), that swearing in stories and narratives, as well as swearing in reactions to stories, modulates humor (Norrick 2012), and that jokes are experienced as funnier when they include swearing (Abbott and Jay 1978; McGhee and Pistolesi 1979). Of particular relevance to this chapter, comic strips including swear words are also considered funnier than those without (Sewell 1984). The combination of comic strips and English swear words creates a mutual feedback loop, such that comic strip context primes the reader for humor, while the swearing elicits a humorous reaction, thus enhancing the humor of the comic strip. In other words, the association with humor of the one reinforces the humor of the other.

6.1 English-language swearing in Swedish

The constant exposure to English both from above and from below serves to secure it as a valid code for communication in Sweden. In general, it can be said that Swedes have both Swedish and English at their disposal as communicative tools, confirming previous assessments of Sweden as a bilingual society (Fergusson 1994; Josephson 2004; Phillipson 1992). Furthermore, English is no longer limited to high status domains or use among the elite but is used in ever-increasing contexts and across socioeconomic class, characterizing social interaction in low status domains as well (Sharp 2007). It is also increasingly common for Swedish and English to co-exist in one and the same communicative context. Much code-switching is in the form of loanwords and the incorporation of idioms or other simple phrases as illustrated in Chapter 5, but even swearing expressions have previously been noted, such as "Shit happens" (Höglin 2002: 56) or "Go to hell" (Sharp 2007: 231, 233). The observation of English-language swearing among otherwise innocuous expressions is significant, as it suggests that swear words and swearing phrases are appropriated indiscriminately.

The practice of using English swear words is not unique to the Swedish context; 'fuck' in particular, and to a lesser extent 'shit', have entered the lexicons of, for example, Norwegian (Andersen 2014), Danish (Rathje 2011), Finnish (Hjort 2017), Dutch (Zenner et al. 2017), and French (Jaffe 2017), in both their native forms and in language-specific orthographic, phonological, morphological, and syntactic adaptations. However, there is a lack of research on or even collected evidence of the use of English swear words specifically in language play and as sources of humor in these or other languages, especially in the medium of comic strips. The examples presented in this chapter help to initiate and establish research on the humorous functions of English-language swearing in foreign or second language contexts. Below, Figure 61 from *Elvis* illustrates the integration of language play and English-language swearing. It also serves as a reminder of how humor is furthermore the product of resolving the opposition and incongruity created by the interaction between the multimodal resources of the comic strip.

Figure 61: Shit vacation.

(61) Shit vacation

>Elvis: (thinking) Wienerschnitzel. The <u>fakking</u> [fucking] **only** positive thing about this shit-vacation.
>
>(Background noise)
>
>Elvis: **Ooww! Go-o-o-d**[36]!

In this example, incongruity within the text can be found in the word *fakking*, an interlanguage spelling of 'fucking', which reflects an orthographical representation of the Swedish pronunciation, and in the word *skitsemester*, which is orthographically and phonetically close to *skidsemester*, "ski trip/skiing vacation". Incongruity within the image can be observed in the opposing depictions of Elvis in the two panels: quietly thinking while clothed, hunched over, and consuming food in the panel to the left; loudly exclaiming while in a state of undress, legs asunder, and voiding his bowels in the panel to the right. Finally, incongruity between the text and image is localized in the word *skitsemester*, or "shit vacation". The Swedish swear word *skit* (Eng: "dirt, crap, shit") can compound with

---

36 The English translation should be understood as the word "God" pronounced with a lengthened vowel (not "good").

adjectives or nouns to serve a qualifying or boosting function, meaning "very", "awful(ly)", or "shit(ty)", for example: *skitmånga* – "very many"; *skitbra* – "really good/great"; *skithungrig* – awfully hungry; or *skitsemester* – "shit(ty) vacation". The comic strip plays with the syntactic vs. semantic qualities of *skit*, requiring the reader to reinterpret the booster function invoked in the first panel to the literal meaning of *skit* which the toilet scene depicted in panel two connotes.

The use of swear words is conventionally associated with abuse, aggression, hostility, pain, frustration, or similar negative emotions and experiences, as illustrated in example (61). There is, however, growing evidence that swearing indexes interlocutor intimacy, expressions of solidarity, or well-being in the communicative context (Adams 2018; Beers Fägersten 2012a; Jay 2009; Stapleton 2010). The apparent polarity between the two general functions of swearing is reflected in the terms "annoyance swearing" and "social swearing" (Montagu 2001), each triggered by generally negative or generally positive, respectively, circumstances or contexts. While annoyance swearing is illustrated in Figure 61, social swearing is featured in Figure 62.

Figure 62: A fucking eternity.

(62) A fucking eternity

> Rocky: You know what? I'll have one of those former Soviet satellite state beers with an unpronounceable name and which takes all night to tap!
>
> Bartender: You mean a Crazkovitche pimplenský prazdroj?
>
> Rocky: My good man, you took the words right out of my mouth!
>
> Bartender: This is going to take a while, it has to be tapped in six rounds and rest five minutes between each one ...
>
> Rocky: Aaaaah! Finally! <u>Wörth waiting a fucking</u> eternity <u>for</u>! Now to blow the hell off of the muffin top and let this shit stream down my throat!

Bartender: No no no!

Bartender: Now you have to wait twenty minutes until the crown has settled and the aroma has really sunk into the beer!

Rocky: Damn, no wonder Dracula was thirsty as hell all the time!

As a bar patron, Rocky evidently evaluates the situation as appropriate for swearing, and does so on four occasions (*fucking, åt helvete, skiten, in i helvete*). These swearing instances may occur in expressions of mild annoyance at the tediousness of tapping a beer, but they are neither directed at the bartender nor intended to abuse or offend him. Instead, the use of swear words in the social setting depicted in example (62) indexes informality and constitutes a sociable overture. Notably, it is only Rocky who swears, whose linguistic freedom to do so is somewhat greater than that of the bartender, who is beholden to a professional register.

Similar to example (61), example (62) illustrates the simultaneous usage of both Swedish and English swear words, suggesting not only compatibility between the two discourse systems, but also no apparent restrictions on or censure of either in the comic strip context, despite the publication of the strip in a daily national newspaper. Before continuing with additional examples, the use of swear words in the medium of daily newspaper comics must first be examined.

6.2 Swearing in the media

A body of research concerned with the evolution of swearing in contemporary Anglophone contexts provides evidence of an increase in swearing and swear word usage in many forms of media (Jay 1992; Hilliard and Keith 2007; Ivory et al. 2009; Kaye and Sapolsky 2004). Furthermore, this development has not gone unnoticed and is occasionally asserted as self-evident and cause for counter-action (Dufrene and Lehman 2002; Hunker and Vanderkam 1999; Maltby 1998; O'Connor 2000). While swear word usage in various social contexts and interpersonal communication varies in terms of salience, appropriateness, and acceptability (Beers Fägersten 2012a), it is generally recognized as a marked feature of language use, typical of non-standard varieties (Anderson and Trudgill 1990; Battistella 2005; Wajnryb 2005) and possessing the potential to cause great offense (Beers Fägersten 2012a; Jay 1992; Jay, Caldwell-Harris, and King 2008). For these reasons, swearing has traditionally been absent from, avoided by, or subject to censorship in the media, largely due to general expectations of the language of the media to embody the standard variety and to be "the most public of languages." (Bell 1983: 30) It is this public aspect of mass media combined with the unknown social composition of its potential consumers which are often at the root of the controversy of swear word usage in the media. It is not suggested that the language of comic strips be equated with the language of the media, but the publication of comic strips in daily newspapers renders them a product of mass media and thus potentially subject to reigning conventions of censorship.

Contemporary Swedish newspaper comic strips provide evidence of not just frequent swear word usage, but also tolerance for and even appreciation of it. The liberal attitude also applies to both native Swedish and non-native English swear words. Figures 63 and 64 feature panel extracts from *Lilla Berlin* and *Rocky*, respectively, representing samples of how native-language swearing occurs in Swedish comic strips.

Figure 63: Ow, damn it!

(63) Ow, damn it!

    Speaker 1: Ow, damn it! Fucking shit.

Figure 64: Oh cock and piss!

(64) Oh cock and piss!

> Rocky: Oh hey, oh ho! Oh cock and piss! Oh damn and shit! Oh hell and damn!

Interesting to note in these examples is the practice of using multiple swear words at once. The utterance of one swear word often triggers the use of even more; when one speaker's swearing turn is followed by swearing in another interlocutor's turn, it is known as "echoic swearing", whereas when one speaker uses many swear words in a single turn, it is referred to as "self-echoic swearing" (Beers Fägersten 2012a). This latter type is particularly associated with laughter reactions (Beers Fägersten 2012a), and for this reason, self-echoic swearing should be considered a predictable element of humorous contexts such as comic strips.

Despite the ease with which swearing can be found in Swedish comic strips, there is, in fact, evidence of self-censorship. Figures 65–67 illustrate different strategies for censoring swear words; Figures 65 and 67 are one-panel extracts from *Berglins*; Figure 66 is from *Lilla Berlin*.

Figure 65: Fitta.

(65) Fitta

>Caption: Go out and pick frost-pinched rosehips! Oh, nothing is more contemplative! Rinse, dry, boil, sift...
>
>Speaker 1: You have a bowl under the strainer, right?
>
>Speaker 2: Wah!
>
>Speaker 2: CUNT!
>
>Speaker 1: Now, Inger ... #Youtoo!

(66) A true "original"!

>Speaker 1: Oh! Isn't it *nice* to get away from town and out in the country?
>
>Speaker 1: Everything is so much simpler here! People are so friendly and open, not so cynical and mean like in town.
>
>Speaker 1: Hi there!
>
>Speaker 2: Eh shut up you damn town tramps from hell!

Speaker 2: You can go to hell you disgusting little X and take your X and stick it up your X with your mother's X X X and X!

Speaker 1: Oh, really so unbelievably **genuine** and **honest**! Not false and ingratiating like in town, but right to the point.

Speaker 1: A true "original"!

Figure 66: A true "original"!.

Figure 67: Are you crazy?

(67) Are you crazy?

> Caption: ... between your own morals and others'.
>
> Speaker 1: Damn ... now I've chipped their paint ... We'll have to write a note so they can get in touch.
>
> Speaker 2: Are you completely @#♣ fucking crazy? I have nine dings of my own! NOW LET'S SPLIT!!

Together, these examples not only detail different strategies of censorship but also show how censorship functions to highlight, not hide, swear word usage. In each, there is no indication that the words were actually censored in the represented talk but, significantly, the affordances of the comic strip medium have been exploited to depict visual censorship for the sake of the reader. In Figure 65, the two Ts look to be scribbled out in the swear word *fitta* ("cunt"). However, the word remains entirely legible and is all the more salient for its partial obfuscation. In contrast, the censorship in Figure 66 is complete, with whole words blocked out. It is not possible to decipher what was actually said. Instead, the readers are invited to use their imagination, and the fact that *helvete* ("hell") and *jävla* ("damn/fucking") are not censored encourages readers to imagine much more offensive words. In this way, the comics artist can effect a level of offense that actual swear words may not have accomplished. In Figure 67, a grawlix is used for similar effect. Here, however, it should be noted that the censorship implies a Swedish word (or words), as the English swear word "fucking" is not censored. The juxtaposition of the grawlix and "fucking" is provocative, particularly for speakers of English, since the word "fuck" is consistently rated as highly offensive and therefore equally reliably subject to censorship. In its unfiltered state and following the grawlix, "fucking" must be interpreted as more acceptable than the censored Swedish word. This particular instance of censorship thus illustrates the status of English swear words in Sweden as not only generally inoffensive, but also socially unproblematic. Swedes are not beholden to the cultural or social restrictions associated with English swear word usage in native contexts, and as such they are free to swear in English with abandon. The result of this freedom is examined in the next set of examples, Figures 68–70.

Figure 68: Turn it down!

(68) Turn it down!

Rocky: I bought a book on tape too, The Heart of Darkness by Joseph Conrad, read by Max von Sydow! Have you read it?

Dog: No, but Max von Sydow has! Turn it on!

Reader: Slowly our boat glided deeper into the jungle, past the stupid niggers who

Dog: Oof! For God's sake turn it down!

Dog: We should maybe listen to a children's book instead? Ture Sventon and Åsa-Nisse i the South Sea?

Rocky: Alwayt these ratists! Let's go have a ticky-bun in the retaurant wagon intead![37]

Rocky: Or are ticky-buns politically incorrect now? Blacklisted together with Napolean pastries, hmm-hmm balls, Nogger ice-cream and China puffs?

Rocky: Uh, I'll just have a marzipan pig, and a mulatto … latte! Just a smooth cup of kaffir … No! A cup of coffee! Black. No, colored coffee, and a cheese sandwich on light bread!

Rocky: And one on dark, on the same plate! I have no problem with that!

Figure 69: Bronx.

(69) Bronx

Monkey: One time we were in Orlando to listen to Prem Rawat, and then I made an explosive fool of myself.

---

37 Rocky imitates Åke Holmberg's literary character Ture Sventon, who is known for occasionally pronouncing [s] as [t].

Monkey: I was maybe seven, and had only seen black people on Kojak[38] ...

Monkey: So when a black man came I got really happy and yelled <u>HI NIGGER</u>!

Monkey: Because that's how black people talked on Baretta! "<u>HEY NIGGER! CRACK THAT CHEESE IN THE BRONK NIGGER</u>! It's CRACK in the shit, I don't CRACK in the Bronx man!"

Monkey: And then the subtitles: "Hello Italian! Will you come along and watch a film?"

Rocky: What did he say then?

Monkey: He said something I didn't understand ...

Monkey: But I can tell you it was fucking chaos in the child-care group ... Horrible trauma to say something well-intended and be met with an uproar and realize what a piece of trash you are!

Rocky: Imagine the trauma for him meeting a Swedish 7-year-old who yells <u>CRACK THAT SHIT IN THE BRONX NIGGER</u>!

In Figure 68, Rocky and Dog are visibly shocked and embarrassed when the narrator pronounces the word *niggarna* (Eng: "the niggers"): they are shown to blush, there is a sudden vocal outburst, and their initial reaction is to lower the volume, suggesting an awareness of the overall public context even though they are alone in their train car. In a definitive act of silencing the offending audio, Dog slams the laptop shut and suggests listening to a children's book instead, naming one example of classic Swedish children's literature. Rocky notes that this literary series has racist elements, which leads them in the ensuing conversation to consider examples of everyday racism in food and drink items. Rocky's reference to "hmm-hmm balls" is an example of self-censorship. Rocky is evidently avoiding naming a chocolate-oatmeal pastry which in the past was called *negerbollar* ("negro balls") and has been marked as socially unacceptable and all but excised from contemporary Swedish. This term has been replaced by *chokladbollar* ("chocolate balls"), which, however, may also encode racist discourse. "Nogger" ice-cream is also seen as problematic, due to its similarity with the word "nigger". By having Rocky confront racist terminology, commit a string of faux pas, and nevertheless claim racial tolerance, strip

---

[38] An American drama series about a New York detective (CBS, 1973–1978).

creator Martin Kellerman manages to play with and mock politically correct language as well as reveal the insidiousness of racism in everyday language.

Example (69) provides an interesting contrast to example (68). Whereas Rocky and Dog exhibit genuine sensitivity to racist terms in the Swedish language, Rocky and Monkey reveal little more than bemusement at the use of the word "nigger" in English. The example illustrates indiscriminate appropriation of media-sourced English, and it also establishes an awareness of inappropriateness in foreign or second language usage. But this comic strip, just like every other example featured in this book, reminds us that comic strip communication occurs on two levels: on the one hand, between the characters depicted in the strips, and on the other hand, between the strips and their readers. It is this second level of communication that is of greatest significance with regards to how language play conveys and fosters linguistic attitudes and ideologies. Comic strips may depict language use in personal, private encounters, but their publication in mass media such as daily national newspapers means that this private context is transferred to a public forum. Comics artists are thus communicating to their readers, encouraging among them an interpretation of depicted events – including language usage – as targets of humor and objects of mirth. In the comic strip context, swearing and the use of racist or offensive language, particularly in English, are contextualized as comical and therefore conveyed to the audience in this way as well.

Some understanding of potential offense, provocation, and controversy is nevertheless evident. Although Monkey claims the innocence of youth, blames his language use on the influence of media and the linguistic model presented in US-American popular culture, and focuses on his trauma of unknowingly speaking inappropriately, Rocky shows an awareness of the one on the receiving end of racist language who cannot know of the mitigating circumstances. By having Rocky consider the perspective of the addressee in his final turn, Martin Kellerman actually appeals to the readers' recognition of themselves or other Swedes as possibly guilty of similar misuses of language. The comic strip conversation represents acceptable language use by Swedes among Swedes, but the overall message of the strip is one of an awareness that the Swedish use of English is at odds with native speaker norms. This is particularly apparent in example (70).

(70) Yeah fo sho!

> Chicken: Now we're going to Roppongi and meeting up with Ichiura and his American friends!

Rocky: Ugh ... I hate Roppongi and I hate speaking English! I can't make jokes and I don't know any fun words ...

Chicken: Well then it's good you get to practice! I'm pretty used to it so for me it's no problem.

Chicken: (on the phone) Hey man, what up motherfucker? Where the fuck are you at?

Chicken: We're just down the fucking street, dog! We're right by this fucking subway joint, you know? Like sandwiches and shit? It's fucked up!

Chicken: Hey man, what's crackulating? You waited long up in this motherfucker? We're kinda late cuz all these fucking whores were all up in our grills talkin bout massage and shit and we're like get the fuck out of my fucking face with that fucking bullshit!

Monkey: Does everybody in Sweden speak English like that?

Chicken: Yeah fo sho nigga! We learn that shit from the fourth fucking grade and shit! It's fucking ... like ... shit!

Monkey: What kind of school did you go to?

Figure 70: Yeah fo sho!

Similar to example (69), example (70) draws on the inherent incongruity resulting from a clash between two discourse systems, English and Swedish. The resolution to the incongruity lies in the recognition and allowance of an unfamiliarity with (or disregard for) native-speaker norms. The humor is not just a function of incongruous speech style with regards to context, but the fact that the speakers are unaware of the incongruity is also humorous. Here, the concept of interdiscourse applies, referring to communication that:

> involves participants with different first languages or different levels of competence in the language(s) used in the interaction, members of different groups and cultures with different assumptions about appropriate speech events and ways of speaking as well as different (cultural) background knowledge – in short, communication across separate discourse systems.
> (Norrick 2007: 389)

Differences and discrepancies between discourse systems increase the potential for incongruities, and thus interdiscourse is particularly ripe for humor. Example (70) illustrates the incongruity resulting from the failure of the Swedish speaker of English to approach native speaker norms. This failure simply suggests that the speaker's level of sociolinguistic competence is inadequate, but does not necessarily entail that the speaker is applying Swedish norms. Specifically, example (70) illustrates a type of humorous interdiscourse that Norrick refers to as Contrast, in which "the humorist creates a persona or character representing an outsider's perspective on some discourse system" (Norrick 2007: 392). Norrick claims that the outside perspective causes "confusion or misunderstanding," which subsequently provides the basis for the incongruity necessary for the humorous interpretation. However, while Norrick focuses on misunderstandings arising from a participant's lack of knowledge of another discourse system, what is essentially humorous about example (70) is the fact Swedes actually have extensive knowledge of English as the 'other' discourse system. Essentially, in this comic, there are two perspectives represented: the Swedish outsider perspective of English and the Swedish insider perspective of Swedish-English. It is therefore proposed that the strategy of Contrast in interdiscourse humor should not only account for an outside perspective on the other's native discourse system (for example, native varieties of English), but also for an insider perspective of contrasting non-native discourse systems (for example, a Swedish variety of English).

Examples (69) and (70) depict Swedish, non-native speakers appropriating what they believe is an acceptable and standard native-speaker speech style. Both examples thus also crucially rely on background knowledge to appreciate the humor, and again, this background knowledge has to do with the variety of English and the kind of Anglophone culture that are most prominent or most attuned to in Swedish society. Example (69) makes explicit reference to television language, thus implicating influences of English from below, while references to learning English at school in example (70) imply that the forces of English from above are equally responsible for national proficiency in English: "We learn that shit from the fourth fucking grade and shit." This particular utterance establishes incongruity on several levels. First, the idea of being an educated speaker is incongruous with the style of speech exhibited; second, knowledge and use of English swear words is incongruous with formal (school) instruction of English; and third, the sanctioned use of swear words is incongruous with children, such as fourth-graders. Finally, this line of dialogue presents an overall incongruity between English from above (what the Swedish reader knows is taught at school) and English from below (what the Swedish reader recognizes as the more likely source of exposure to English-language swearing). Via an outsider perspective, the comic mocks the native, swear word-laden discourse system, and via an insider perspective, the comic mocks the contrastively inappropriate Swedish, non-native discourse system. While Chicken represents an example of a Swedish, non-native speaker of English in example (70), it is Rocky who provides the insider perspective by reacting to his friend's swearing via facial expressions, conveying an evolution from dubiousness to discomfort to anxiety, culminating in his fleeing the scene in the last panel.

6.3 Swearing as code-switching

The examples presented thus far establish that swearing in Swedish may be enacted with both Swedish and English swear words. The use of English, however, constitutes a code-switch, and the use of English swear words can therefore be considered a "swearing-switch". Representing the essence of the use of English-language swear words for humorous purposes in Swedish, swearing switches draw on background knowledge of (1) the stereotype of Anglophone (especially US-American) popular culture as characterized by frequent swearing, (2) the taboos of swearing that persist in native Anglophone cultures, and (3) the tendency for Swedish speakers to appropriate the fictional use of swear words while being unaware of or even unconcerned with these associated taboos. The analyses show how the humor of swearing-switches derives from incongruities, which in turn establish interdiscourse clashes. The incongruities can only be resolved by applying background knowledge in the form of Swedish stereotypes of English speakers and Anglophone cultures. Ultimately, humor is claimed to be derived from recognizing oneself as a product of imported Anglophone culture in the form of a non-native, Swedish speaker of

English. The following two strips exemplify the mindful consumption of swearing in Anglophone popular culture and the subsequent act of appropriation. Figure 71 is a single-panel extract from *Berglins*; Figure 72 is from *Rocky*.

Figure 71: Fuck! Vroom!

(71) Fuck! Vroom!

>Speaker 1: Okay, now we've seen aging men as swearing lobster fishers, aging men as fiendishly swearing goldminers and aging men as frantically swearing lumberjacks ... shall we go to bed?

>Speaker 2: Wait ... now it's aging men as truck drivers, swearing beyond all reason out in the frozen tundra!

>Speaker 1: Ah ... "Ice road truckers"!

>Television: Fuck! Vroom! Fuck! Vroom!

(72) Fucking fuck!

>Rocky: Cuba Goodie Junior has such a special look that he can never play another person.

Monkey: He looks like Gizmo in the Gremlins.

Rocky: You watch <u>The People vs O.J. Simpsons</u> S01E01 [season 1 episode 1] and along comes Gizmo wobbling out from the murder scene. You're all I don't remember Cuba Goodie Junior was involved in this mess?

Monkey: They really nailed the casting of the one playing Cuba Goodie Junior.

Television: <u>Fuck!</u>

Rocky: <u>Fucking fuck! It's that guy from Jerry McGuyver!</u>

Rocky: Cuba Goodie Junior's fate is worth a mini-series of its own. He was an American football star and guard at Guantánamo before he became a movie star!

Monkey: And then it all ended with his wife getting murdered by O.J. Simpsons!

Figure 72: Fucking fuck!

The couple in example (71) make clear that one of the most defining characteristics of American television series is the practice of swearing, performed in such a way as to warrant evaluations of "fiendish", "frantic", and "beyond all reason". Concluding this fourth and final panel of the strip on the theme of "evening TV-viewing" is a sound-bite from the series "Ice Road Truckers", confirming the impression that American television programming (and, by plausible extension, American society) is nothing more than aging men saying "fuck".

Example (72) also features media dialogue in the form of the word "fuck" as part of the strip's text. Similar to example (71) (and also the final turn of example (50) in Chapter 5), the media dialogue is integrated into the strip as a conversational turn. This swearing turn seems to trigger Rocky,[39] who then performs a swearing switch, thereby engaging in both echoic and self-echoic behavior by uttering "Fucking fuck!" This strip thus illustrates the process of appropriating English swear words via media consumption.

6.4 Swearing as the 'other'

Swearing-switches in Swedish comic strips serve as a commentary not only on the paradoxically complicated use of swear words in native-English contexts, but also on the innocent failure or deliberate unwillingness of Swedes to adhere to native-speaker conventions. Humor is a function of incongruity in the form of intercultural contrasts which, in turn, are a function of background knowledge with regards to native English (outsider) and Swedish-English (non-native insider) norms. To appreciate fully this non-native insider perspective, the concept of background knowledge needs to be developed. Here, the Encryption Theory of Humor (Flamson and Barrett, 2008) is applicable. Flamson and Barrett's model builds upon Sperber and Wilson's (1986/1995) theory of relevance (as does Yus (2003)) and the concept of encryption (citing Piper and Murphy (2002)), and proposes that the successful production and appreciation of humor depends on background knowledge being used as a "key" to encode and decode a message:

> [I]n a successful joke, both the producer and the receiver share common background knowledge – the key – and the joke is engineered in such a way (including devices like incongruity) that there is a nonrandom fit between the surface utterance and this background knowledge that would only be apparent to another person with the background knowledge. Humor therefore guarantees or makes highly likely that specific, hidden knowledge was necessary to produce the humorous utterance, and that the same knowledge is present in anyone who understands the humor. The encryption theory bears a strong resemblance to what are commonly known as "inside jokes": jokes that only those "in the know" can produce and get. (Flamson and Barrett 2008: 264)

Much of the humor experienced from swear word usage is believed to be the result of an unexpected obscenity at an inappropriate moment (Zelvys 1990). Offensive and obscene swearing (Fine 1979) can evoke laughter, which serves to lessen social distance and increase a sense of community or solidarity. The shared awareness of Anglophone swearing practices and the attitudes (often

---

39 The speaker is identified as Rocky based on the location of the tail of the speech balloon corresponding to Rocky's location on the sofa.

hypocritical) towards swearing combined with their own general indifference to the potential force of English swear words allows Swedes to target English-language swearers and swearing as a source of humor. This is illustrated by Figure 73, in which Rocky and a friend are accosted outside of Santa Rosa Plaza, California, by what is apparently an American.

Figure 73: Fucking fags!!!

(73) Fucking fags!!!

> Rocky: This is really such a cuddly society where there's always something horrible happening.
>
> Rat: Yeah, school shootings are probably like a regular free period here.
>
> Dog: FUCKING FAGS!!! FUCK YOU!!!
>
> Rocky: I think he meant us!
>
> Rat: Yeah, what the hell do you think? We're walking with little bags of Italian delicacies on the way from the Snoopy museum to our gay cottage!
>
> Rat: Street cred zero!
>
> Rocky: Just la la laaa ♪♪ get my head sliced off with a samurai sword …
>
> Rat: "If those fucking fags would have been carrying samurai swords this tragedy could have been avoided."

The portrayal of the American as an aggressive, slobbering bully who hurls obscenities at unsuspecting strangers is not particularly flattering, but it is one which Anglophone popular culture has made familiar, and the mockery is blatant. But it is the depicted reaction to the outburst that is most noteworthy: the baseball cap flying off Rocky's head and Rat's hair standing on end indicate that the two are taken aback, startled, and perhaps even shocked. In the third panel, Rocky's surprise is confirmed, as he comes to realize that he and his friend were the targets of the epithet. The dialogue in the first panel establishes an awareness of "horrible" things happening at any time in the United States, and for this reason it cannot be so surprising to be accosted in the street. Instead, it seems that it is the content of the verbal assault which prompts the suitably "cartoonish" reaction. In the fourth panel, the processing of the encounter by Rocky and Rat suggests that violence and swearing as stereotypical characteristics of American society have been confirmed, and the swearing they were exposed to has been appropriated and repurposed for comical effect. This comic strip thus illustrates an awareness of the potential force of English swear words in an Anglophone context at the same time as it establishes a delight in the immunity to this force experienced by Swedes, by virtue of their non-native speaker status.

The swearing expressions included in example (73) constitute examples of annoyance swearing, and they rank among those that are consistently rated by native speaker study populations as being highly obscene or offensive; other such expressions include "fuck off" and "(mother)fucker" as a vocative or exclamation (Beers Fägersten 2012a). Swearing of this type is both infrequent (Beers Fägersten 2012a) and highly unexpected in formal but even casual social situations (Johnson and Lewis 2010). Such expressions are not normally associated with humor, and they are conventionally subject to strict censorship in Anglophone media. In Swedish media, however, their use is not only permitted, but English-language swearing of this type is promoted as particularly humorous by virtue of its saliency in comic strips, illustrated by the following examples from *Zelda, Berglins,* and *Stockholmsnatt* (Figures 74–76).

(74) Fuck you Charlotte

> Speaker 1: Oh my Go-o-o-o-d[40] how cozy it is to eat lunch altogether girls! Just like in Sex and the City!
>
> Speaker 2: I call being Carrie Bradshaw!
>
> Speaker 3: No, I want to be Carrie!

---

40 The English translation should be understood as the word "God" pronounced with a lengthened vowel (not "good").

Figure 74: Fuck you Charlotte.

Speaker 1: You are without a doubt Samantha! Emotionally cold man-eater in a superficial industry!

Speaker 2: Fuck you Charlotte, you prudish mouse!

Speaker 1: "Charlotte"?

Speaker 3: I'm still the most like Carrie!

Speaker 4: Ugh! Can we talk about something else? I hate Sex and the City! It's a piss-awful, hypocritical, Mr. Right-idolizing, materialistic shit series that is disconnected from reality and encourages anorectic fashion blogging and passivity!!!

Speaker 2: Oh, a typical Miranda!

Speaker 3: Yeah, totally!

Speaker 4: What? I don't want to be the ugly one!

Figure 75: Guppy.

(75) Guppy

    Caption: But what do you give to the one who has everything?

    Speaker 1: May I tempt you with the <u>very</u> latest? These small luminous rascals have been injected with neon colors! Like tattooed fishies.

    Speaker 2: No way!! Then I want a guppy that has "<u>Fuck off</u>" on it!

(upper-right text: True! What did you think?)

Figure 76: Fuck you!

(76) Fuck you!

> Speaker 1: Excuse me, but what exactly are you doing ... ? You're not really thinking about using that sweaty selfie as your profile picture on Facebook, right? That is just so embarrassing, have you lost all of your ambitions or what ... Do you even remember who you once were?
>
> Speaker 2: Hey now, I've run the Healthy Huff and Puff[41] in under an hour ...
>
> Speaker 2: And by the way, who are you?
>
> Speaker 1: I'm just your 16-year-old self, don't you recognize me anymore? Or do you no longer want to recognize me anymore?
>
> Speaker 2: I see, is there something wrong with the Healthy Huff and Puff now or what?!!
>
> Speaker 2: There aren't many my age who can run it in 58:47. Hello there ...
>
> Speaker 1: <u>Fuck you!</u>

In contrast to examples (69)–(73), the swearing-switches in examples (74), (75), and (76) do not highlight interdiscourse humor as an incongruity due to an intercultural clash. In fact, there is neither an explicit nor implicit reference to English, nor an obvious trigger for situational code-switching. The general lack of reference to English (with a possible exception of example (74) which is about the US-American sit-com *Sex and the City*) makes these swearing-switches all the more interesting, as they illustrate how English-language swearing occurs in Swedish without any preliminary priming or cuing, suggesting development toward complete appropriation. In contrast to the previous examples, however, these swearing-switches function as pragmatic borrowing (Andersen 2014: 18), understood as "the direct borrowing of forms which serve pragmatic functions in the [source language]." The pragmatic force of the swearing expressions "fuck you" and "fuck off" could perhaps be achieved by a similar Swedish swearing expression, for example, *dra åt helvete* ("go to hell"), which calls into question the necessity of or motivation for a switch to English. However, by featuring the

---

[41] A made-up name for an outdoor fun-run, a loose translation to English would be "The Healthy Huff and Puff". The word *friskus* is most likely formed from the adjective *frisk*, meaning "healthy"; *flåset* means "the huffing and puffing", from the verb (*att*) *flåsa* meaning "(to) breathe heavily; huff and puff".

swearing-switch, these comic strips simultaneously index the extent to which English-language swearing is integrated in Swedish and further establish the pragmatic functions of English-language swearing in Swedish.

Example (75) and especially example (76) also illustrate how English swearing expressions often are relied upon to deliver the humor in Swedish comics by virtue of being invoked in the final speaker turn, i.e., the crucial punchline position. In example (76), the speaker of the punchline is not even depicted in the final panel; the "Fuck you!" speech balloon provides the terminal punctuation.

In Chapter 5, a series of examples illustrate how code-switches to English repeatedly occur in punchline position in contemporary Swedish comic strips; the same applies to swearing-switches, as exemplified in the following series of *Elvis* comic strips (Figures 77–79).

Figure 77: Subject: Romantic film.

(77) Subject: Romantic film

> Caption: Subject: Romantic film
>
> Elvis: I can spare you the time. First, they're going to mess it up and not get together, and then she'll realize that it's him she really loves and not the other guy. And then it'll be them for always, the end!
>
> Wife: Well **THANKS** for ruining the film!!
>
> Wife: Do you know how I think your film is going to end? The hero is going to survive, first he'll get beat up, but just when it looks hopeless he'll come back and win.
>
> Elvis: … ?
>
> Wife: And it's the same for **ALL** the action movies you will ever see, <u>fucker</u>.

Figure 78: Maddafakka!

(78) Maddafakka

> Elvis: (**cough**) (spit!)
>
> Elvis: Haha, did you see? I gobbed it out the window! Did it fly!
>
> Wife: Yeah, that wasn't so smart. You learn that already as a kid, not to spit upwind.
>
> Elvis: What do you mean, it went well … hah
>
> Wife: Whatever, we're here now.
>
> Elvis: Oh it's a tight squeeze …
>
> Elvis: **MADDAFAKKA**!! [motherfucker]

Figure 79: Lanzarote.

The placement of swearing-switches in punchline position encourages an understanding of the comic strips as deliberately promoting English-language swearing as humorous. Even in examples with non-swearing punchlines, the preceding swearing-switches serve to set up the punchline and are thus equally integral to this conventional signaling of humor. The result is that swear words and swearing expressions that in native Anglophone cultures are first and foremost associated with offensiveness, are subject to censure, and are rare occurrences in public discourses, undergo a transformative process in Sweden via language contact and borrowing. The result is that a "hostile and aggressive" (Andersen 2014: 25) swearing expression such as "fuck you", "fuck off", or "(mother)fucker" can be repurposed as humorous.

6.5 New norms of English-language swearing

In this chapter, examples of Swedish-language comic strips featuring English-language swearing- switches have been presented as a evidence that the use of English swear words in the comic strip context both establishes and capitalizes on English-language swearing as humorous. Comic strips encourage their readers to expect humor, and previous research associates swearing with humor. The use of swear words in comic strips thus contributes to a mutual feedback loop (Trotta 1998, 2010), whereby the comic strips frame swearing as funny, and swearing enhances the humor of comic strips. With regards to the specific case of English-language swearing in Swedish, it must be remembered that the English language holds a privileged position in Swedish society as a result of forces from above and, more significantly, from below (Preisler 1999b). Despite lacking any official status, English can be considered a second language in Sweden (Fergusson 1994; Josephson 2004; Philipson 1992), and as such, it gives rise to frequent and extensive code-switching and borrowing (Höglin 2002; Sharp 2007), including the use of English-language swear words.

English-language swearing in Swedish-language comics as exemplified in the featured examples represents interdiscourse humor (Norrick 2007) based on incongruity (Yus 2003) in the form of intercultural clashes (Norrick 2007). However, while Norrick (2007: 398) claims that code-switching "affiliates the speaker with the system switched to", the examples suggest that the affiliation should account for a native/non-native distinction. In code-switching from Swedish to English, speakers are not aligning with the native-speaker discourse system of English, but with the non-native discourse system of Swedish English. Shared experiences, similar exposure, and common histories enhance humor and make it more effective (Raskin 1985: 5), such that "the sense of funniness, or mirth, that results is an internal pleasurable affective signal that indexes shared underlying knowledge and attitudes, and produces a positive evaluation of the producer" (Flamson and Barrett 2008: 265). Swedes share common background knowledge with regards to English. Despite years of formal instruction and deliberate strategies to institutionalize English for internationalization and socioeconomic progress, English from below wields more powerful influence on Swedish speakers of English. This reality is encrypted in the comic strip, and the members of the Swedish speech community who laugh at this are in on the joke, which is that Swedish speakers of English are not necessarily unaware of native-speaker norms concerning swear word usage, but are simply immune to these. Indeed, there is at least general if not acute awareness of native-speaker inhibitions or restrictions, even if these are not experienced first-hand. English swear words borrowed into other languages are of course subject to semantic bleaching, whereby their strength in the recipient language is reduced (Dewaele 2010b; Peterson 2017). For this reason, the suggestion that Swedes are unlikely to experience "reluctance, offense or impropriety with regards to [English] swear word usage" (Beers Fägersten 2014a: 78) is in line with other observations of foreign or second language speakers with regards to swear word usage (Dewaele 2004, 2010a; Jay and Janschewitz 2008).

Indeed, Swedes enjoy swearing in English specifically in ways (e.g., abusive swearing) and in social contexts (e.g., in public or in the media) that are at odds with native-speaker standards for appropriateness (Beers Fägersten 2012b, 2014a, 2017a, 2017b). Thus, the Swedish practice of swearing in English, that is, engaging in swearing-switches, capitalizes on the fundamental incongruity of two discourse systems that operate under different norms for appropriateness: English used in native language contexts, and English used in non-native contexts. As Monro (1951: 248) stated, "humor is inappropriateness", and indeed many of the swearing-switches featured in the example Swedish comic strips illustrate a range of inappropriate behavior – but perhaps only from an English-speaker perspective. Inappropriateness is due to incongruity in the form of an intercultural clash but, crucially, it is the common background knowledge of both the Swedish and the English discourse systems and their respective cultural norms that provides a key to its resolution. Swedes have appropriated English swear words in a way that allows them to laugh not only at the native English discourse system and culture, but more importantly, at their own non-native discourse system and culture as well.

7 Face the facts

By way of concluding this book, we first look back on what has been done, in order to establish the context of the final set of analyses, which in their turn will allow us to consider how language play in Swedish contemporary comic strips gives us a glimpse of future forms of English and Swedish. In Chapter 1, language play was defined as the deliberate and creative manipulation of language for fun and for entertainment. Language can be the object or medium of play, and language play may serve as a framing device and/or characterize interaction that is already framed as play. As an artistic medium and as a communicative context, comic strips both literally and discursively frame talk-in-interaction as play, and thus the combination of language play and comics constitutes suitable conditions for humor. Humor is largely a result of the incongruity (and subsequent resolution) of language play as the deliberate manipulation of linguistic form, which the multimodality of the comic strip context makes all the more salient.

In Chapter 2, Swedish newspaper comic strips were introduced along with the argument that they are characterized by an over-representation of what are known as moment-to-moment panel transitions. In other words, Swedish comics tend to be multi-panel strips that depict little to no change in setting or action from panel to panel. While such transitions would be considered a rarity on the international comics landscape (where visual story telling dominates), they are so common in contemporary Swedish comic art as to constitute a national characteristic. Moment-to-moment panel transitions impose a slower pace on the action unfolding in a comic strip, providing the reader with both time and space to linger within a particular moment. In contemporary Swedish comic strips, this time and space is saliently devoted to detailed depictions of (often lengthy) conversations between comic strip characters. Thus a second defining characteristic of Sweden's contemporary newspaper comic strips is their tendency to have a high degree of dialogue density. Indeed, it is an overt focus on talk-in-interaction that necessitates an over-reliance on moment-to-moment panel transitions; the one begets the other.

Since conversation comprises the main focus of Swedish comic strips, it also represents their main source of humor. Humor is not, however, simply a matter of the topic of conversation, but rather a function of the representation both of comics characters as engaged users of language and of their idiolects. Not only do comics artists play with language to represent comics characters and their interactions, but also, within the social context depicted in the comic strip, the characters themselves actively engage in play with and in language.

The examples presented so far establish play with language as more common in Swedish comic strips than play in language, whereby the former applies to manipulations of linguistic forms and the latter to playful behavior enacted in a target language (Bell 2012: 191). Both types of language play apply to two levels of communication: one between the comics characters within the comic strip, and one between the artist and the readers within the medium of comic art. The material affordances of the comics medium allow comics artists to depict language play by visually representing not just playful behavior and activity but also creative manipulations of linguistic forms. Consequently, humor resulting from language play applies to both what is said and how. The comic strip as a medium provides the comics artist with the opportunity for reflection, planning, and editing. The final, published product thus represents choices made with regards to the propositional content of communication, and deliberate manipulation of the material resources of the comic strip context with regards to representations of linguistic form.

Chapter 2 established that the focus in contemporary Swedish comic strips is language, such that humor is delivered textually more so than via purely visual means, which mostly serve to support the depiction of the form, structure, and progression of talk-in-interaction. In Chapter 3 and Chapter 4, cultural and linguistic stereotypes of Swedish dialects and foreign languages, respectively, were invoked via play with language, primarily in the form of manipulated linguistic forms to represent non-standard pronunciations, lexical items, and syntax. The analyses in Chapter 3 focused on the representation of non-standard, regional varieties as well as non-dialectal variation; the examples of foreign language play included in Chapter 4 focused on the representation of linguistic incompetence. In Chapter 5 and Chapter 6, play with language was similarly exemplified by representations of non-standard English, while play in English was illustrated by code-switches to fixed phrases, idioms, media quotations, or swearing expressions, often in punchline position. Chapter 5 explored the widespread use of English in Swedish comics as a reflection of the general pervasion of English in Swedish society, while Chapter 6 examined the humorous use of English swear words. In each of these chapters, the simultaneous use of standard Swedish as well as one or more codes, i.e., the practice of code-switching, could be observed in various manifestations, such as inter- and intrasentential switches to other native regional dialects, to invented varieties of Swedish, or to various foreign languages, as well as English. The code-switches help to make salient linguistic contrasts, and the analyses have shown that resulting incongruities and interdiscourse clashes are mined for humor.

In addition to highlighting incongruities, code-switching has also been analyzed as operationalizing both disparagement humor and self-deprecating humor. Linguistic and cultural stereotypes of the "other" code and of its speakers are invoked for the purpose of mockery in comic strips via language play. At the same time, attempts at mockery are often attentuated by evident flaws and imperfections in parody, such that the perpetrator of mockery becomes instead the object of it.

The act of code-switching has been called a "skilled performance" (Myers-Scotton 1993: 6), one that showcases a speaker's multicompetence, understood as the combined knowledge of one's first language as well as additional languages (Cook 1991). However, in many of the analyses presented so far, it has been argued that code-switching among comics characters instead highlights their linguistic incompetence in the targeted code; the incompetent performances are meant to be appreciated as humorous by the (multi)competent reader. Multicompetence must therefore be understood first and foremost as a characteristic of the comics artists, whose linguistic acuity and knowledge of multiple codes is reflected in sophisticated language play. In other words, a high degree of proficiency and of multilingual awareness is required to represent recognizable linguistic incompetence. This, too, must be acknowledged as a skilled performance.

Siegel (1995: 100) notes that various studies of code-switching have identified the practice as being connected to humor in three closely related and not always mutually exclusive ways: (1) a code-switch can indicate that joking is about to take place, (2) a code-switch can in and of itself index humor, or (3) the code to which a speaker switches may be associated with humor. For example, in his own research, Siegel (1987, 1995) shows how switches from Fijian to Hindi reliably signal that joking is taking place. In other studies (McClure and McClure 1988; Stølen 1992; Woolard 1988), language play and linguistic creativity have been shown to occur within the language switched to. Examples of the third kind of humorous code-switching include switches to other dialects associated with speakers one wishes to mock, mimic, or ridicule (Apte 1985, Macaulay 1987; Saville-Troike 1989). With regards to code-switching in comic strips, one must also consider the mutual feedback effect: existing associations between code-switching and humor may explain the frequency of code-switching in Swedish comics, but it may also be that the association between comics and humor serves to assign a humorous function to code-switching. The play frame is mutually enforced.

According to Siegel (1995: 102), "Once the 'funniness' of a particular language, dialect, or style has become conventionalized, its use by speakers of other varieties is sure to get a laugh." The examples presented so far in this book have illustrated humor via play with a variety of Swedish dialects and foreign languages, but English must nevertheless be singled out as the current *de facto* language of play in Swedish society as represented in contemporary Swedish comic strips. While Chapter 5 and Chapter 6 have examined aspects of English language play in Swedish comic strips, the exploration must continue in the present chapter in order to account more fully for variables of usage. The previous chapters have only reflected the native context and perspective of English language usage – in other words, English as it is generally used by Swedes in interaction with other Swedes. By way of concluding the book, this final chapter considers how Swedes are represented in comics as using English outside of their social networks and beyond their national borders, for example, in interaction with native speakers of English or with other speakers of English as a non-native language. Such interactions also feature the Swedish perspective on non-Swedish native and non-native varieties of English, illustrating additional cultural and linguistic stereotypes that enable disparagement and mockery. The chapter examines English language play in Swedish comics with regards to how Swedes creatively play with English (as opposed to using fixed phrases or quoting), how Swedes use English with non-Swedes (as opposed to how they use English amongst themselves), how Swedes perceive other people's use of English, including native varieties and non-native varieties, and how the Swedish language shows evidence of anglification.

7.1 Creative English

Chapters 4 and 5 have established that English is a valid code for communication in Sweden, such that despite its foreign language status, it serves second language functions. The distinction between English as a foreign language (EFL) and English as a second language (ESL) is a significant one with regards to a discussion of non-native language play versus errors. Deshors et al. (2016: 137) argue that the widespread view of EFL as norm-dependent and ESL as norm-developing has resulted in "a division of innovations and errors" such that emergent deviations are more likely to be considered innovations in an ESL context and errors in an EFL context. The problem with such an approach is that foreign language users may be less likely to be credited for linguistic creativity (Bamgbose 1998, in Deshors et al. 2016).

The analyses included in Chapter 5 suggest that the proficient and idiomatic usage of English in Swedish in-group communication attests to its status

7.1 Creative English — 159

as a second language, while the non-idiomatic and non-normative use of English indicates a foreign language. The following examples from *Rocky* allow us to re-visit this dichotomous representation, building on language play as re-production and re-contextualization of formulaic language to now include language play as free-form creative production. Figure 80 and Figure 81 feature language play in the form of spontaneous rhyming games.

Figure 80: Sock it!

(80) Sock it!

> Rocky: Watch now! Eight ball in the corner pocket, on a rocket!
>
> Dog: Sock it!
>
> Rocky: Fock it!
>
> Dog: You sank the white, now you have to add a ball! And I get a free shot on top of it all!
>
> Dog: In the corner I call here goes the one-ball!
>
> Dog: Hi-yah!
>
> Rocky: The twelve on the six on the four ... hmm-hmm, something, party some more ... Nah, wait, I'll come up with something.
>
> Dog: Ah, too slow are your thoughts, I'll wait by the slots.[42]

---

[42] Jack Vegas is a brand of video lottery terminal, similar to a slot machine.

Figure 81: Bros goes before hoes!

(81) Bros goes before hoes!

> Rocky: You have hardly met any of my friends! We should have a beer with Smacks and his girlfriend some day!
>
> Cat: I didn't think you HAD any friends! You're never busy when I call!
>
> Rocky: It's just a coincidence that you always call right when I was thinking about leaving anyway. I have a ton of friends and I'm always hanging out with them!
>
> Rocky: <u>Bros goes before hoes!</u>
>
> Cat: <u>But when hoes phones, bros goes home!</u>
>
> Rocky: <u>Nose! Hoes phones when bros goes homes before!</u>
>
> Cat: <u>Okay, if you say so's…</u>
>
> Rocky: <u>Hoes with pantyhose on their toes blows bros does on clothes!</u>
>
> Rocky: Elektro-helios[43]!

In both examples, rhyming is initiated in similar ways, namely, via language that is formulaic: "eight ball in the corner pocket" or inspired by a formulaic phrase: "bros (goes) before hoes". Thus, the switch to English is facilitated by the recitation of a familiar phrase. The pursuant rhyming sequences depart from the formulaicity and reflect true creative production in the form of meaningful content within the formal aural parameters. In example (80), Dog's use of the phrase "sock it" reveals an ability to parse the sounds of the single lexeme "rocket" so

---

43 A Swedish appliance company.

as to create a rhyming phrase consisting of two lexemes, while Rocky creatively adapts the phrase "fuck it" to this rhyming scheme. Similarly, violation of grammatical rules (e.g., *hoes phones; *bros goes) is necessary to maintain the rhyming scheme in example (81), as are ungrammatical inflections for plural, such as in *nose (as a plural of "no"), *homes, and *so's. In both examples, language play is depicted as a game, with the interlocutors taking turns and building upon each other's contributions. Finally, the English-language play in both examples transitions to Swedish, suggesting compatibility and equality between the languages and their perceived communicative potential.

In stark contrast to the framing of English-language play as a spontaneous, collaborative, and even fun activity that is compatible with Swedish-language interaction, Figure 82 presents the use of English as an isolating and anxiety-inducing exercise.

Figure 82: I say toast!

(82) I say toast!

> Cat: What are you doing?
>
> Rocky: My little sister is getting married, I'm trying to come up with what to say in my speech...

Cat: Are **you** giving a speech?!

Rocky: Well I have to! When my other sister got married I chickened out ... And then as punishment she's getting married to an Englishman, so I have to hold the speech in English!

Cat: (reading) "Dear sister. I am your brother. You are getting married today to your husband Michael. He is my swooger.[44] He is a photografer. You have a shop. May you take many pictures and shop together for all eternity ... "

Cat: (reading) "When you was little it was very nice, because you made me happy when I was sad, and also your sister too. Now you are old and smart and beautiful. And your sister also ... "

Cat: (reading) "I like your husband. I also like your sisters husband. If you have trouble you can call me. Or if you don't have trouble also. Let me propoast a toast to Fanny and Michael. (Cheers)"

Cat: That will be great, what are you worried about?

Rocky: uuuugh ...

Speaker: Now Rocky will make a speech ...

Rocky: A-ahem! I am brother! I ... ..say ... toast!

In this example, Rocky makes explicit his anxiety about speaking in English, going so far as to frame it as punishment. A similar sentiment was expressed in example (70) of Chapter 6, where Rocky revealed his distaste for speaking English due to a lack of vocabulary and inability to make jokes. Yet considering the great extent to which Rocky uses English proficiently, meaningfully, and humorously throughout the *Rocky*-comic strip collection (only a fraction of which is included in this book), Rocky's proclaimed reluctance defies comprehension. It is only when one considers the context in which he is to speak English that a likely explanation becomes clear: similar to example (70) of the previous chapter in which the use of English was to accommodate an American, in example (82), above, the use of English is necessitated by the presences of an "Englishman", in other words, a native speaker of English. This single contextual variable suffices to trigger Rocky's linguistic incompetence as an EFL-speaker, evidenced by the

---

44 An anglicization of Swedish *svåger*, Eng: brother-in-law.

plethora of errors and awkward expressions in his prepared text and ultimately confirmed by his unsuccessful and nerve-racking performance. Language play and innovation are certainly evident in, for example, the conversion of "shop" to a verb in "may you take pictures and shop together" and the rhyming in "let me propoast a toast", but overall the speech is rudimentary.

The differences between the play with language illustrated in examples (80) and (81) and the linguistic struggles depicted in example (82) must be considered in relation to the comic strip medium. Working within this medium, Martin Kellerman and other comics artists have the opportunity to fashion and adjust their texts to their own satisfaction. While depicted talk-in-interaction may be inspired by actual communicative events, texts should be assumed to have undergone editing for the sake of efficacy, verbal artistry, and humor. It follows that, although unplanned and unwanted mistakes in, for example, type-setting are sure to occur, a reader should proceed from the assumption that errors in texts are deliberate and meaningful. All three examples illustrate deliberate language play on the part of Martin Kellerman, but within the contexts of the strips, the reader is encouraged to interpret examples (80) and (81) as proficiency in the form of linguistic innovation and example (82) as incompetence in the form of linguistic errors. In Chapter 5, these differences were suggested to reflect the use of English as a second language versus a foreign language, respectively.

Deshors et al. (2016) claim that persistent ideologies and analytic orientations among researchers serve to perpetuate the labeling of similar instances of linguistic creativity as innovations in ESL and errors in EFL. Swedish comic strips provide evidence that laymen operate according to similar assumptions: in an all-Swedish context, language play suggests the use of English as a second language whereas error-ridden interaction with native speakers aligns with the use of English as a foreign language. The native Swedish, in-group environment is presented as a safe space for Swedes to perform an English-speaker identity, recite a media text, or engage in linguistic creativity, while native English, out-group environments cause anxiety and increase one's awarenes of his or her non-native status and lack of creative rights in English. However, while the representation of English ultimately confirms the persistent and opposing interpretations of deviations, Swedish comic strips provide compelling evidence that the distinct depiction of both innovations and errors requires a high degree of linguistic proficiency, one that may be deployed to a speaker's advantage in presenting their choice of an ESL- or EFL-speaker identity.

7.2 Performing the native speaker

Examples (80)–(82) illustrate how English-language play in comic strips can represent Swedish speakers aligning with English as a second or foreign language. Figure 83 and Figure 84, below, feature the use of English to perform as speakers of native varieties, and are included in order to emphasize the contrast in the depiction of Swedish varieties of English presented so far, and other non-native varieties of English presented later in the chapter.

Figure 83: You poofta!

(83) You poofta!

> Rocky: ♪ You lied to me! You badibadibadibaloo! You lied to me![45]
>
> Speaker 2: Mark Morrisson ... what a fucking fool!
>
> Speaker 2: He went to jail because he waved around his pistol wherever he went!
>
> Rocky: But he was from England! You sure can't wave guns around in London!
>
> Rocky: And how did they get him in jail if he was the only one in the country with a gun!? They're all "Oy! Is the bobby! Drop the old blagger or I'll pop you over the knob end wiv mi billy club, you poofta!"
>
> Speaker 2: Maybe he got captured by insurgent peasants with torches and pitchforks?
>
> Rocky: "Bloody freeze or I'll blow mi whistle really loud an mook up yer earing-g!"

---

[45] Mark Morrison, "Return of the Mack".

7.2 Performing the native speaker — 165

Figure 84: I'm loving these shoes?

(84) I'm loving these shoes?

> Rocky: I woke up super early today! Made the most of it and watched cable-tv, I don't have that at home …
>
> Rocky: I saw a show about a stylist named Rachel …
>
> Rocky: She's a stylist to the stars in LA. Everyone in LA has sunglasses and talks without moving their face. And everyone has that robot voice …
>
> Rocky: I'm like so stressed out?
>
> Rocky: My cell is going crazy today? Everything sounds like a question! I'm loving these shoes?
>
> Rocky: I talk like Stephen Hawking asking a questiöööön? The universe is like expanding?
>
> Rocky: I'm going for a warm autumn date look? With lots of paljetts [sequins] and pumps and punky pants?
>
> Dog: I'm trying to read about Libya here …
>
> Rocky: I don't need your negative energy right now? My cell is like going crazy?

In both of the examples above, place-naming establishes the context for the subsequent code-switch to English and its corresponding regional variety: "England" and "London" in example (83) and "LA" in example (84). Additionally, verbal, non-verbal, and semiotic cues indicate the pending code-switch serves as a performance of imitation. In example (83), Rocky prefaces the code-switch with the quotative "they're all", he adjusts his facial expressions, and quotation marks enclose the English-language text. In example (84), the coming code-switch is primed by the mention of "everyone ... talks" and "everyone has that robot voice", which is similarly accompanied by adjusted facial expressions. In these examples, Rocky voices a native-speaker 'other' in the spirit of a performance. Body language and facial expressions in particular contribute to the presentation of the voicing as a performance of language play. Characteristic features of pronunciation are indicated by non-standard spellings such as "wiv", "poofta" and "earing-g" in example (83) and "questiöööm" in example (84).

In the previous chapters, analyses highlighted the strategies employed to depict talk-in-interaction that featured regional Swedish dialects and the use of other languages. Often, the goal was determined to be less a disparagement of the represented variety and more a mockery of the actual speaker's own incompetence. Humor was thus a function of incongruities created by an imperfect renditions. The language play and linguistic creativity wielded to portray incompetence can be observed in examples (83) and (84), now directed at achieving accurate depictions. This raises the question of how humor as a function of language play can be achieved by depictions of both poor performances (as in examples throughout Chapter 4 and Chapter 5, as well as example (82), above) and accurate imitations (as in examples (83) and (84))? In effect, language play in both cases trades on incongruities: just as the accurate portrayal of non-proficient, non-native varieties exploits incongruities with standard, correct, or native forms, the accurate immitation of a native speaker is incongruous with the speaker's true, non-native identity. The English-language play in contemporary Swedish comic strips alternates between these established incongruities, but also applies to depictions of English-language interaction with speakers of other languages, as examined in the next section.

7.3 Many Englishes

The examples presented so far in this and previous chapters have featured language use by Swedish people almost exclusively with other Swedish people. Even in non-Swedish contexts, use of foreign languages and English has taken place in in-group interactions, with few exceptions. This section explores the use of English by other speakers, allowing for an examination of many varieties of English. Figure 85, from *Stockholmsnatt*, depicts an interaction taking place between a tourist and a rental car representative in Belek, Turkey.

Figure 85: Flück öff.

(85) Fück öff

Caption: Belek, Turkey

Speaker 1: So that just has to be the most depressing sight of charter tourism ... He's now been sitting in there for a week just staring straight out into the lobby without anything to do. We should almost rent a car and just leave it in the parking lot to be nice.

Speaker 2: Well wait, would you rather work as a bartender at a hotel like this? A constant line of all-inclusive drunks pink as pigs and ordering cheap booze in Dutch ...

Speaker 3: Fünf Piña Coladas und eine Tüte Kartoffelchips! [Five piña coladas and a bag of potato chips!]

Speaker 4: Fück öff ... [fuck off]

Speaker 2: Well, in his heart he's probably the happiest man in the eastern Mediterranean.

Example (85) represents a return to the theme of English-language swearing, although here it outside of the Swedish context. Instead, what seems to be a Turkish local uses an English-language swearing expression in response to German-speaking tourists who mistake him for a bartender. The mention of "ordering cheap booze in Dutch" as well as the use of German in panel 3 could be interpreted as disapproval of tourists unwilling to engage in linguistic accommodation by using English as a *lingua franca*. The fact that the Turkish representative does so confirms the evaluation of the situation as appropriate for English *lingua franca* interaction. His response, however, suggests a knowledge of English possibly limited only to swearing expressions and, moreover, a local variety of such, as represented by the spelling of "fuck off" with umlauted vowels characteristic of the Turkish language.

Example (85) thus serves as a first introduction to the depiction, in Swedish comic strips, of linguistic variation in the form of other people's varieties of English, specifically in English *lingua franca* interaction; examples (86)–(89), corresponding to Figures 86–89, continue the exploration.

Figure 86: Dis is for dis.

(86) Dis is for dis

>Bird: Dis is dö living room, eh? TV, eh? Computer wit internet, eh? End e estereo, eh? [And a stereo] Wit CD, eh?
>
>Rocky: Ok, I understand …
>
>Bird: Kitchen, eh? Dis is gas stove, eh? Turn on here, eh? And dis is for dis, dis is for dis, dis is for dis, dis is for dis, **no**, **dis** is for dis, dis is for dis and **dis** is for dis, eh?
>
>Rocky: Eh?
>
>Frog: Hehe …
>
>Bird: Under dis painting, eh? You have safety box, eh?
>
>Rocky: Very clever.
>
>Frog: Unless the thief is a fan of Diego Rivera.
>
>Bird: Dis flower is plastic, eh? Don't put water, eh? Understand?
>
>Dog: Does she think we're idiots?

In example (86), Rocky and his friends are vacationing in Buenos Aires, Argentina; it can thus be assumed that (female) Bird, as their local AirBnB host, is a speaker of Spanish and what is represented can be accounted for as a Spanish or Latin American variety of English. Support for this claim can be found in Bird's first turn, which includes the distinctly Spanish epenthetic 'e' before word-initial 's' in "estereo". However, most notably characterizing the representation of Bird's variety is an abundance of simple declaratives, frequent comprehension checks via the use of "eh" as a tag question, and the pronunciation of "this" as [dis]. This last feature in particular should be noted as typical of many varieties of English. The consonant sounds normally represented in spelling by the letters 'th' are known as dental fricatives, one voiceless, [θ], heard word-finally in "with", and one voiced, [ð], heard word-initially in "this". Producing these sounds can be difficult for non-native speakers, who tend to replace them with the voiceless alveolar stop [t] or its voiced counterpart [d], respectively as illustrated by Bird's use of "wit" and "dis". Such substitution does not seem to be interpreted in face-to-face interaction as unintelligible errors, effectively eliminating any need for distinction. For this reason, the consonant sounds [θ] and [ð] are not included in the 'core' phonology of *lingua franca* English (Jenkins 2000). thus establishing this feature as typical of *lingua franca* English.

Bird's repetitive syntactic pattern punctuated by "eh" and "dis" in example (86) help to create an identifiable variety of English, the distinct features of which are conducive to imitation (for example, Rocky's use of "eh" in panel 2) and mockery (in the form of the comic strip itself). In Figure 87, phonological properties of *lingua franca* English are similarly made orthographically salient in the text.

Figure 87: Yez!

(87) Yez!

> Bird: Hey! How are you tomorrow? Ha ha ha ha haa! It's beer o'clock, ya? Haa ha ha! Cheerz!
>
> Frog: Cheers! HAHAHA HA HA HA HA!!!
>
> Bird: You guys are not wery social, are you? I zee you here every day, never talking to anybody, jast sitting trinking beer yez?

Bird: Evrabody elz knowz evrabody here, just chillz, hangz around, getz drank ha ha ha ha haa!

Bird: I've been trinking cosmic shakes for two dayz straight now! MASHROOMZ! You mazt try, you completely ezcape reality HA HA HA HA!

Rocky: I've never felt the need to escape reality, until just now ...

Bird: Yez!

Bird: Zatz why you should be more social! you should come to yoga hut tomorrow, you go deep inside yourself and it'z so chill man you know?

Rocky: Can you teach me how to go deep inside my own asshole and become a douche bag?

According to Seidlhofer (2004: 215), "phonology is a comparatively closed system, and virtually all [English lingua franca] users speak the language with some trace (more or less pronounced, so to speak) of their [first language] accent." The nationality of (male) Bird in example (87) is not made explicit, but if it is the case that his use of *lingua franca* English should include a trace of his first language accent, then the salient phonological features of his depicted talk (rendered as interlanguage spelling) should provide some indications. First, the abundant use of the letter 'z' in environments where the letter 's' would be expected suggests a systematic voicing of the alveolar fricative [s] as [z]. Furthermore, 'z' is used in the first word of Bird's panel 4 turn, "Zatz why you should be more social!" Here, 'z' replaces the letters 'th', corresponding to [ð], yet another alternative pronunciation for this non-core consonant sound. Furthermore, Bird's use of English includes instances of the interdental, voiced fricative [v] pronounced as the glide [w] in "not wery social" (panel 2), the devoicing of [d] in "trinking" (panel 3), and the lowering of the mid, back vowel [ʌ] to front, low [a] in "getz drank", "mashroomz" and "you mazt try". Based on the depiction of these phonological features of *lingua franca* English, a plausible guess would be that Bird is a speaker of German or another Germanic language.

A comparison of examples (86) and (87) illustrates how typical features of *lingua franca* English appear in depictions of linguistic variation while the depictions themselves reflect distinct varieties, reflecting the speaker's first language. Figures 88 and 89, below, provide two additional portrayals of English as used in *lingua franca* interaction.

Figure 88: This good bar?

(88) This good bar?

>Speaker 1: This good bar?
>
>Speaker 2: Yes shitgood! Hav you manny for beer?
>
>Speaker 1: You want beer yes?
>
>Speaker 3: We buy you beer yess..
>
>Speaker 2: Cool!
>
>Caption: Five minutes later
>
>Speaker 1: Hahahaha bartender is funny man! He from **Spain**..we speek Engliss to him and he: que?
>
>Speaker 2: Ke?
>
>Speaker 1: Yes que! Like **Manuel**!
>
>Speaker 2: Manuel?
>
>Speaker 1: Manuel work Fallty Tower [Fawlty Towers]! With funny man **Yon Klees** [John Cleese]!
>
>Speaker 2: Uh … dö tall guy on Monte Pyton [Monty Python]?
>
>Speaker 3: Bassyl Fallty [Basil Fawlty] ha ha ha ha ha ha
>
>Speaker 1: Yes yes Monti Pyton! Hahahaha! Yon Klees is minister silly walk!

(HAHAHAHA HAHA HA HA)

Speaker 2: Damn fool..

Speaker 3: <u>Yess very silli</u>! Hahahahahaha

The comic strip in example (88) has been extracted from multi-strip suite in which a range of interactions take place in the outside seating area of a bar. In this series, the male and female couple (Speaker 1 and Speaker 3) were presented as tourists in Stockholm hailing from what Speaker 2 referred to as "Risifrutti", seemingly implying an Asian country. The English-language interaction between all three speakers further suggests the couple's (likely Southeast) Asian origin by exhibiting several different features distinguishing their respective varieties of English. Predictably, Speaker 2 mixes Swedish and English, evident in "*skit*good" in panel 1 and in "dö [the] *lång snubbe* on Monte Pyton" in panel 3. The depiction of Speaker 2's use of English also indicates particular features of pronunciation represented by interlanguage spellings, such as "manny" for "money" and "dö" for "the".[46] In contrast, turns by Speaker 1 and 3 include no code-mixing, but instead suggest that their variety of English is characterized by simple sentence structures ("We buy you beer"), occasional omission of the copula ("This good bar?") or third person singular inflection ("Manuel work Fallty Tower"), and the use of declaratives in place of interrogatives ("You want beer yes?"). All of these practices are listed as distinctive grammatical features of New Englishes (Crystal 2012), noted specifically in Asian varieties of English (e.g., Malaysian English, see Baskaran 1994).

Figure 89 features yet another representation of Asian English. In this strip, Rocky is on vacation in Thailand and interacts with what appears to be a local, although neither the nationality of this interlocutor nor the exact variety of English is made explicit. The dialogue is transcribed as it appears in the comic strip, and possible translations of unintelligible utterances are provided in brackets.

---

46 Martin Kellerman has a penchant for representing non-native pronunciations of "the" in this way, as he did in Example 59 and in a number of other strips in the *Rocky*-repertoire.

Figure 89: Hello papa!

(89) Hello papa!

> Bird: Hello papa! Ok? Ha ha ha!
>
> Rocky: Yes yes hello hello ...
>
> Bird: You? Ha ha! Eh, go bis? [Go beach?] Eez bangrow for eat. [?Leave bungalow for eat.] Ne? [right?] Ha ha! Kapum, shlimp? [Yes, ?shrimp]
>
> Rocky: I don't know what you are babbling about, but I go beach, I go eat, I go to bungalow, I go to sleep, everyday same!
>
> Bird: Slee bis? [Sleep beach] Ha ha ha, no! You riw eez bangrow? [You will ?leave bungalow!] Ha ha ha, no!
>
> Rocky: Yes, but now I go to the beach, but shit in it, it doesn't matter!
>
> Bird: Ha ha vey goo! [very good] Tomollo motobye watafar? [Tomorrow motorbike waterfall] Ha ha!
>
> Rocky: Yes, tomorrow is a fucking motorbike waterfall ...

Bird's second turn (panel 2) in example (89) includes two instances of code-switching, indicating that the variety of English depicted is presumably Southeast Asian if not specifically Thai; first, the discourse particle *ne*, which can function as a tag question in, for example, Japanese and Chinese, and is similar to the Thai particle *ná* (Cook 1999); and second, the turn-final *Kapum, schlimp?* which shares some similarities with the Thai phrase affirmation[47] ครับ ผม, the pronunciation of which could feasibly be approximated as "kapum". In addition

---

47 This phrase may also function as a tag question or an expression of gratitude.

to some of the same features of an Asian variety of English presented in example (88) (such as simple sentence structure, copula deletion, and declaratives used as interrogatives), example (89) depicts specific features of pronunciation, such as consonant cluster reduction (Kirkpatrick 2011) in "slee bis" and "motobye". Most salient, however, is the alternation between the sounds [l] and [r], evident in the non-standard spellings of "bungrow", "tomollo", and "watafar" ("bungalow" "tomorrow" and "waterfall"). These forms draw from and perpetuate the stereotype of Asian varieties of English as indiscriminately conflating the two sounds, and in fact some Asian languages do not distinguish between them (Saito and Lyster 2012) or do not produce these sounds in the same phonetic environments that they are produced in English (Hall-Lew and Starr 2010), such as word-finally, reflected in "riw" as possibly corresponding to English "will".

That Swedish comics artists' representations of Latin American, European, and Asian varieties of English include features confirmed as characteristic by lingusitic research is testimony to their abilities to both recognize and depict distinguishing aspects of *lingua franca* culture, syntax, and pronunciation. More importantly, the fact that these depictions, along with those of Swedish English and native varieties of English included in examples (80)–(84), constitute comic strip content affirms a general predisposition to finding not just linguistic variation funny but also imitation of it. There reigns, in other words, an unbiased approach to mining all linguistic variation and the imitation thereof for humor in contemporary Swedish comic strips. Furthermore, as established in Chapter 3 and Chapter 4, even own's own attempts at imitation, especially flawed ones, can be ridiculed. The next two comic strips are additional examples of *lingua franca* English, illustrating explicit mockery of the 'other' (Figure 90) and implicit mockery of oneself (example (91)).[48]

Figure 90: Have you heard.

---

48 Permission to reprint the figure corresponding to example (91) was not granted.

(90) Have you heard

> Rocky: Have you heard about Finland's Secretary of State, when he was in England and wanted to order two cups of tea from room service?
>
> Rat: What, are we telling jokes now? Are we so old?
>
> Rocky: No, it's a true story! Rippo told it.
>
> Rat: Rippo! What the hell happened to that bastard? He hasn't been seen since confirmation!
>
> Rocky: Anyway, he was staying in room 32 and wanted two cups of tea, but he was so bad at English and called <u>room service</u> and said: <u>Tö tä tö tötö tö</u>![Two teas to thirty-two]
>
> Rat: How about this one: Have you heard about the Dane, the Frenchman and the Bellman? They went into a bar, then the pig said, "I told you so!"

In example (90), Rocky initiates his account of the Finnish Secretary of State using wording that is reminiscent of a joke. Although he clarifies his impending story as true, the joking frame has nevertheless been invoked, and the comic strip's readers have thus been primed for a punchline according to the premise of a Finnish politician ordering tea in England. The humor of the non-joke is anchored to the evaluation of the politician's proficiency in English as "so bad." With this information, the readers are equipped to resolve the incongruity between the information revealed in Rocky's turn in panel 3 ("staying in room 32 and wanted two cups of tea") and the nonse-string "tö tä tö tötö tö". The mockery of language use is explicit and directed exclusively at pronunciation. This focus establishes a pattern, in that the depictions of *lingua franca* English as 'other' varieties of English in Swedish comic strips are mostly achieved via the use non-standard spellings to represent distinct features of pronunciation.

In contrast to the explicit mockery in example (90) of the *lingua franca* English of the 'other', an example from *Zelda* which focuses on the Swedish variety of English as a *lingua franca* invites a self-deprecatory interpretation. This particular example was included in *Zelda: Kampen fortsätter* (2012, page 95), within a suite of strips chronicling Zelda's experiences backpacking through Southeast Asia. However, since its original publication, the strip has been removed from circulation of later editions of the album, and permission to reprint was therefore not granted. For this reason, only the text is included, accompanied by a description of the panel illustrations. In the first panel, a full moon shines on a dancing Zelda, foregrounded among a crowd of, presumably, other backpackers who are also dancing and partying. In the second panel, a rising sun shines on the same partiers, sleeping or lying naked in a heap among empty bottles, while a sole male figure in the background lugs a full trash bag and carries an empty bottle. A sign hanging askew from a tree branch reads, "FULL ~~MOON~~ SVENSK PARTY". In the third panel, Zelda is photographing three brown-skinned children. And finally, the fourth panel depicts Zelda reviewing the photos in her camera, while another female, presumably a fellow backpacker/tourist, lies beside Zelda, smoking. Original usages of English are underlined.

(91) <u>Full</u> svensk <u>party</u>

Panel 1

Caption: So with abundant travel funds (that I am liberally borrowing from) we have covered half of Southeast Asia in just 14 days and are now on the paradise island Koh-Lon-Tay where we are honoring Mother Earth's cycles at a <u>full moon party</u>!

Zelda: Wohooo, I love being abroad and away from all those inhibited Swedes!

Crowd: Me too!

Panel 2

Caption: But we're not just <u>party girls</u>, we are actually crazy about nature and local inhabitants too. Karma[49] and I strongly believe in eco-tourism!

Zelda: <u>Hey don't throw that bottle in the nature, give it to the native so he can</u> panta <u>it and support his family!</u>

Panel 3

Caption: My inner journey is also in full swing! I'm finding a lot of inspiration here in Asia and I've begun taking photos a bit, mostly kids and rugged old people, they're so genuine! Like, innocent!

Zelda: <u>Okay, just look sad and you will get this banana! Mmm, ba-na-naaa!</u>
No, not money! You think I'm rich or something? I'm just as poor as you. I'm a <u>backpacker</u>.

Panel 4

Caption: People here are really nice and tell me I have talent! Not at all like the overbearing elitists at art school!

---

49 The name of Zelda's friend.

> Zelda: ... and this is a picture of a little boy I met in the Philippines, and here is his friend Leif, a Swedish småbarnspappa from Skövde! What a small world!
>
> Speaker 2: Yeah, that's so sweet! Creativity is so beautiful man! Like the rainbow!

While the first panel indicates that Zelda is mostly encountering other Swedes on her journey, the subsequent panels establish her need to use *lingua franca* English to converse with locals and other tourists. Overall, it is Zelda's own self-righteousness, disrespect, and naïveté that are offered as objects of self-mockery. However, most noteworthy in this example with regards to Zelda's language usage is the inclusion of two Swedish words, *panta* in Zelda's second turn and *småbarnspappa* in her fourth turn. To the Swedish readership, presence of these Swedish words within the English text is appreciated as humorous due to the incongruity created by such code-mixing in the depicted context, which gives no indication that the addressees understand Swedish. Initially, a reader may assume that Zelda mixes in these Swedish words due to her own lexical gaps. But on further consideration, it may be the case that the Swedish terms are deliberately used to compensate for a gap in the English lexicon. Indeed, the single words *panta* and *småbarnspappa* correspond to multi-word expressions in English, "(to) return for deposit" and "father of young children". The asymmetry reflects yet another potential incongruity that can enhance the humor, but the use of singular Swedish words in this way (or anglified Swedish words, such as "swooger" in example (82), and "paljetts" in example (84)) also helps to distinguish and disparage the Swedish variety of *lingua franca* English.

7.4 Anglicisms in Swedish

Chapters 5 and 6 examined the extensive use of English in Swedish-language communication in Swedish comic strips in the form of code-switching. The present chapter explores the creative use of English as a second language, the error-ridden use of English as a foreign language, and distinct varieties of English used as a *lingua franca* with and by speakers of other languages. In nearly every case, the presence of English is obvious, even if pronunciation respellings or interlanguage spellings are employed for the purpose of depicting specific accents. Some examples, however, have blurred the lines between English and Swedish as two codes comprising two distinct lexicons: example (41) in Chapter 5 featured a mixing of Swedish and English that defied identification of a matrix language; example (61) in Chapter 6 presented a near-total linguistic appropriation of the word "fucking" in "*det fakking enda positiva med den här skitsemestern*"; example (82) and example (84) of the present chapter include, respectively, the anglified words "swooger" and "paljetts"; example (89) shows the use of an English word-for-word translation of the Swedish idiom *skit i det*, "shit in it", meaning "forget about it; don't worry about it"; and example (88) and example (91) feature the inclusion of Swedish words (*lång snubbe* and *panta*, *småbarnspappa*, respectively) in *lingua franca* English. Each of these instances indicates a compatibility between English and Swedish that facilitates mixing. The examples presented in this section thus allow for an examination of more subtle results of the influence of English on Swedish, namely the loan translations, or calques, of English "face the facts" and "give me a break". Figure 91 is a panel extract from *Rocky*; Figure 92 is a panel extract from *Berglins*. Figure 93 is a single-panel *Elvis*-comic; Figure 94 is a two-panel extract from *Lilla Berlin*.

Figure 91: *Rocky*: Face the facts.

(92) Face the facts

> Rocky: You just have to face the facts [*fejsa fakta*], if you've lived in a house once, then you don't have any reason to be in the forest!
>
> Frog: Wait now ... didn't we walk past this skeleton an hour ago?
>
> Rocky: I'm cold and hungry ...

Figure 92: *Berglins*: Face the facts.

(93) Face the facts

> Caption: After the shock, sorrow & processing comes a new orientation.
>
> Speaker: You have to face the facts [*fejsa fakta*] & accept the situation: Hello good-looking! Today we're staring Nordic walking!

Figure 93: Fucking brejk.

(94) Fucking brejk

Speaker 1: Come on, give it your all! Stop loafing around, get to wor-

Elvis: That sure is some damn badgering! I'm doing as well as I can you know, so give me a <u>fucking</u> break! [*ge me ett fucking brejk*]

Speaker 2: (thinking) It was bound to happen. Sooner or later..

Figure 94: Give me a break.

(95) Give me a break

Speaker 1: (reading) "Madeleine Larsson is only 18 years old but has already been named this year's shooting star entrepreneur. She has studied at Harvard, started three businesses and runs a center for deaf dolphins on the verge of extinction."

Speaker 1: I mean **give me a break** [*ge me en paus*], I can't take it!

Speaker 1: Here you can barely graduate highschool before these splendiferous teenagers come breathing down your neck!

The inclusion of more than one loan translation and more than one example for each serves to establish the effects of the influence of English as more widespread than what a single example from a single source may manage to convey.

Furthermore, a comparison of the examples demonstrates that the appropriation of some expressions as calques entails a more straight-forward process than others. The examples suggest that the calque of "face the facts" is simply *fejsa fakta*, while the expression "give me a break" allows for more variation. In example (93), the use of *fejsa fakta* aligns with the theme of the comic strip, "Face to face", in which the depicted figures confront their own outward signs of aging, especially those visible in one's visage. In example (94), the phrase *ge mig ett fucking brejk* adheres very closely to the English-language expression, but the inclusion of "fucking" as obviously English-sourced provides a humorous incongruity with the Swedish form of the phrase in which it is inserted. In example (95), the translation of the phrase as *ge mig en paus* manages to render the expression wholly Swedish, but nonetheless identifiable as originally English. This, too, creates an incongruity: that between the underlying English expression and the surface form as Swedish, further emphasized by the intonation and raised volume indicated by italics and bold type.

Considering the extent to which code-switching to English occurs in Swedish-language interaction and particularly in Swedish comic strips, the question arises as to why examples (92)–(95) do not simply feature a code-switch as opposed to a loan translation. One possible answer to this question encourages a view on the long-term promotion and active use of English across all domains in Swedish society as having succeeded in establishing such use as manifest. Whereas English-language communication may previously have enjoyed a high degree of saliency and indexed modernity, the shine of novelty may now be dulling such that the pendulum is swinging away from overt and frequent usage. In other words, so established is the use of English and the practice of code-switching that to not code-switch may have acquired its own indexical value. Instead, the use of loan translations of easily identifiable fixed phrases and idioms signals awareness and knowledge of English, but also reflects greater interactive engagement: loan-translations arguably constitute a form of covert code-switching on the part of the speaker, which in turn triggers the listener to identify the underlying English-language source. Since both speaker and listener must draw from shared background knowledge with regards to both Swedish and English discourse systems, covert code-switching is an activity of potential enjoyment and humor. Just as overt code-switching to English entails incongruity in the form of the juxtaposition of two codes or discourse systems, covert code-switching via loan translations can also produce incongruity by virtue of Swedish words imposed on an English-language structure. Figures 95 and 96 (corresponding to examples (96) and (97)), from *Elvis* and one panel from *Rocky*, respectively, illustrate how this phenomenon represents a further development of code-switching and impacts upon the Swedish language.

7.4 Anglicisms in Swedish — 183

Figure 95: Chicken race!

(96) Chicken race!

    Elvis: Come on now! There's no party without a **chicken race**!

    Elvis: Do you dare keep up with the drinking tempo or are you **chickening out**!

    Speaker 2: Maybe ...

    Elvis: "Maybe"?? Are you a man or a chicken, Jocke? Cluck-uck-uck-uck-uck!

    Speaker 2: Okay, okay.!

    Elvis: Cheers!

    Others: Cheers!

    Elvis: (swallows)

    Others: (swallows)

    Elvis: Cheers!

    Others: Cheers!

    Elvis: (swallows)

    Others: (swallows)

    Elvis: Cheers!

    Others: Cheers!

    Others: Okay, Elvis, we give up! You **win**! Any words from the master?

Elvis: Poa blrrfh ka kaeh koh..

Speaker 3: What did he **say**?

Speaker 4: Don't know, sounded almost like he was **clucking**!

In this example, Elvis's first turn includes a code-switch to English, made extra salient by bold-face type. The pronouncement of English-language "chicken race" establishes the 'chicken' theme of the strip, which Elvis maintains in his next turn in the phrase *chickar ni out*, also emphasized via bold-face lettering. This is a translation of the verb phrase "to chicken out", with Swedish morphology on the borrowed verb form, *chickar* and the Swedish second-person plural pronoun, *ni*, but a retention of the English particle, "out". Elvis is responsible for invoking the 'chicken' theme, and there seems to be a transition from a wholly English code-switch in his first turn, to code-mixing of English and Swedish in his second turn until, finally, Speaker 4 takes up the 'chicken' theme once again to deliver the punchline, but entirely in Swedish, with the Swedish word for "clucking". Example (96) shows how Swedish language play can first be instigated via a code-switch to English, then incorporate both English and Swedish via code-mixing, and thereafter continue in Swedish via thematic maintenance. Significantly, example (96) illustrates how language play in Swedish comic strips can extend beyond single, isolated instances of creativity to encompass a comic strip in its entirety by serving as a cohesive device.

Figure 96: A little something like this …

(97) A little something like this …

> Rocky: Now I'm going to play a song from my hometown! It's an Ulf Lundell song, that I've written myself, it goes a little something like this …
>
> Rocky: (strumming)

The loan-translation in question in Figure 96 (example (97)) refers to "*den går en liten nånting så här*", which is not recognized as an idiomatic phrase in Swedish, but rather is a word-for-word translation of English "it goes a little something like this." This type of loan-translation from English represents a form of language play that goes one step further than code-switching by both invoking and encoding (i.e., translating) English. The reader must recognize the phrase or idiom in the source language to understand that a code-switch was only partially enacted: the underlying phrase is in English while the turn itself is in Swedish. The code-switch is, in effect, hidden within the Swedish translation. Consequently, it could be argued that the risks but also the rewards of such covert code-switching are greater than those for overt code-switching in terms of the associated appreciation, enjoyment, and humor.

Referring to loan-translations as covert code-switching is appropriate only insofar as the underlying English-language source maintains recognizabililty. Loan-translations otherwise reflect a transformative process known as loan nativization (Trask 2000), which impacts upon the recipient language, ushering in changes that, over time, may be mistaken for native forms such that the connection to English as the source language is not just covert but ultimately rendered unrecognizable.

We conclude this section with a final example from a comic strip that is not comprised in the collection of contemporary Swedish newspaper strips featured in this book, but a newspaper strip nonetheless, and one that is too rich in data to exclude from the present analytical focus. *Pondus* is a Norwegian comic strip created by Frode Øverli which is featured in a number of national and local newspapers in Norway, Denmark, and Sweden, including *Dagens Nyheter*, *Aftonbladet*, and *Göteborgs-Posten*. Populating the strip are two main recurring characters, the eponymous Pondus and his friend Jocke, both middle-aged men who like soccer, beer, and hard rock. In Figure 97 (example (98)), Jocke and Pondus communicate exclusively in English loan-translations; the transcript of the first four panels and the final turn in panel 6 reflects a word-for-word translation of the text, which itself is a word-for-word translation of a series of English-language idioms and popular slang expressions.

Figure 97: What's up, homeboy?

(98) What's up, homeboy?

>Jocke: What's up, homeboy? Has any new shit hit the street?

>Pondus: Oh yeah, you'd better believe it, dog! Special import is in the house! White Snake kicks ass! Big time!

>Jocke: Sweet! You're the main man! White Snake kicks as much ass as Deep Purple, Judas Priest, Motorhead, Thin Lizzy and Fan Heller [hell no]!

>Pondus: Fan Heller?

>Jocke: Van Halen!

>Pondus: Smart ass! But why isn't Kiss on your hot list?

>Jocke: Kiss? Not worthy! White trash with bad make-up!

>Pondus: **No** way!

>Jocke: Way!

Pondus: **No** way!

Jocke: Way!

Pondus: You want a piece of me?

Jocke: Bring it on, homeboy! Bring it on!

Pondus: Give us your best shot, fat face!

Jocke: Hahaha! Okay! Let's give up!

Pondus: Just as well. I was close to using the mother-word!

Jocke: Just for the record ... **then** you would have gone down, homeboy!

Pondus: Peace, dog, peace!

To the Swedish-speaking reader, the text is blatantly – nearly disturbingly – non-idiomatic; the oddity of the expressions baffles. Swedish readers would face difficulties in comprehension before recognizing the underlying English-language source as the basis. Once that realization is made, participation in the game that such language play entails is facilitated and can actually be enjoyed as humorous, as readers succeed in resolving the incongruity of Swedish words imposed on English-language structures and can subsequently identify the original expressions. The speakers in example (98) make the game all the more challenging by translating even proper names, attributing propositional content to monikers (for example, names of rock bands such as "Kiss" and "Deep Purple"), thereby requiring readers not only to retrieve the English-language source but also to draw from their background knowledge in order to make sense of the references. The goal of the comic seems to be to exaggerate the extent to which the English language actually does or plausibly can impact upon the Swedish vernacular. Indeed, although in the fifth panel the speakers overtly call a truce to their escalating quarrel, the implication is that they have exhausted their repertoire of loan-translations. Ultimately, however, each manages to encode one more slang expression, suggesting a sustainability to the practice. It is up to the readers to decide whether this *Pondus*-comic strip constitutes a criticism or approval of English-language influence.

7.5 Lingua ludica

The comic strips featured in this chapter and throughout the book, *Rocky*, *Fucking Sofo*, *Lilla Berlin*, *Berglins*, *Elvis*, *Stockholmsnatt*, and *Zelda*, comprise a collection of contemporary Swedish humor strips originally published in broadsheet or tabloid newspapers. As such, they constitute a genre of comic strips colloquially referred to as "the funnies" (Inge 1990) which have humor as their communicative goal. Each of the strips is also notably characterized by an abundance of text, most often in the form of detailed depictions of conversation. Due to the salient, cross-strip focus on language usage and talk-in-interaction, contemporary Swedish humor strips emerge as predictable sites of language play.

Common to each of the comic strips is the recurring practice of engaging in language play to establish an incongruity which profers a humorous resolution in the form of a punchline. The comics medium lends itself well to language play in that incongruity can occur between images, between texts, or between text(s) and image(s). Furthermore, aural aspects of face-to-face interaction can be visualized, such that what would not necessarily be heard can at least be seen, resulting in an incongruity between sight and sound. Indeed, as many examples in this book testify to, some language play in talk-in-interaction can only be seen, which further confirms the multimodal comic strip medium as the quintessential site for language play. The chapters of this book have explored language play as a creative exploitation of linguistic variation, including play with native Swedish dialects and with foreign languages, as well as with English as a foreign language, second language, and *lingua franca*. Even though the comics target a native Swedish audience, they reflect the Swedish society as being characterized by a dominance of English and Anglophone popular culture. Consequently, English has emerged as the *de facto* language of play in contemporary Swedish comic strips.

Chapters 4–7 have highlighted the practice of code-switching to English (including the use of idioms, swear words, and media-sourced English) and the use of loan-translations as recurrent in Swedish comic strips, as is the phenomenon of turn-final usage of English in conversational Swedish to index a joking framework. The examples have highlighted the importance of Anglophone popular cultural literacy to the appreciation of the humor of the recognizable, and how contemporary English may impact upon the Swedish language. Examples have also demonstrated the fluid status of English as a second language or foreign language in Sweden: despite arguments for and evidence of Sweden as a Swedish-English bilingual society (Sundqvist 2009; Viberg 2000), Swedish comic strips encourage a view of English as variously and, significantly, selectively used as a second language (with Swedes), as a foreign language (with native-speakers) and as a *lingua franca* (with speakers of other languages). Common to the use of each of these varieties is the practice of language play, which encourages a consideration of the role of English on the broader, international linguistic landscape.

As a global language, English can neither be conceptualized as one variety nor can it be claimed as the property of one nation, population, or speech community. The many users of English around the world have, over a period of time, adapted English to their own purposes and continue to leave their own marks on the language. Many varieties of English now exist, and while these are perhaps distinguished by their differences, it is their similarities that prevent complete linguistic chaos. Variation that impedes communication would, after all, defeat the purpose of a global language and a *lingua franca*.

The use of English as a *lingua franca* tends to correspond to specific communicative functions and domains, serving to establish norms. Phillipson (2008: 250) has identified several such domain-based categories of English as a *lingua franca*, including the following:
- *lingua economica* (the corporate globalisation imperative)
- *lingua cultura* (the specific values and norms of a society, country, group, or class, needing exploration in foreign language teaching)
- *lingua academica* (an instrument for international collaboration in higher education)
- *lingua emotiva* (the pull of Hollywood, global advertising, pop culture, and how such grassroots identification with English ties in with top down promotion of the language)
- *lingua bellica* (the language of military aggression)

Additionally, due to the wide reach of *lingua franca* English, Phillipson claims that its subtractive use, that is, when *lingua franca* English threatens the survival or prestige of other languages, renders it a *lingua frankensteinia* (Phillipson 2009). The use of English as a second and foreign language and as a *lingua franca* in contemporary Swedish comic strips challenges the Frankensteinian evaluation of English and highlights the need for another *lingua franca* category, namely, English as a *lingua ludica*. The examples presented in this book have established language play in Swedish and a range of foreign languages as characteristic of Swedish comic strips and, consequently, strongly associated with humor. Examples of specifically English-language play in second language, foreign language, and *lingua franca* communication have furthermore established the essential role of speakers' native languages to effecting the linguistic incongruities vital to language play, thereby serving to defend against the use of English as a linguistically predatory practice. English-language play may serve, in other words, preservatory purposes. Finally, the use of English as a *lingua ludica* illustrated in English-language play in contemporary Swedish comic strips serves as a reminder that English *lingua franca* communication need not reflect a domain-specific purpose, but may simply provide an outlet for or inspire linguistic creativity. Overall, this book has aimed to convince its readers of the importance of play in social interaction and the joys of playing with any language.

Bibliography

Abbott, Michael & Timothy Jay. 1978. *Why dirty words make jokes funny*. Unpublished manuscript. North Adams, Massachusetts: North Adams State College.
Adams, Michael. 2016. *In praise of profanity*. Oxford: Oxford University Press.
Alford, Finnegan & Richard Alford. 1981. A holo-cultural study of humor. *Ethos* 9(2). 149–164.
Andersen, Gisle. 2014. Pragmatic borrowing. *Journal of Pragmatics* 67. 17–33.
Andersson, Lars-Gunnar. 2016. Är engelska vårt andraspråk? *Göteborgs Posten*, 2016-06-24. https://www.gp.se/debatt/är-engelska-vårt-andraspråk-1.3195572 (accessed 24 February 2020).
Andersson, Lars-Gunnar & Peter Trudgill. 1992. *Bad language*. New York: Penguin.
Andersson, Per J. 2017. Resebarometern 2017-Turkiet och USA förlorare, Grekland vinnare. *Vagabond* 2017-05-17. http://www.vagabond.se/artiklar/artiklar/20170517/resebarometern-2017-/ (accessed 24 November 2018).
Androutsopolous, Jannis. 2000. Non-standard spellings in media texts: the case of German fanzines. *Journal of Sociolinguistics* 4. 514–533.
Apte, Mahadev. 1985. *Humour and laughter: An anthropological approach*. Ithaca: Cornell University Press.
Attardo, Salvatore. 2014. Incongruity and resolution. In Salvatore Attardo (ed.), *Sage encyclopedia of humor studies*, 383–385. Thousand Oaks: Sage Publications.
Attardo, Salvatore, Christian F. Hempelmann, & Sara Di Maio. 2002. Script oppositions and logical mechanisms: Modeling incongruities and their resolutions. *Humor* 15 (1). 3–46.
Attardo, Salvatore, & Victor Raskin. 1991. Script theory revis(it)ed: Joke similarity and joke representation model. *Humor-International Journal of Humor Research* 4 (3–4). 293–348.
Auer, Peter. 1988. A conversation analytic approach to code-switching and transfer. In Monica Heller (ed.), *Codeswitching*, 151–186. Berlin: Mouton de Gruyter.
Bakhtin, Mikhail. 1984. *The dialogical principle*. Translated by Wlad Godzich. Minneapolis: University of Minnesota Press.
Bamgbose, Ayo. 1998. Torn between the norms: Innovations in world Englishes. *World Englishes* 17(1). 1–14.
Barrett, Jeanelle. 2000. Dialect, stereotype, and humor: Linguistic variation and its place in humor studies through the lens of Mark Twain's dialect humor. PhD diss., Purdue University.
Bascom, William R. 1955. Verbal art. *The Journal of American Folklore* 68 (269). 245–252.
Baskaran, Loga. 2008. Malaysian English: Phonology. *Varieties of English* 4. 278–291.
Bateman, John. 2014. *Text and image: A critical introduction to the visual/verbal divide*. London: Routledge.
Bateson, Gregory. 2006. A theory of play and fantasy. In Katie Salen and Eric Zimmerman (eds.), *The game design reader: A rules of play anthology*, 314–328. Cambridge, Massachusetts: MIT Press.
Battistella, Edwin. 2005. *Bad language: Are some words better than others?* Oxford: Oxford University Press.
Bauman, Richard. 1975. Verbal art as performance 1. *American anthropologist* 77 (2). 290–311.
Bechdel, Alison. 2007. *Fun home: A family tragicomic*. Boston: Houghton Mifflin Harcourt.
Beerman, Ursula. 2014. Humor styles. In Salvatore Attardo (ed.), *Sage encyclopedia of humor studies*, 364–365. Thousand Oaks: Sage Publications.

Beers Fägersten, Kristy. 2012a. *Who's swearing now? The social aspects and pragmatic functions of conversational swearing*. Newcastle-upon-Tyne: Cambridge Scholars Publishing.
Beers Fägersten, Kristy. 2012b. Fucking svenska! *Språktidningen*. October. 54–56.
Beers Fägersten, Kristy. 2014a. The use of English swear words in Swedish media. In Marianne Rathje (ed.), *Swearing in the Nordic countries*, 63–82. Copenhagen: Dansk Sprognævn.
Beers Fägersten, Kristy. 2014b. Comic strips. In Salvatore Attardo (ed.), *Sage encyclopedia of humor studies*, 155–156. Thousand Oaks: Sage Publications.
Beers Fägersten, Kristy. 2017a. The role of swearing in creating an online persona: The case of YouTuber PewDiePie. *Discourse, Context and Media* 18. 1–10.
Beers Fägersten, Kristy. 2017b. FUCK CANCER, fucking Åmål, aldrig fucka upp. In Kristy Beers Fägersten & Karyn Stapleton (eds.), *Advances in swearing research: New languages and new contexts*, 65–86. Amsterdam: John Benjamins.
Beers Fägersten, Kristy. 2017c. English-language swearing as humor in Swedish comic strips. *Journal of Pragmatics* 121. 175–187.
Bell, Allan. 1983. Broadcast news as language standard. *International Journal of the Sociology of Language* 40. 29–42.
Bell, Nancy. 2012. Formulaic language, creativity, and language play in a second language. *Annual Review of Applied Linguistics* 32. 189–205.
Bell, Nancy, & Anne Pomerantz. 2015. *Humor in the classroom: A guide for language teachers and educational researchers*. London: Routledge.
Belz, Julie A. 2002. Second language play as a representation of the multicompetent self in foreign language study. *Journal of Language, Identity, and Education* 1 (1). 13–39.
Blom, Jan-Petter & John Gumperz. 1972. Social meaning in linguistic structure: code-switching in Norway. In John Gumperz and Dell Hymes (eds.), *Directions in sociolinguistics*, 407–434. New York: Holt, Rinehart and Winston.
Bryant, Chad. 2006. The language of resistance? Czech jokes and joke-telling under Nazi occupation, 1943–45. *Journal of Contemporary History* 41 (1). 133–151.
Cabau-Lampa, Beatrice. 1999. Decisive factors for language teaching in Sweden. *Educational Studies* 25. 175–186.
Cabau-Lampa, Beatrice. 2005. Foreign language education in Sweden from a historical perspective: status, role and organization. *Journal of Educational Administration History* 37. 95–111.
Carrier, David. 2000. *The aesthetics of comics*. University Park: Penn State Press.
Carter, Ron. 2004. *Language and creativity: The art of common talk*. London: Routledge.
Chong, Dennis, & James N. Druckman. 2007. Framing theory. *Annual Review of Political Science* 10. 103–126.
Cohn, Neil. 2013. *The visual language of comics: Introduction to the structure and cognition of sequential images*. London: A&C Black.
Cook, Guy. 2000. *Language play, language learning*. Oxford: Oxford University Press
Cook, Haruko M. 1999. Particles. *Journal of Linguistic Anthropology* 9 (1-2). 181–183.
Cook, Vivian J. 1991. The poverty-of-the-stimulus argument and multicompetence. *Interlanguage Studies Bulletin (Utrecht)* 7 (2). 103–117.
Crumb, Robert. 1996. *American splendor presents Bob and Harv's comics*. New York: Four Walls Eight Windows.
Crystal, David. 1998. *Language play*. London: Penguin Books.
Crystal, David. 1996. Language play and linguistic intervention. *Child Language Teaching and Therapy* 12 (3). 328–344.

Crystal, David. 2012. *English as a global language*. Cambridge: Cambridge University Press.
Dahlberg, Hans. 1999. *Hundra år i Sverige: Krönika över ett dramatiskt sekel*. Stockholm: Bonnier.
Davies, Catherine Evans. 2014. Dialect humor. In Salvatore Attardo (ed.), *Sage encyclopedia of humor studies*, 201–203. Thousand Oaks: Sage Publications.
Davies, Christie. 2004. Victor Raskin on jokes. *Humor-International Journal of Humor Research* 17(4). 373–380.
Davies, Christie. 2011. Logical mechanisms: A critique. *Humor-International Journal of Humor Research* 24 (2). 159–165.
Deshors, Sandra C., Sandra Götz & Samantha Laporte. 2016. Linguistic innovations in EFL and ESL: Rethinking the linguistic creativity of non-native English speakers. *International Journal of Learner Corpus Research* 2 (2). 131–150.
Dewaele, Jean-Marc. 2004. The emotional force of swearwords and taboo words in the speech of multilinguals. *Journal of Multilingual and Multicultural Developement* 25 (2–3). 204–222.
Dewaele, Jean-Marc. 2010a. "Christ fucking shit merde!" Language preferences for swearing among maximally proficient multilinguals. *Sociolinguistic Studies* 4. 595–614.
Dewaele, Jean-Marc. 2010b. *Emotions in multiple languages*. Palgrave Macmillan, New York.
DuFrene, Debbie & Carol Lehman. 2002. Persuasive appeal for clean language. *Business Communication Quarterly* 65 (1). 48–55.
Duncan, Randy. 2012. Image functions: Shape and color as hermeneutic images in "Asterios Polyp". In Matthew Smith & Randy Duncan (eds.), *Critical approaches to comics: Theories and methods*, 61–72. London: Routledge.
Dundes, Alan. 1987. At ease, disease-AIDS jokes as sick humor. *American Behavioral Scientist* 30 (3). 72–81.
Dundes, Alan & Thomas Hauschild. 1988. Auschwitz jokes. In George Paton, Chris Powell, Luciano Venezia & Kelly Frailing (eds.), *Humour in society: Resistance and control*, 56–66. London: Macmillan.
Ezell, Jennifer. 2012. Hitler walks into a bar: The Nazi in American humor. PhD diss., The George Washington University.
Eisner, Will. 1985. *Comics & sequential art*. London: W.W. Norton & Co.
Fergusson, Charles A. 1994. Note on Swedish English. *World Englishes* 13(3): 419–424.
Ferguson, Mark & Thomas Ford. 2008. Disparagement humor: A theoretical and empirical review of psychoanalytic, superiority, and social identity theories. *Humor-International Journal of Humor Research* 21 (3). 283–312.
Fine, Gary, 1979. Obscene joking across cultures. *Journal of Communication* 26 (3). 134–140.
Flamson, Thomas & Clark Barrett. 2008. The encryption theory of humor: A knowledge-based mechanism of honest signaling. *Journal of Evolutionary Psychology* 6 (4). 261–281.
Ford, Thomas E. 2015. The social consequences of disparagement humor: Introduction and overview. *Humor* 28 (2). 163–169.
Freud, Sigmund. 1905. *Der witz und seine beziehung zum unbewussten*. Frankfurt: Fischer.
Gardner, Jared. 2012. *Projections: Comics and the history of twenty-first-century storytelling*. Palo Alto: Stanford University Press.
Gersten, Russell, Nancy C. Jordan & Jonathan R. Flojo. 2005. Early identification and interventions for students with mathematics difficulties. *Journal of Learning Disabilities* 38 (4). 293–304.
Göteborgs Posten. Kellerman och Koch pristagare. 14 April 2010. http://www.gp.se/kultur/kultur/kellerman-och-koch-pristagare-1.1000607 (accessed 14 November 2019).

Groensteen, Thierry. 2007. *The system of comics*. Jackson: University Press of Mississippi.
Grosjean, Francois. 1982. *Life with two languages: An introduction to bilingualism*. Cambridge, Massachusetts: Harvard University Press.
Haberland, H. 2005. Domains and domain loss. In Bent Preisler, Anne Fabricius, Hartmut Haberland, Susanne Kjærbeck & Karen Risager (eds.), *The consequences of mobility: Linguistic and sociocultural contact zones*, 227–237. Roskilde: Roskilde University, Department of Language and Culture.
Håkansson, Gabrielle. 2007. Framtidens språk. Om hundra år pratar svenskarna som Rocky. *Dagens Nyheter* 2007.07.10 https://www.dn.se/arkiv/kultur/framtidens-sprak-om-hundra-ar-pratar-svenskarna-som-rocky/ (accessed 24 November 2019).
Hall-Lew, Lauren & Rebecca L. Starr. 2010. Beyond the 2nd generation: English use among Chinese Americans in the San Francisco Bay area. *English Today* 26 (3). 12–19.
Harris, Richard Jackson, Abigail J. Werth, Kyle E. Bures & Chelsea M. Bartel. 2008. Social movie quoting: What, why and how?. *Ciencias psicologicas* 2 (1). http://www.redalyc.org/html/4595/459545421004/ (accessed 24 November 2019).
Haugen, Einar. 1987. *Blessings of Babel: bilingualism and language planning. Problems and pleasures*. Berlin: Mouton de Gruyter.
Hayman, Greg, & Henry John Pratt. 2005. What are comics? In Lee B. Brown & David Goldblatt (eds.), *Aesthetics: A reader in philosophy of the arts* (Second Edition), 419–424. New Jersey: Prentice Hall.
Hellquist, Elof. 1948. *Svensk etymologisk ordbok*. Malmö: Gleerups.
Hempelmann, Christian F., & Salvatore Attardo. 2011. Resolutions and their incongruities: Further thoughts on logical mechanisms. *Humor-International Journal of Humor Research* 24 (2). 125–149.
Highmore, Ben. 2002. *Everyday life and cultural theory: An introduction*. London: Routledge.
Hillenbrand, Fritz Karl Michael. 1995. *Underground humour in Nazi Germany, 1933–1945*. London: Routledge.
Hilliard, Robert & Michael Keith. 2007. *Dirty discourse: Sex and indecency in broadcasting*. Malden, Massachusetts: Blackwell.
Hilmes, Michele. 1997. *Radio voices: American broadcasting, 1922–1952*. Minneapolis: University of Minnesota Press.
Hjort, Minna. 2017. Swearing in Finnish: folk definitions and perceptions. In Kristy Beers Fägersten & Karyn Stapleton (eds.), *Advances in swearing research: New languages and new contexts*, 233–258. Amsterdam: John Benjamins.
Hobbes, Thomas. 1996 [1951]. *Leviathan*. New York: Oxford University Press.
Höglin, Renée. 2002. *Engelska språket som hot och tillgång i Norden*. Copenhagen: TemaNord.
Holm, Kjell. 2006. *Antiliksomism. Språkförsvaret*. Available at: http://www.språkförsvaret.se/sf/?id=900 (accessed 24 November 2019).
Honeybone, Patrick, & Kevin Watson. 2013. Salience and the sociolinguistics of Scouse spelling: Exploring the phonology of the contemporary humorous localised dialect literature of Liverpool. *English World-Wide* 34(3). 305–340.
Hughes, Alex. 1999. *Heterographies: Sexual difference in French autobiography*. Oxford: Berg.
Huizinga, Johan. 1980. *Homo Ludens: A Study of the Play Element in Culture* (PDF) (3rd ed.). London: Routledge & Kegan Paul Ltd. (accessed 29 October 2019).
Hult, Francis. M. 2012. English as a transcultural language in Swedish policy and practice. *Tesol Quarterly* 46 (2). 230–257.

Hunker, Paula & Laura Vanderkam. 1999. Proliferating profanities. *Insight on the News*, 20 September 1999. 30.
Inge, M. Thomas. 1990. *Comics as culture*. Jackson: University Press of Mississippi.
Ivory, James, Dmitri Williams, Nicole Martins & Mia Consalvo. 2009. Good clean fun? A content analysis of profanity in video games and its prevalence across game systems and ratings. *CyberPsychology & Behaviour* 12 (4). 457–460.
Jaffe, Alexandra. 2017. Fuck in French: evidence of "other-language" swearing in France and Québec. In Kristy Beers Fägersten & Karyn Stapleton (eds.), *Advances in swearing research: New languages and new contexts*, 87–106. Amsterdam: John Benjamins.
Jakobson, Roman. 1960. Linguistics and poetics. In Thomas. A. Sebeok (ed.), *Style in language*, 350–377. Cambridge, MA: MIT Press.
Jay, Timothy. 1992. *Cursing in America*. Philadelphia: John Benjamins.
Jay, Timothy, 1999. *Why we curse: A neuro-psycho-social theory of speech*. Amsterdam: John Benjamins.
Jay, Timothy. 2018. Swearing, moral order, and online communication. *Journal of Language Aggression and Conflict* 6 (1). 107–126.
Jay, Timothy, Catherine Caldwell-Harris & Kendall King. 2008. Recalling taboo and non-taboo words. *The American Journal of Psychology* 121 (1). 83–103.
Jay, Timothy & Kristin Janschewitz. 2008. The pragmatics of swearing. *Journal of Politeness Research. Language, Behavior, Culture* 4 (2). 267–288.
Johnson, Danette Ifert & Nicole Lewis. 2010. Perceptions of swearing in the work setting: An expectancy violations theory perspective. *Communication Reports* 23 (2). 106–118.
Jenkins, Jennifer. 2000. *The phonology of English as an international language*. Oxford: Oxford University Press.
Josephson, Olle. 2004. *Ju: Ifrågasatta självklarheter om svenskan, engelskan och alla andra språk i Sverige*. Stockholm: Norstedts.
Josephson, Olle. 2014. The Swedish Language Council and English as a lingua franca. *Sociolinguistica: Internationales Jahrbuch für Europaeische Soziolinguistik* 28 (1). 105–122.
Kaye, Barbara & Barry Sapolsky. 2004. Talking a 'blue' streak: Context and offensive language in prime time network television programs. *Journalism and Mass Communication Quarterly* 81 (4). 911–927.
Kirkpatrick, Andy. 2011. English as an Asian lingua franca and the multilingual model of ELT. *Language Teaching* 44 (2). 212–224.
Kotsinas, Ulla-Britt. 1994. Snobbar och pyjamastyper: Ungdomskultur, ungdomsspråk och gruppidentiteter i Stockholm, in Johan Fornäs, Ulf Boëthius, Michael Forsman, Hillevi Ganetz & Bo Reimer (eds.), *Ungdomskultur i Sverige*, 311–336. Stehag, Sweden: Brutus Östlings Bokförlag Symposion.
Kotsinas, Ulla-Britt. 2002. *Ungdomsspråk*. Stockholm: Hallgren & Fallgren.
Krapp, George. 1926. The psychology of dialect writing. *The Bookman* 63. 522–527.
Kunzle, David. 1973. *The early comic strip: Narrative strips and picture stories in the European broadsheet from c. 1450 to 1825*. Berkeley: University of California Press.
Labrie, Normand & Carsten Quell. 1997. Your language, my language or English? The potential language choice in communication among nationals of the European Union. *World Englishes* 16 (1). 3–26.
Lantolf, James P. 1997. The function of language play in the acquisition of L2 Spanish. *Contemporary Perspectives on the Acquisition of Spanish* 2. 3–24.

Lee, Micky. 2000: Crossing boundaries: From code-switching to voice-quoting: An alternative approach to code alternation. Paper presented at American Association of Applied Linguistics, Vancouver, Canada, 11–14 March 2000.

Lefèvre, Pierre. 2000. Narration in comics. *Image [&] Narrative* 1 (1). http://www.imageandnarrative.be/inarchive/narratology/pascallefevre.htm (accessed 24 November 2019).

Lefèvre, Pierre. 2009. The construction of space in comics. In Jeet Heer & Kent Worcester (eds.), *A comics studies reader*, 157–162. Jackson: University Press of Mississippi.

Li, Wei (ed.). 2005. *The bilingualism reader*. New York: Routledge.

Lindström, Fredrik & Marcos Hellberg. 2006. *Svenska dialektmysterier*. Stockholm: Sveriges television.

Lindström, Fredrik. 2010. Fredriks fynd: e och ä. *Språktidningen*. http://spraktidningen.se/artiklar/2010/06/e-och (accessed 24 November 2019).

Lindström, Fredrik. 2019. *100 svenska dialekter*. Stockholm: Bonnier Fakta.

Lipman, Steve. 1991. *Laughter in hell: The use of humor during the holocaust*. Northvale, New Jersey: J. Aronson.

Macaulay, Ronald. 1987. The social significance of Scottish dialect humor. *International journal of the sociology of language* 65. 53–63.

Magnussen, Anne. 2000. The semiotics of CS Peirce as a theoretical framework for the understanding of comics. In Hans-Christian Christiansen (ed.), *Comics and culture: Analytical and theoretical approaches to comics*, 193–207. Copenhagen: Museum Tusculanum Press.

Maltby, David. 1998. Swearing can be a curse in many settings: Foul mouths are just bad business. *The Kansas City Star*, 22 November 1998, p. D1.

Martin, Rod. 2007. *The psychology of humor: An integrative approach*. Burlington, Massachusetts: Elsevier Academic Press.

Martineau, William H. 1972. A model of the social functions of humor. In Jeffrey Goldstein (ed.), *The psychology of humor: Theoretical perspectives and empirical issues*, 101–125. Cambridge, Mass: Academic Press.

McCarthy, Anjanie, Kang Lee, Shoji Itakura & Darwin W. Muir. 2008. Gaze display when thinking depends on culture and context. *Journal of Cross-Cultural Psychology* 39 (6). 716–729.

McCloud, Scott. 1993. *Understanding comics: The invisible art*. Northampton, Massachusetts: William Morrow.

McClure, Erica & Malcome McClure. 1988. Macro- and micro-sociolinguistic dimensions of code-switching in Vingard (Romania). In: Monica Heller (ed.), *Codeswitching: Anthropological and sociolinguistic perspectives*, 25–51. Berlin: Mouton de Gruyter.

McGhee, Paul & Edie Pistolesi. 1979. *Humor: Its origin and development*. San Francisco: WH Freeman.

Mella, Orlando, Fereshteh Ahmadi & Irving Palm. 2013. *Mångfaldsbarometern 2013*. Gävle: University of Gävle.

Meskin, Aaron. 2007. Defining comics? *The Journal of Aesthetics and Art Criticism* 65 (4). 369–379.

Monro, D. H. 1951. *Argument of humor*. Melbourne: Melbourne University Press.

Moore, Alan, Dave Gibbons & John Higgins. 1987. *Watchmen*. New York: Warner Books.

Muysken, Pieter. 2000. *Bilingual speech: A typology of code-mixing*. Cambridge: Cambridge University Press.

Myers-Scotton, Carol. 1988. Code-switching as indexical of social negotiations. In Monica Heller (ed.), *Codeswitching*, 187–214. Berlin: Mouton de Gruyter.

Myers-Scotton, Carol. 1993. *Social motivations for codeswitching*. Oxford: Clarendon Press.
Negus, Keith, & Michael J. Pickering. 2004. *Creativity, communication and cultural value*. London: Sage.
Norrick, Neal. 2007. Interdiscourse humor: contrast, merging, accommodation. *Humor* 20 (4). 389–413.
Norrick, Neal. 2012. Swearing in literary prose fiction and conversational narrative. *Narrative Inquiry* 22 (1). 24–49.
Norrick, Neal. 2014. Conversation. In Salvatore Attardo (ed.), *Sage encyclopedia of humor studies*, 175–179. Thousand Oaks: Sage Publications.
Norrick, Neal. 2017. Language play in conversation. In Nancy Bell (ed.), *Multiple perspectives on language play*, 11–45. Boston/Berlin: Walter de Gruyter.
O'Connor, James. 2000. *Cuss control: The complete book on how to curb your cursing*. New York: Three Rivers Press.
Oring, Elliott. 1987. Jokes and the discourse on disaster. *Journal of American Folklore* 100. 276–286.
Oring, Elliott. 2011. Still further thoughts on logical mechanisms: A response to Christian F. Hempelmann and Salvatore Attardo. *Humor-International Journal of Humor Research* 24 (2). 151–158.
Oring, Elliott. 2016. *Joking asides: The theory, analysis, and aesthetics of humor*. Boulder: University Press of Colorado.
Parkvall, Mikael. 2009a. *Sveriges språk: vem talar vad och var? Rapporter från Institutionen för lingvistik vid Stockholms universitet*. Stockholm: Stockholm University.
Parkvall, Mikael. 2009b. *Lagom finns bara i Sverige och andra myter om språk*. Stockholm: Schibsted.
Pennycook, Alastair. 2007. 'The rotation gets thick. The constraints get thin': Creativity, recontextualization, and difference." *Applied Linguistics* 28.4. 579–596.
Peterson, Elizabeth. 2017. The nativization of pragmatic borrowings in remote language contact situations. *Journal of Pragmatics* 113. 116–126.
Philipson, Robert. 1992. *Linguistic imperialism*. Oxford: Oxford University Press.
Phillipson, Robert. 2001. English or "no" to English in Scandinavia? *English Today* 17 (2). 22–28.
Phillipson, Robert. 2008. Lingua franca or lingua frankensteinia? English in European integration and globalisation 1. *World Englishes* 27 (2). 250–267.
Phillipson, Robert. 2009. English in globalisation, a lingua franca or a lingua frankensteinia? *TESOL Quarterly* 43 (2). 335–339.
Piper, Fred & Sean Murphy. 2002. *Cryptography. A very short introduction*. Oxford: Oxford University Press.
Pope, Rob. 2005. *Creativity: Theory, history, practices*. London: Routledge.
Preisler, Bent. 1999a. Functions and forms of English in a European EFL country. In Tony Bex & Richard Watts (eds.), *Standard English: The widening debate*, 239–267. London: Routledge.
Preisler, Bent 1999b. *Danskerne og det engelske sprog*. Roskilde: Universitetsforlag.
Preisler, Bent 2003. English in Danish and the Danes' English. *International Journal of the Sociology of Language* 159 (1). 109–126.
Preston, Dennis. 1982. Ritin fowklower daun rong: Folklorists' failure in phonology. *Journal of American Folklore* 95. 304–326.
Raskin, Richard. 1992. *Life is like a glass of tea: Studies of classic Jewish jokes*. Aarhus: Aarhus University Press.

Raskin, Victor. 1985. *Semantic mechanisms of humor*. Boston: D. Reidel.
Raskin, Victor. 1992. Humor as a non-bona-fide mode of communication. *Deseret Language and Linguistic Society Symposium* 18 (1). 87–92.
Rathje, Marianne. 2011. Fuck, fandme og for pokker. Danske bandeord i tre generationers talesprog. *Språk och stil* 21. 81–109.
Reyes, Iliana. 2004. Functions of code switching in schoolchildren's conversations. *Bilingual Research Journal* 28 (1). 77–98.
Rieber, Lloyd P., Lola Smith, & David Noah. 1998. The value of serious play. *Educational Technology* 38. 29–36.
Ruch, Willibald. 1992. Assessment of appreciation of humor: Studies with the 3 WD humor test. *Advances in personality assessment* 9. 27–75.
Saito, Kazuya, & Roy Lyster. 2012. Effects of form-focused instruction and corrective feedback on L2 pronunciation development of/ɹ/by Japanese learners of English. *Language Learning* 62 (2). 595–633.
Sandelin, Anna. 2013. Skandinaviska för nybörjare. Svenska institutet. https://svenskaspraket.si.se/skandinaviska-for-nyborjare/ (accessed 24 November 2019).
Saraceni, Mario. 2003. *The language of comics*. London: Psychology Press.
Saville-Troike, Muriel, 1989. *The ethnography of communication: An introduction* (Second edition). Oxford: Blackwell.
Schneider, Edgar. 2011. 2011. *English around the world. An introduction*. Cambridge: Cambridge University Press.
Schneider, Greice. 2010. Comics and everyday life: From *ennui* to contemplation. *European Comic Studies* 3 (1). 97–109.
Seidlhofer, Barbara. 2004. Research perspectives on teaching English as a lingua franca. *Annual review of applied linguistics* 24. 209–239.
Selinker, Larry. 1972. Interlanguage. *International Review of Applied Linguistics* 10. 209–231.
Sewell, Edward. 1984. Appreciation of cartoons with profanity in captions. *Psychological Reports* 54. 583–587.
Sharp, Harriet. 2001. *English in spoken Swedish. A corpus study of two discourse domains*. Stock- holm: Almqvist and Wiksell International.
Sharp, Harriet. 2007. Swedish–English language mixing. *World Englishes* 26 (2). 224–240.
Sherzer, Joel. 2014. Speech play. In Salvatore Attardo (ed.), *Sage encyclopedia of humor studies*, 727–730. Thousand Oaks: Sage Publications.
Siegel, Jeff. 1987. *Language contact in a plantation environment: A sociolinguistic history of Fiji*. Cambridge: Cambridge University Press.
Siegel, Jeff. 1995. How to get a laugh in Fijian: Code-switching and humor. *Language in society* 24 (1). 95–110.
Simpson Paul. 2003. On the Discourse of Satire: Towards a Stylistic Model of Satirical Humour. Amsterdam and Philadelphia: John Benjamins.
Sköld, Matilde. 2010. Lena Ackebo tittar närmare på Sofo. *DN På Stan*. http://www.dn.se/pastan/mer-pa-stan/lena-ackebo-tittar-narmare-pa-sofo (accessed 24 November 2019).
Smith, Peter K., & Anthony Pellegrini. 2008. Learning through play. *Encyclopedia on early childhood development* 24 (8). 61.
Smyers, John Otis. 2016. "Here's looking at you, kid:" An empirical study of the social movie quoting phenomenon. PhD diss., Kansas State University.
Smyth, Willie. 1986. Challenger jokes and the humor of disaster. *Western Folklore* 45 (4). 243–260.

Special Eurobarometer 243. 2006. *Europeans and their languages*. The European Commission. http://ec.europa.eu/public_opinion/archives/ebs/ (accessed 24 February 2020).
Special Eurobarometer 386. 2012. *Europeans and their languages*. The European Commission. http://ec.europa.eu/public_opinion/archives/ebs/ebs_386_en.pdf (accessed 24 November 2019).
Sperber, Dierdre & Dan Wilson. 1986 [1995] *Relevance: Communication and cognition*. Oxford: Blackwell.
Spiegelman, Art. 1986. *Maus: A survivor's tale*. New York: Pantheon.
Spurgeon, Tom. 2005. A short interview with Martin Kellerman. *The Comics Reporter*. http://www.comicsreporter.com/index.php/resources/interviews/3434/Håkansson2007%20Accessed%20November%2024 (accessed 24 November 2019).
Stapleton, Karyn. 2010. Swearing. In Miriam Locher & Sage Graham (eds.), *Interpersonal pragmatics*, 289–306. Berlin: Mouton De Gruyter.
Stølen, Marianne, 1992. Codeswitching for humour and ethnic identity: Written Danish-American occasional songs. *Journal of Multilingual and Multicultural Development* 13. 215–228.
Sundqvist, Pia. 2009. Extramural English matters: Out-of-school English and its impact on Swedish ninth graders' oral proficiency and vocabulary. PhD diss., Karlstad University.
Swann, Joan, & Janet Maybin. 2007. Introduction: Language creativity in everyday contexts. *Applied Linguistics* 28 (4). 491–496
Teleman, Ulf. 2003. *Tradis och funkis: Svensk språkvård och språkpolitik efter 1800*. Stockholm: Norstedts.
Thorén, Caroline. 2009. Bernspriset till Martin Kellerman. *Dagens Nyheter*, 20 May 2009. https://www.dn.se/kultur-noje/bernspriset-till-martin-kellerman/ (accessed 14 November 2019).
Trask, Robert Lawrence. 2000. *The dictionary of historical and comparative linguistics*. London: Psychology Press.
Trotta, Joe. 1998. Ethnolinguistic identity in Metropolitan New York City dialects. In Hans Lindquist, Staffan Klintborg, Magnus Levin & Maria Estling (eds.), *The major varieties of English. Papers from MAVEN 97*, 101–110. Växjö: Acta Wexionensia.
Trotta, Joe. 2010. Whose rules rule?: Grammar controversies, popular culture and the fear of English from below. *Nordic Journal of English Studies* 9 (3). 41–65.
Vandergriff, Ilona, & Carolin Fuchs. 2009. Does CMC promote language play? *Calico Journal*, 27 (1). 26–47.
Vandergriff, Ilona, & Carolin Fuchs. 2012. Humor support in synchronous computer-mediated classroom discussions. *HUMOR: International Journal of Humor Research* 25(4). 437–458.
Varnum, Robin & Christina T. Gibbons. 2001. *The language of comics: Word and image*. Jackson: University Press of Mississippi.
Venezia, Tony. 2011. Harvey Pekar's anti-epiphanic everyday. *The Comics Grid*. http://www.comicsgrid.com/2011/06/harvey-pekar-everyday/ (accessed 24 November 2019).
Viberg, Åke. 2000. Tvåspråkighet och inlärning av språk i och utanför skolan. *Språk 2000: 18. Kursplaner, betygskriterier och kommentarer*, 27–41. Stockholm: Skolverket.
Wajnryb, Ruth. 2005. *Expletive deleted: A good look at bad language*. New York: Free Press.
Warren, Caleb, & A. Peter McGraw. 2014. Appreciation of humor. In Salvatore Attardo (ed.), *Sage encyclopedia of humor studies*, 52–54. Thousand Oaks: Sage Publications.

Westman, Margareta. 1996. Har svenska språket en framtid? In Lena Moberg & Margareta Westman (eds.), *Svenska i tusen år: Glimtar ur svenska språkets utveckling*, 182–194. Stockholm: Norstedts.

Wolff, Harold A., Carl E. Smith & Henry A. Murray. 1934. The psychology of humor: A study of responses to race-disparagement jokes. *Journal of Abnormal and Social Psychology* 28. 341–365.

Woolard, Kathryn, 1988. Codeswitching and comedy in Catalonia. In: Monica Heller (ed.), *Codeswitching: Anthropological and sociolinguistic perspectives*, 53–76. Berlin: Mouton de Gruyter.

Yus, Francisco. 2003. Humor and the search for relevance. *Journal of Pragmatics* 35 (9). 1295–1331.

Zeigler-Hill, Virgil & Avi Besser. 2011. Humor style mediates the association between pathological narcissism and self-esteem. *Personality and Individual Differences* 50 (8). 1196–1201.

Zelvys, V.I. 1990. Obscene humor: what the hell? *Humor* 3. 323–332.

Zenner, Eline, Tom Ruette & Emma Devriendt. 2017. The borrowability of English swearwords: an exploration of Belgian Dutch and Netherlandic Dutch tweets. In Kristy Beers Fägersten & Karyn Stapleton (eds.), *Advances in swearing research: New languages and new contexts*, 107–138. Amsterdam: John Benjamins.

The comic strips featured in this book have been published in the following volumes

Ackebo, Lena. 2010. *Fucking Sofo*. Stockholm: Kartago.
Ackebo, Lena. 2012. *Vi ses i Sofo*. Stockholm: Kartago.
Berglin, Jan & Maria Berglin. 2011. B*ronto Berglin: Samlade serier av Jan & Maria Berglin 1999–2008*. Stockholm: Galago.
Cronstam, Maria & Tony Cronstam. 2010. *Elvis: Tillsammans sen 2000. 2000–2010*. Malmö: Egmont.
Ekman, Ellen. 2014. *Lilla Berlin Del 1, So last year*. Stockholm: Kolik.
Ekman, Ellen. 2014. *Lilla Berlin Del 2, Mina vänner*. Stockholm: Kolik.
Ekman, Ellen. 2015. *Lilla Berlin Del 3, Leva life*. Stockholm: Kolik.
Ekman, Ellen. 2015. *Lilla Berlin Del 4, Cute overload*. Stockholm: Kolik.
Ekman, Ellen. 2016. *Lilla Berlin Del 5, Netflix och chill*. Stockholm: Kolik.
Kellerman, Martin. 2008. *Rocky 10 år - samlade serier 1998–2008*. Stockholm: Kartago.
Kellerman, Martin. 2013. *Rocky - samlade serier 2008–2013*. Stockholm: Kartago.
Kellerman, Martin. 2018. *Rocky - samlade serier 2013–2018*. Stockholm: Kartago.
Neidestam, Lina. 2009. *Zelda*. Stockholm: Kartago.
Neidestam, Lina. 2012. *Zelda: Kampen fortsätter*. Stockholm: Kartago.
Neidestam, Lina. 2013. *Zelda: Zelda vs. patriarkatet*. Stockholm: Kartago.
Neidestam, Lina. 2015. *Zelda: uppbrott och utbrott*. Stockholm: Kartago.
Neidestam, Lina. 2016. *Zelda: täckning saknas*. Stockholm: Kartago.
Neidestam, Lina. 2017. *Zelda: allt är normalt*. Stockholm: Kartago.
Thungren, Stefan and Forshed, Pelle. 2015. *Tio år med Stockholmsnatt. Samlade serier 2005–2015*. Stockholm: Kartago.

Index

accent 10, 16, 40, 42, 44, 46, 57, 58, 120, 171, 178
– non-standard 122
Arabic 11, 62, 64, 66, 67, 88, 90
aural 10, 11, 28, 34, 37, 44, 45, 54, 58, 80, 87, 160, 188

Berglins 21, 23, 37, 91, 94, 95, 131, 142, 146, 179, 188
Berlin 22, 23, 25, 37, 75, 76, 77, 98, 100, 101, 110, 117, 130, 188
bilingual 16, 95, 97, 124, 126, 188
bisociation 5
borrowing 12, *See also* loan nativization

ceceo 83, 85
censor 131, 134
censorship 12, 130, 131, 134, 135, 146
code-switching 1
– asymmetrical 98
– inter-sentential 95, 98
– intra-sentential 95, 98
– situational 124, 150
– unidirectional 98
cognitive dissonance 9
cohesive device 184
comic strip 1–13, *See also* humor strip
creativity 4, 5, 10, 13, 14, 17, 30, 34, 36, 44, 47, 62, 95, 117, 157, 158, 163, 166, 190

Danish 11, 62, 67, 68, 69, 70, 71, 88, 90, 126
dialect humor 10, 11, 35, 44, 45, 48, 49, 50, 51, 54, 56, 59, 63, 87, 88
dialect spelling 10, *See also* regiolectal spelling
dialogue 10, 20, 26, 27, 28, 34, 39, 41, 45, 46, 97, 115, 120, 141, 143, 146, 155, 173
discourse clash 141, 156

Elvis 21, 23, 37, 112, 127, 151, 182, 188
English
– as a foreign language 95, 158, 163, 178, 188

– as a lingua franca 13, 120, 168, 170, 171, 175, 176, 178, 179, 188, 189, 190
– as a lingua ludica 188
– as a second language 95, 158, 163, 178, 188
– from above 108, 141
– from below 108, 141, 154
– punchline 12, 101, 107
eye-dialect 1, 10, 12, 16, 40, 44, 117, 123

Finnish 64, 67, 90, 126, 176
forced lexical reanalysis 120
formulaic phrase 100, 160
frame 3, 4, 8, 9, 162
Fucking Sofo 22, 23, 27, 37, 40, 41, 44, 47, 117, 188
funnies 8, 188

gag-a-day 9, *See also* single panel
General Theory of Verbal Humor (GTVH) 6, 7
German 11, 62, 67, 68, 73, 74, 88, 90, 168, 171
Gothenburg 10, 47, 48, 49, 50, 53
grawlix 135

humor
– adaptive 88
– affiliative 64, 88
– dialect 10, 11, 35, 44, 45–47, 48, 49, 50, 51, 54, 56, 59, 63, 87, 88
– disparagment 11, 63, 64, 66, 74, 82, 87, 88, 157
– interdiscourse 140, 153
– maladaptive 88
– self-deprecating 88, 123, 157
– self-disparagement 11, 88
– self-enhancing 88

idiom 12, 73, 98, 100, 101, 107, 117, 122, 124, 126, 156, 158, 179, 182, 185, 187, 188
inappropriateness 138, 154
incompetence 11, 63, 67, 71, 80, 82, 87, 88, 89, 156, 157, 162, 163, 166

incongruity 5, *See also* script opposition
in-group 17, 19, 64, 95, 117, 123, 158, 163, 166
intercultural clash 150, 153, 154
interdiscourse clash 141, 156
interlanguage spelling 12, 123, 127, 171, 173, 178
Italian 11, 19, 71, 73, 74, 76, 85, 88

juxtaposition 5, 6, 42, 123, 135, 182

knowledge resource 6, 7

language
– contact 1, 35, 62, 82, 95, 153
– foreign 1, 11, 35, 47, 63, 64, 71, 73, 74, 76, 77, 81, 82, 83, 85, 86, 87, 88, 89, 91, 95, 108, 124, 156, 158, 188, 189
– matrix 98, 178
– medium of play 3, 155
– minority 64, 90, 95
– object of play 3, 61, 88
– play 1–13, 14, 16, 17, 20, 30, 34, 35, 36, 44, 45, 46, 47, 51, 53, 56, 57, 58, 59, 60, 61, 62, 69, 71, 74, 88, 89, 94, 95, 97, 98, 105, 107, 117, 123, 124, 126, 138, 155, 156, 157, 158, 159, 161, 163, 164, 166, 184, 185, 187, 188, 189
Law of Jante 11
Lilla Berlin 22, 23, 25, 37, 98, 100, 101, 110, 117, 130, 131, 188
linguistic creativity 1, 5, 10, 163
loan nativization 16, 17, 185
loan translation 179, 181, 182
ludic 4, 13

Malmö 10, 22, 47, 48, 51, 53
medium 3, 7, 10, 19, 21, 27, 45, 69, 74, 80, 84, 87, 88, 89, 126, 134, 155, 156, 163, 188
meta-communication 4, 8, 9
meta-language 47, 49, 50, 56, 64, 71, 82, 83, 87
mimicry 46, 47, 48, 49, 50, 51, 54, 56, 59, 63, 67, 87

mockery 10, 11, 15, 19, 46, 47, 63, 77, 80, 115, 123, 145, 157, 158, 166, 170, 175, 176, 178
moment-to-moment panel transition (MMPT) 33, 45, 80, 155
multicompetence 87–89, 157
mutual feedback loop 27, 125, 126, 153

native 10, 11, 12, 15, 62, 64, 67, 79, 81, 82, 87, 89, 90, 93, 95, 115, 117, 120, 122, 123, 124, 126, 130, 135, 138, 140, 141, 144, 146, 153, 154, 156, 158, 162, 163, 164, 170, 175, 185, 188, 189
native speaker 12, 67, 81, 82, 87, 89, 90, 117, 124, 138, 140, 141, 146, 158, 162, 163, 164, 166, 170
Nazi 76, 77
non-native 11, 12, 13, 67, 87, 89, 115, 117, 122, 123, 130, 140, 141, 144, 153, 154, 158, 163, 164, 166, 170
non-native speaker 12, 67, 89, 117, 140, 141, 170
non-standard
– accent 42
– orthography 10, 11, 44, 51, 54, 56, 57, 71, 117, 120, 122
– spelling 16, 37, 40, 54, 57, 166, 175, 176
norms 12, 40, 117, 124, 138, 140, 144, 153–154, 189
Norwegian 11, 62, 67, 68, 69, 71, 88, 90, 126, 185

out-group 124, 163
Östermalm 42, 43, 47

panel
– single 19, 21, 22, 24
– transition 33
performance 3, 4, 13, 85, 88, 89, 115, 120, 124, 157, 163, 165, 166
play
– definition 2
– frame 4, 8, 71, 155, 157
– in a language 3
– with a language 3

Pondus 185, 187
popular culture 1, 12, 15, 108, 120, 125, 138, 141, 142, 145, 188
prolonged moment 34
pronunciation respelling 16, *See also* eye-dialect
punchline 12, *See also* punchline English

regional dialect 10, 35, 36, 37, 44, 46, 47, 48, 53, 54, 56, 57, 58, 61, 71, 156
resolution 7, 9, 25, 140, 154, 188
Rocky 18, 20, 21, 23, 25, 26, 33, 35, 37, 42, 43, 44, 45, 46, 47, 49, 54, 56, 58, 62, 63, 65, 67, 69, 71, 87, 88, 89, 130, 142, 159, 162, 179, 182, 188

Scania 51
script opposition 5, 6, 7, *See also* serial narrative
script-based semantic theory of humor (SSTH) 5, 6, 7
simultaneity 5
skånska 51, 53, 54
Södermalm 22, 40, 42, 43, 47
Spanish 11, 63, 74, 81, 88, 90, 169
Special Eurobarometer 81, 90, 91
speech
– play 2
– style 37, 40, 140, 141

stereotype 14, 22
– linguistic 35, 36, 48, 49, 51, 53, 54, 56, 57, 58, 61, 62, 63, 65, 67, 71, 87, 156, 157, 158
Stockholm 10, 21, 23, 36, 37, 39, 40, 41, 42, 43, 44, 47, 49, 75, 81, 173
stockholmska 37, 41, 42, 44
Stockholmsnatt 21, 23, 37, 95, 166, 188
strip *See* comic strip
superiority theory 11, 63, 88
swearing
– annoyance 128, 146
– echoic 131
– self-echoic 131, 144
– social 128
– switch 141, 144, 150, 151, 152, 153, 154

taboo 12, 58, 59, 77, 141
talk-in-interaction 7, *See also* dialogue
Thai 174
transition 23, 33, 45, 80, 155, 161
– moment-to-moment panel 33, 45, 80, 155
– panel 33, 80, 155

Umeå 10, 47, 56

verbal art 3, 13, 163

www.ingramcontent.com/pod-product-compliance
Lightning Source LLC
Chambersburg PA
CBHW030653230426
43665CB00011B/1069